"Visually stunning, *The New Wildcrafted Cuisine* is incredibly impressive, a tour de force, a masterpiece. At long last, an author has truly captured the power and sophistication that wild foods can impart to both our diets and our lives."

—Stephen Harrod Buhner, author of *The Lost Language of Plants* and *Sacred and Herbal Healing Beers*

"This gorgeous book will make you salivate and dream. Pascal Baudar is exploring important culinary terrain in his coastal California bioregion, incorporating the incredible diversity he forages into a broad array of foods and drinks in exciting, elegant, and clever ways. Beyond the particulars of what he can harvest there—some which you or I might find where we live, but much of which is very different—it is his methods, ideas, and aesthetics, all of which can be applied much more broadly, that are truly inspirational."

—Sandor Ellix Katz, author of *The Art of Fermentation* and *Wild Fermentation*

"*The New Wildcrafted Cuisine* takes wild foraging to a gourmet level of creativity. I am delighted by Pascal's ingenuity of wild combinations and impressed by his experience demonstrating the vast potential of culinary artistry. Pascal clearly articulates the procedures and details of transforming wild ingredients into practical recipes, thereby making the gifts of nature more accessible to us all."

—Katrina Blair, author of *The Wild Wisdom of Weeds*

"As a Southern California native, I grew up with the terroir that I eventually would incorporate into my cuisine at Girasol. Pascal was my spark. The first day Pascal walked through our back kitchen door with a cornucopia of foraged California wild plants and 'Old World' recipe vinegars and beers, I knew I had found my voice. Pascal's seemingly infinite knowledge and passion for what grows in the desert region we live in has truly inspired me. This book is one of a kind, a walk off the beaten trail and an exploration of true wild flavors. Chefs who truly care about finding new ways of expression and commitment to 'time and place' cooking will undoubtedly be captivated by it."

—CJ Jacobson, executive chef, Girasol restaurant; winner of *Top Chef Duels*

"Pascal's book contains some of the most unique and innovative ideas that you'll ever find for using wild flavors. Clear instructions accompany each recipe, along with striking photos of the ingredients and finished products."

—Samuel Thayer, author of *The Forager's Harvest* and *Nature's Garden*

The New Wildcrafted Cuisine

Exploring the Exotic Gastronomy of Local Terroir

PASCAL BAUDAR

Chelsea Green Publishing
White River Junction, Vermont

Project Manager: Patricia Stone
Project Editor: Benjamin Watson
Copy Editor: Susan Davidson
Proofreader: Laura Jorstad
Indexer: Shana Milkie
Designer: Melissa Jacobson

Printed in the United States of America.
First printing March, 2016.
10 9 8 7 6 5 4   20 21 22

Our Commitment to Green Publishing
Chelsea Green sees publishing as a tool for cultural change and ecological stewardship. We strive to align our book manufacturing practices with our editorial mission and to reduce the impact of our business enterprise in the environment. We print our books and catalogs on chlorine-free recycled paper, using vegetable-based inks whenever possible. This book may cost slightly more because it was printed on paper from responsibly managed forests, and we hope you'll agree that it's worth it. *The New Wildcrafted Cuisine* was printed on paper supplied by Versa Press that is certified by the Forest Stewardship Council.®

Library of Congress Cataloging-in-Publication Data
Names: Baudar, Pascal, 1961– author.
Title: The new wildcrafted cuisine : exploring the exotic gastronomy of local terroir / Pascal Baudar.
Description: White River Junction, Vermont : Chelsea Green Publishing, [2016]
  | Includes bibliographical references and index.
Identifiers: LCCN 2015037455| ISBN 9781603586061 (hardcover) | ISBN 9781603586078 (ebook)
Subjects: LCSH: Cooking (Wild foods) | Seasonal cooking. | LCGFT: Cookbooks.
Classification: LCC TX652 .B333 2016 | DDC 641.5/64—dc23
LC record available at http://lccn.loc.gov/2015037455

Chelsea Green Publishing
85 North Main Street, Suite 120
White River Junction, VT 05001
(802) 295-6300
www.chelseagreen.com

CONTENTS

FALL: The Seeds Time

What Is This Book About?

The New Wildcrafted Cuisine is not about wild food identification, although you will see many photos of the plants, fruits, and berries I use. There are already so many books on the subject of identifying plants that it is much better for you to buy one specific to your local environment.

I have included some recipes, but this book is not really about cooking either. As with plant identification, numerous books and resources on the subject of cooking wild foods exist online. Another recipe for nettle soup or pesto would be redundant when there are already so many delicious ones to be found online.

This book is about exploring from a culinary perspective what the wilderness is so generously gifting to us and about how to create interesting ingredients that will represent your local terroir as a forager, cook, or chef. To some degree it fills a gap between foraging and cooking.

You can also think of it as a good companion to plant identification books. Hopefully you will find some interesting, unusual, and additional uses for your regular forages, such as the use of stems, leaves, rocks, and so on. This may not be covered in some of the other books.

Although I live in Southern California and thus use the bounty from my local wilderness, there are many ideas and methods presented here that you can use regardless of where you live. Quite a few of the plants I mention (or closely related species) can be found around the world.

If I have a goal with this book, it's to inspire people to explore more deeply the tremendous bounty nature offers all of us—twigs, leaves, sap, barks, dirt, insects, and much more.

As I finish writing this book I am painfully aware that I'm barely scratching the surface on the possibilities and uses of local edible plants. I have much more to learn myself and still need to experiment with many plants that are found in the desert that is local to my home.

I could have written many more pages, but one has to stop somewhere. I've tried to be as comprehensive as possible and show a variety of interesting uses for foraged ingredients. My sincere wish is that, after reading this book, you will develop the same passion and creative urge that I have, to research and experiment in your own local wilderness and to safely try new things—new methods and ingredients that define you and your terroir. It is truly a wild, creative, and fulfilling endeavor that has changed my life.

Out there, you will find an amazing world of endless flavors and ingredients waiting for you. Jump in, and share what you do with others.

Happy exploring!

My Personal Quest for Local Flavors

When I was growing up in the 1970s as a kid in Belgium, foraging was a normal part of life. Living in a tiny farming town with very limited entertainment, my favorite pastime was wandering the woods. There was always something you could discover or make from scratch to entertain you. I could make my own bow and become the Robin Hood of my local forest for a few hours, or I could pick up beautifully colored rocks for my collection. Foraging was just a natural part of my entertainment. During my wanderings I would come across delicious wild edibles such as hazelnuts, chestnuts, or various wild edible berries and help myself liberally to these tasty free gifts.

I think the valuable lesson I learned at the time was that food and delicious flavors could be found everywhere and that foraging was a normal activity, not something unusual and weird. It was part of living in a country setting.

As a teen I wanted to become a *garde forestier* (akin to a forest ranger in the United States). At the time I had some very vague ideas about what their duties might entail, but the notion of wandering the woods for a living was awesome in my mind. Unfortunately I had no idea how to qualify for such a job. I enrolled in a school that I thought was teaching the subject of plants and biology; instead, I was learning how to become a farmer.

Domesticating plants was never on my agenda, so I left after a year. I decided to follow my other passion, which was art, and enrolled in the Academy of Fine Arts in Tournai, Belgium where I learned drawing, painting, sculpting, and photography. I developed a profession as a graphic artist, which I pursued until very recently.

Looking back, I don't have any regrets; I believe the path I took was meant to be and made me who I am today. Art is still very much part of my life—I view foraging and creating from wild ingredients as a true art form. There are endless amounts of aesthetics and creations you can make with the gifts that nature offers us.

My passion for exploring the local wilderness in search of flavors started in the late 1990s. At the time, being mostly interested in outdoor survival skills, I attended numerous classes and workshops with various instructors in Southern California, Arizona, and Oregon.

As part of their curriculum, some instructors would teach about edible wild plants, and it wasn't unusual for our classes to make very basic dishes with local plants, such as salads, porridges, or simple infusions. While some were quite good, very often the resulting flavors and textures were in the realms of "I would eat that in a survival situation if that's all I had."

As I continued attending classes, I became more intrigued by the possibility of using our local edible and aromatic plants beyond creating what I call survival food. Some of the plants had incredible flavors, but nobody I knew locally was really doing anything more refined with them beyond these basic survival dishes.

A good example of a plant with amazing flavor is black mustard, which has some very pronounced wasabi-like tastes, but in the classes I attended it was mostly eaten cooked or prepared raw as part of a wild food salad. One wild food instructor even told me it wasn't edible because it was too spicy!

One day I decided to experiment with the flowers using a recipe for making mustard I found in a culinary book. Using my stone grinder (*molcajete*), I crushed the flowers with vinegar, white wine, salt, and a bit of honey and made a beautiful yellow paste. The end result was somewhere between wasabi and artisanal Dijon mustard. It was truly the most delicious mustard I had ever eaten. A spark ignited at that moment—I think this was the first time I realized that wild food could be truly gourmet food and should be approached with that perspective.

In the early 2000s, I started experimenting with preserving and cooking wild edibles. I attended over four hundred classes and workshops with anyone who could provide me with information about cooking, preserving food, and foraging wild plants. I also spent time with native people learning how to process acorns and cook traditional foods.

I had great fun during these years. I did a lot of traveling, and I made some really bad concoctions—and some interesting ones too. I started playing with native and wild food using traditional and modern methods of preservation such as pickling, fermentation, dehydration, smoking, and pressure canning. And I was doing a great deal of research to find more local edible, medicinal, and aromatic plants.

My friend, the author and survival/wild food instructor Christopher Nyerges, was instrumental in teaching me about local wild edibles during these years, and I probably attended over two hundred of his classes.

The next level of my education in wild foods came when I met my partner, Mia Wasilevich, who is an accomplished and truly talented chef. We've been living together for over six years now, and she really opened my eyes to what's possible in terms of flavors. Together we are culinary accomplices, with Mia creating a lot of refined and sophisticated dishes while I concentrate on researching plants and developing new ingredients and preserves.

Four years ago I decided to follow my passion for foraging and wildcrafted food. I quit my job as a graphic artist and I've not looked back since. So far it's been the most fulfilling adventure of my life. I've made countless new friends, worked with some of the most talented chefs in the United States, and to this day I still feel like a little kid in a candy store. The learning and fun never stop.

Why Foraging?

Having hosted countless wild edible and aromatic plant identification classes for many years, I find it interesting to see what motivates people to forage.

Some people are interested in the survival aspect of foraging. In case the whole society goes down, they would be able to find food for themselves and their family or exchange food with others. Knowledge of what's edible and what's not is definitely a very important skill, making you a valuable person during dire times, someone others want to have around to help with their own survival.

However, the vast majority of people who come to my classes and workshops are not survivalists. They want to connect more with nature, understand where our food used to come from, look for an alternative to the regular store-bought foodstuffs, have access to more nutrient-rich foods, and consume fewer chemicals and pesticides. They're also interested in becoming more independent and gaining the ability to create their own ingredients, such as cheese, mustard, beers, and wines. There is even an actual movement called *rewilding*, in which advocates are striving to return to a more wild or natural state and undo the human domestication of our modern society.

From my perspective, this is not an unhealthy view. The reality is that most urban dwellers have become disconnected from the food they consume and are forced to simply buy it prepackaged at the local grocery store. Many of them would not even know how to start growing their own food or would contemplate with disgust the possibility of killing and butchering an animal.

If you think about it, it's really a fascinating trend. As a species we humans started as hunters/gatherers, then became farmers, and now we are simply becoming consumers. In the process, we are losing our freedom of choice and have become limited by what is made available to us. A good example of this dwindling choice is potatoes. Presently only seven types of potatoes are commonly available at the supermarket, but did you know that there are actually over seven thousand types of potatoes in the world?

The same limitations and lack of freedom to choose apply to many other foods. The lettuce selection made available to me in a commercial grocery store is reduced to maybe ten varieties. But nature can actually provide me with a much wider variety and more interesting flavors. At the right time of the year I can forage more diverse, interesting, and delicious ingredients than what the store is offering. Last spring, it only took me 20 minutes to create for my students a delicious wild food salad composed of dandelion, sow thistle, chickweed, chervil, watercress, wild lettuce, mustard, radish flowers, lamb's quarters, and miner's lettuce.

In this process of domestication, we are also losing precious knowledge. For example, through my research I found that natives on the West Coast once foraged over a hundred types of wild seeds; yet none are available at the store today except for chia. And the chia you can purchase is not even the local wild variety. West Coast peoples probably foraged for many more seeds than what my research turned up, but that knowledge and their preparation methods have been, for the most part, lost.

For many of us who are now learning about local edible plants and foraging, there is a very tangible pleasure to be found in wandering through the local wilderness, foraging seasonal wild edibles, and creating from scratch an incredible dish that could not be found anywhere else in the world. You get a feeling of independence from the regular food system, a sense of freedom and choice.

In addition to people seeking this kind of independence, I also get a decent number of foodies, home cooks, and professional chefs in my classes who are interested in being part of the foraging "movement"—searching for wild edibles has become trendy these last few years. Some come to a few classes and realize that foraging is actually *a lot* of work; some people stick around because they discover a passion for it.

On my part, although I probably have a touch of the rewilding urge going on, over the years I have become more and more involved in a quest for local flavors. So far it's truly been a fascinating and endless journey. The more I learn, the more I realize I'm just getting started. It is quite a humbling experience, but it's also very exciting knowing that you have a future full of discoveries and the ability to create new ingredients.

I find that this knowledge also grows exponentially. For example, if you know how to make wild beers, you can create interesting vinegars with them. With the vinegars you can make very unique mustards with local seeds, along with sauces, shrubs (vinegar-based drinks), and pickled wild seeds. You can also use the vinegars to preserve or infuse many foraged ingredients and to curdle cheese, and that's just a beginning. The opportunities for exploration are endless.

Recently I was invited to speak about foraging as part of a panel for "The Taste," an annual food festival in Los Angeles. Out of curiosity, I spent a few hours beforehand looking at what wild edibles some trending restaurants in the city were using in their dishes. I came up with around 30 different items, ranging from common and well-known edibles such as dandelion, chickweed, fennel, and watercress to more exotic ingredients such as yarrow or black sage.

As a comparison, I decided to take a look at what plants and other wild raw ingredients I've discovered and collected so far over the years and came up with around four hundred. From that base alone, there is already an almost infinite number of potential culinary creations I can make through various processes such as lacto-fermentation, pickling, brewing, winemaking, salting, dehydrating, or just plain regular cooking.

From a culinary perspective, there is a whole universe of flavors waiting to be rediscovered in wild foods.

The Gift of Foraging: Harmony and Balance

The greatest gift I've probably received from my foraging activities is a true sense of balance, harmony, and freedom.

I feel the most aware and alive when I'm in the forest or the wilderness. It's actually quite Zen-like, in that I can tune out the noise of modern civilization and simply be there in the moment. Gone are the financial worries, the alarming news that radio or TV is spouting off on a continuous basis, the commuting, the concept of having to work, the dealing with sometimes complex human interactions, the constant noise surrounding us, and so on.

Instead of prompting a "storm watch," as it's called in the local Los Angeles TV newscasts, I welcome the rain as a precious ally and provider of life.

The "civilized" world, the chatter in your head, the crushing sense of time—everything seems to just slow down and cares disappear after a short while. You can simply be present in the moment and experience the environment fully and with all your senses: smell, touch, hearing, taste, and sight. It's an amazing state of awareness. You can be picking wild lettuces knowing that the alarmed bird 400 yards away is telling you that something has disturbed him—maybe a predator, or another human. You can discern that the noise you hear from 10 yards away is a lizard slowly making its way through the decomposing leaves, not a snake. You can smell slight hints of fennel in the air, which tell you some oyster mushrooms may be nearby. The list goes on. With experience, you can even close your eyes and by smell alone identify many of the plants surrounding you. By tuning out, you let the forest talk to you.

As you get to know the plants and understand their world, you realize that you're truly surrounded by pure, unadulterated life forces and, with time, your relationship with their environment becomes more intimate. You become simply part of the environment as a human being, not trying to dominate plants and place them neatly in rows after rows over endless acres of sorry-looking land. You understand nature is not trying to dominate or scare you, either. It's a symbiotic relationship. I try to do my best to make my activity highly sustainable; sometimes I take care of human trash and restore water flows, remove or manage invasive foreign plants, and even plant native seeds if necessary.

Through accumulated knowledge, research, observation, and interaction with them, the plants will gladly reveal their deepest secrets and speak your language. For one of my friends, an herbalist, that language is medicinal. As a forager, the plants talk to me about flavors, smell, texture, color, touch, and many other sensory perceptions related to food.

The Quest for a True California Cuisine

I've trained and worked with many chefs and talented cooks. During my classes and workshops I often tell them that if they want to truly be innovative, they need to try setting aside their culinary education and take the time to let these new ingredients talk to them as if it were the first time they had to cook something.

Sure, you can easily make acorn pastas, wild food pizzas, nettle ravioli, lamb's quarter pesto, a Vietnamese roll or a Thai salad with fresh wild greens, and countless other ethnic-inspired dishes using foraged ingredients, but is that really the best use of the ingredient? You can use French, Italian, and Asian recipes or cooking techniques with them, but what about creating a California cuisine? What kind of cuisine would actually express the most of what our local terroir has to offer?

Similarly, if you live in another state or country, what unique creations can you make with what nature is providing you locally to create a true taste of place?

It's not easy to explore this question, because our tendency is to rely on our previous knowledge and experience. But I think that by making this exploration there is the potential to go much further in creating a true and original modern-day wild and native cuisine. Well-known restaurants featuring local wild food, like Noma, Fäviken, or D.O.M. in Brazil, have become what they are because they went deeper and further in their approach to wildcrafted or local ingredients and, in the process, created something new.

These restaurants and others have also made wild food very trendy in the culinary world, and I've seen many places trying to emulate them when creating dishes. But if you study their cuisine, they are what they are because of their own creativity, location, culture, and what their environment provides. Trying to be Noma or Fäviken in Southern California, Seattle, or New York City is kind of pointless because we have little in common in terms of ingredients, history, climate, and culture.

What are the real flavors of contemporary Southern California, the true cuisine?

I don't know and I don't think it has been created yet—it's still wide open for creative interpretation and exploration—but from my perspective, you won't find it by importing food from other countries or purchasing ingredients at the local farmer's market or supermarkets.

For example, one might ask what is a Southern California beer? Should it be a beer made locally with regular hops and grains, or one made with actual local native resources, such as wild plants and grains? If you compare these two beers, which one would truly taste like our terroir?

Will you experience the local flavors if you make a salad using purchased ingredients at the farmer's market? Some may argue that, yes, the farmer's market is a good representation of our local produce, but the flavors will be vastly different than a salad made using foraged ingredients such as chickweed, miner's lettuce, native watercress, speedwell, and countless other delicious wild greens. Again, which one is a true representation of our terroir?

Add to that salad a dressing made with our local cactus pears and vinegar made from a forest beer (turned into vinegar by using local *Acetobacter aceti* bacteria) and I think we're getting closer to tasting the true local

flavors. Heck, you can even go further and incorporate local black walnuts or pinyon pine nuts and sprinkle it with a spice blend made from chaparral aromatic herbs.

What about the original native cuisine? Where can you eat acorns in a Los Angeles restaurant? Properly cooked, acorns are delicious, so why can't you find them on local menus? The same goes for screwbeans, palo verde beans, and mesquite.

How deep can you go? Reptiles? Insects? Oaxacan cuisine—not too far from Southern California, if you think about it—is not shy about using what we might consider to be unusual ingredients. They're actually not really unusual; the ingredients are just part of Oaxaca's culture and environment.

What about seeds? There are over one hundred edible seeds in the local wilderness but practically none are found in the local cuisine. Where can I find black sage, clarkia, primrose, plantain, or white sage seeds incorporated into a dish in a restaurant?

Why can't we find all these native ingredients in our local cuisine? It is cost? lost knowledge? lack of culinary experience with them? the amount of time it takes to forage them? not enough demand? Would it be too expensive for the customer?

Probably we can't find native ingredients in our local restaurants for every reason just mentioned, but I don't believe for a minute that food-savvy customers would not be interested in these foods. There isn't any real demand for this cuisine because it isn't there in the first place, and most people are not even aware of it. The motto "Eat local" is a nice marketing slogan created to sell farmers' produce, but it does not raise awareness of our untamed, wild, and true flavors.

The "local" cuisine has too often fallen victim to farming and food globalization. I don't think this phenomenon is just happening in Southern California; it quite widespread in North America.

Don't take me the wrong way: I'm far from being an extremist, and I have really nothing against small local farming and having your own garden. A large percentage of my diet actually consists of organically grown local food.

But I think there is the possibility of a happy marriage between locally grown food and wild flavors as an example of a true local cuisine, one that embraces everything a particular place has to offer.

My point is this: We are missing a tremendous amount of cultural and culinary identity by not exploring and creating a cuisine that would integrate all the flavors our untamed terroir has to offer. I don't care where you live—Oregon, New York, Georgia, or anywhere else—the use of wild food should not be considered a trend or some bizarre or unusual practice. Instead, it should be an integral part of the local culinary experience and something to be proud of.

As for where I live—Southern California—let the culinary fun begin! I'm not a chef or even a cook: I see myself more as a culinary explorer, and even after all these years wandering in the woods, mountains, chaparral, and desert in the quest for ingredients, I know I'm just scratching the surface in terms of what's possible culinary-wise.

If this book makes a humble contribution to the creation of a true local cuisine, or simply brings awareness to readers interested in food—helping them understand that nature can offer a truly incredible bounty of nutritious and flavorful food outside the regular channels—it's all worth it.

Foraging Ethics and Caveats

Many of the books about plant identification will have guidelines for foraging ethics. Read them carefully and follow them. Respect the rules. I've done my best and, so far, after 16 years of local foraging, I've not encountered any problems. Never pick rare or endangered native plants, and do your best to help them propagate. Do your research and find out if specific plants are legal to harvest.

Think sustainability. Don't uproot plants if it's unnecessary and don't take too much in a specific area, even if they seem plentiful. If I find a field of nettles, wild onions, or watercress, I try to never forage more than 20 percent so that I can come back year after year and enjoy the gift nature is offering me. I have seen fields of edible or aromatic plants being destroyed for dubious commercial uses; it is truly pointless and destructive.

As a forager, you must assume the role of being a steward of the land. If you do so, the rewards will be plentiful.

As a general rule, always approach a new food source sensibly. Although from my experience it is extremely rare, there is always the possibility that your body may experience an allergic reaction to a new plant or ingredient. For instance, I once saw a person have a slight allergic reaction to amaranth. It's better to eat only a small quantity of any new food and see how your body likes it. The same rule applies to both wild and conventional foods. Also, if you are allergic to shrimp, approach entomophagy (eating insects) cautiously.

Some plants can induce specific actions (laxative, diuretic, hormonal, etc.), stimulate the uterus, or have abortive effects. Although the following list is quite incomplete, here are some plants that would not be recommended for eating or drinking if you are pregnant. As you learn about new herbs and plants, always check them out carefully to see if they may have toxic, allergic, or other effects. This information is often available online.

SOME HERBS AND PLANTS TO AVOID IF YOU ARE PREGNANT:

Black cohosh (*Cimicifuga racemosa*)
Buckthorn (*Rhamnus frangula*)
California sagebrush (*Artemisia californica*)
Cotton root (*Gossypium hirsutum*)
Feverfew (*Tanacetum parthenium*)
Ginseng (*Panax ginseng*)
Goldenseal (*Hydrastis canadensis*)
Horehound (*Marrubium vulgare*)
Horsetail (*Equisetum arvense*)
Juniper (*Juniperus*, which I assume would include our local California juniper berries)
Licorice (*Glycyrrhiza glabra*)
Motherwort (*Leonurus cardiaca*)
Mugwort (*Artemisia vulgaris* and others)
Sages (*Salvia*, including white sage, black sage, etc.)
Tansy (*Tanacetum vulgare*)
White fir (*Abies concolor*)
Wild rhubarb (*Rumex hymenosepalus*)
Wormwood (*Artemisia absinthium*)
Yarrow (*Achillea millefolium*)

WINTER
The Forest Time

Winter Recipes

I started this book with winter because it is really the beginning of foraging season in Southern California. It's one of the few states where you can forage all year long.

We usually get some rain in November (maybe in October, if we get lucky) and pretty soon after that chickweed, miner's lettuce, mustards, and stinging nettle start to appear. While most of the country is under snow, it is truly the time of plenty and a forager's dream. We are able to collect edible plants months ahead of many other states. The year's end makes my work so much easier too, as the temperatures are milder.

From my perspective, winter is all about the forest; it's when the forest becomes truly alive. This is what this section is all about.

We'll look at ways to use interesting forest ingredients for cooking, brewing primitive beers, making delicious cheeses, mixing aromatic forest blends, and preserving some of the bounty nature is offering us, such as herbs, acorns, mushrooms, and much more.

I've included photographs of many of the plants I forage from December to March. You can refer to these photos when you look at recipes: Most should be there, and if not, check the Resources section for books on plant identification.

As you'll see, I'm not just gathering edible plants. As I walk through the forest, there are many other interesting things that can be collected and used for culinary purposes; see Cooking with Dirt, Sticks, Bark, Leaves, Sap, and Stones on page 83.

Tasting the Forest

The inspiration for exploring the flavors of the local forests came to me four years ago. It was the middle of November and I was foraging for Melisse, a restaurant in Santa Monica.

We had a couple of rainy days prior to my foraging hike. That morning, the air was permeated with thousands of amazing smells from the local aromatic plants and the fall leaves slowly decomposing on the ground.

It was quite breathtaking. I remember stopping in the middle of the trail, closing my eyes, and breathing in slowly to analyze all the scents. Overall it was musky from the fall leaves on the ground and the organic decomposition from the topsoil; I could detect lots of earthy qualities you sometimes experience when you smell a wild mushroom. There were quite a few aromatic tones as well: the wonderful scent of mugwort and sagebrush, and a hint of fennel—probably from some nearby oyster mushrooms.

It was like listening to music but through the sense of smell, each plant being an instrument and a specific sound working together in harmony to create an awe-inspiring symphony.

Right there, in the middle of that trail, I decided to try to re-create the experience in my foraging and culinary/preserving work. I walked the trail for over an hour, finding and foraging the plants responsible for my olfactory nirvana: grass, specific rotten leaves, oyster mushrooms, decomposing oak wood, turkey tail mushrooms, mugwort, California sagebrush, yerba santa, black sage, fig leaves, and more.

By the end of the walk, I had my first experimental "forest blend" with over 20 ingredients. In retrospect, aside from the fact that I knew the plants were not poisonous or harmful, I didn't really know what I was doing, and my proportions were all wrong. That day I cooked some potatoes in my forest blend, which ended up tasting quite bitter and not very palatable. But I could see the potential, and I was determined to work on it until I was successful.

Over the last few years I have become much more experienced in creating these forest blends by tweaking the proportions of the various ingredients and creating a harmony among the various flavors. Each forest blend is unique, depending on the intended purpose and the seasons. I use the blends for cooking, to make ice cream, to infuse vinegars, and even to make beers.

Sometimes I have been successful at re-creating the flavors of whole environments, such as my mountain-forest-infused vinegar, which tastes deliciously of pine, white fir, and California juniper. It's a constant work in progress, and to this day I continue working at it and improving the blends.

On Edible Versus Unpalatable and Poisonous

I consider the act of creating forest blends to be advanced foraging. You can start with a few plants that you know well, but to make complex blends requires a bit more sophisticated knowledge.

As with any foraging, you *must* know what you are doing. Only pick plants, leaves, and other matter that you can positively (100 percent) identify, and know the properties of the plants, from both a culinary and a medicinal perspective. Dosages are often crucial. A particular plant could be used sparingly as a spice, for instance, but could make you sick if eaten in large amounts. This is nothing new, by the way; it's also true of some more conventional spices or plants that you buy at the store. Nutmeg is a good example. Nutmeg has psychoactive effects when ingested in large quantities and can make you quite ill. In extreme cases it is deadly. In small amounts, however, nutmeg is an excellent and useful spice.

While you may be tempted to pick up some beautiful and fragrant autumn leaves from the forest ground to experiment with, you will need to know the poisonous plants in the environment as well. One leaf of poison oak or poodle-dog bush (*Eriodictyon parryi*) in your blend is already too much. Here in Southern California we have deadly plants such as poison hemlock (*Conium maculatum*), white snakeroot (*Ageratina altissima*), and the castor bean plant (*Ricinus communis*). Some potentially harmful plants can smell very good—like jimsonweed (*Datura stramonium*), which smells similar to peanut butter—but this plant is highly psychotropic and can kill you as well.

If you pick up decomposing fall leaves, don't use them if you're not 100 percent sure what they are. As you accumulate more knowledge about plants, you will gain more freedom and creativity.

Knowing what plants not to include in a blend is one thing, but what makes a plant edible?

Edibility is an interesting concept. The dictionary definition of *edible* is "fit to be eaten, especially by humans." It's often used to contrast with unpalatable or poisonous examples.

When I was learning about wild food, the vast majority of instructors would stick to the most well-known edible plants (although they were all new to me), but anything that was considered unpalatable was usually skipped. I learned about amaranth, yucca, mesquite, and countless other edible plants and berries, but outside of that realm, the potential culinary uses of interesting ingredients such as mugwort, sagebrush, unusual seeds, tree leaves, barks, unripe berries, grasses, insects, and many roots were not usually part of the education.

The truth is that many plants, trees, roots, unripe berries, and so forth are edible but usually not used because they are unpalatable as is. The taste is too bitter, the texture is too tough or too woody, they're not digestible without processing, or the flavors are too strong.

Over the years my definition of *edible* has changed quite significantly. If something that I can gather in the wild is not poisonous or harmful in any way, I simply assume that I may have not found a culinary use for it yet. In fact I may not always be successful in doing so, but often the inedible properties can be altered through such simple processes as boiling, candying, frying, roasting, or fermenting. Experimenting is the fun part, and a large part of what Mia and I do.

These days it's not unusual for me to even forage barks that once roasted, are used to create smoked vinegars by simply placing the roasted bark in the vinegar for several weeks. I can make ten different smoked vinegars using the barks of various local trees, such as mesquite, oak, and figs. Each of these vinegars has a slightly different flavor.

Once you have accumulated enough expertise about the edible and medicinal properties of an environment, you will perceive it with completely different senses. The forest, chaparral, desert, and mountains become vast universes of aromas and flavors begging to be discovered and used. It is also ever changing with the seasons. You just need to learn, explore, experiment, and have fun in the process!

Some of the plants and ingredients I currently use in my forest and other environment blends include:

Australian bushberries (dehydrated)
Black sage
Blackberry leaves
California bay
California juniper berries and wood
California sagebrush
Chervil (burr-chervil)
Cottonwood leaves
Currant (berries and sometimes leaves)
Dates (from local palm trees)
Epazote
Fennel
Figs (leaves and fruits)
Fragrant everlasting
Grass
Lemonade berries
Magnolia leaves or flower petals
Manzanita berries
Mormon tea (ephedra)
Mugwort
Mushrooms (turkey tail and oyster)
Pine needles
Pineapple weed (wild chamomile)
Prickly pear cactus
Purple sage

Rose hips
Seeds (black mustard, mugwort, etc.)
Stinging nettle
Sweet alyssum
Sweet white clover
Toyon berries (dehydrated)
White fir needles
White sage
Willow leaves
Wright's cudweed
Yarrow
Yerba santa
Various wild mints
    (seven different kinds)
Various stems (horehound,
    mugwort, sages, etc.)
Various barks, sometimes roasted
    (oak, sycamore, etc.)
Various roots (radish, mustard, etc.)
Insects (ants for lemon flavors,
    cochineal for color)
Organic honey from the local forest
    or mountains
Lerp sugar (honeydew excreted
    from insects)

This process is simple, yet easy to overcomplicate. It's all about proportions, balance, harmony, and knowing the purpose of the blend.

When a chef asks me to create a forest or mountain blend, my first question is: "For what purpose?" If he intends to cook meat with beer and a forest blend, my choices for the blend will be very different than if he intends to cook pears, which are much sweeter and require a different blend of ingredients.

The blend's purpose (making beer or infused vinegar, for example) or the main ingredient to be cooked dictates what the blend should be composed of. The photo on page 13 shows a forest blend I made for Chris Jacobson of Girasol restaurant here in Los Angeles. Chris worked briefly at Noma in Denmark, a restaurant widely known for locally foraged ingredients and for launching the Nordic food movement. Since he opened Girasol, Chris has been very passionate about foraging and quite adventurous with wild ingredients in his kitchen.

This blend is used to cook pears. Pears are quite sweet, so I know that their taste will balance and harmonize well with bitter ingredients. I also added plenty of aromatics to infuse the fruits. There is no set recipe; this blend was composed of the following ingredients:

40% forest grass—grassy/green flavors
15% fall leaves (mostly willow and a bit of cottonwood)—
    bitter and musky flavors
25% aromatics (mugwort, sagebrush, wild fennel,
    rabbit tobacco [Wright's cudweed], black sage)
15% fig leaves—fruity and fig flavors
5% fresh turkey tail mushrooms—earthy and musky flavors

If I were making a blend for a beer using the same seasonal forest ingredients, I probably would have used the following ratio for 1 gallon (3.75 l):

40% (0.3 ounce/9 g) grass
30% (0.2 ounce/6 g) dry mugwort
20% (0.2 ounce/6 g) fall leaves (decomposing leaves are
    even better for musky flavors)
5% (0.05–0.1 ounce/3 g) mushrooms, such as turkey tails
5% (0.05–0.1 ounce/3 g) other aromatics (California
    sagebrush, fennel, white sage, etc.)

Each environment (forest, mountain, desert, and coastline) can likely give you a minimum of ten plants or other ingredients to start with. The blends don't have to be complex to taste delicious. My favorite mountain blend is composed of only four ingredients: white fir and pine needles, manzanita, and California juniper berries.

Learn and research your local environment and try different blends. The various combinations of all these flavors is limitless.

Pears cooked in forest floor.

GOAT (OR LAMB, RABBIT, OR BEEF) COOKED IN FOREST FLOOR

The fact that I brew various primitive beers using wild plants and forest ingredients made it only natural that I would use my beers for cooking.

This dish began as an exploration into the flavors of my local forest and has become a classic during our private dinners. You can use various types of meat but I really like using goat or lamb. Here in Southern California, late fall and winter are the best seasons to forage the components, but I also dehydrate and keep some for use during the dry summer and early fall. You get the best flavors with fresh ingredients, though.

The basic recipe is pretty loose, and you can play around with your own forest ingredients; to some degree it's an intuitive process and you'll get better over time as you make various blends. My first attempts were . . . well, let's just say that they needed work. Take the time to experiment before you actually serve this dish to guests.

Ingredients

2 pounds (900 g) goat shoulder, cut into large chunks; you can also use shanks
Olive oil
2 cloves garlic, crushed
1 large onion, chopped roughly
A large handful of forest floor mix, roughly composed of mostly fresh green grass, two to three mugwort leaves, fall leaves (I use willow and cottonwood), a few mushrooms (turkey tail, oyster), and a very small amount of sagebrush, yarrow, and other strong aromatics; so the blend is (approximately):

    60% forest grass (fresh and green is much better)
    10% mugwort leaves
    15% fall leaves (decomposing ones are even better for musky flavors)
    10% mushrooms (oyster/turkey tail/others)
    5% other aromatics (California sagebrush, fennel, yarrow, black sage, and so forth)

1 California bay leaf (or you can use 2 regular bay leaves)
2 bottles (16 ounces/375 ml each) mugwort or forest beer*
Honey, salt, and pepper to taste

Procedure

1. Heat the oven to 300°F (150°C).
2. Season the meat chunks with salt and pepper. Heat the olive oil in a Dutch oven or similar cookware over medium-high heat. Add the meat chunks or shanks and brown on all sides. When browned, add the garlic and onion and cook an additional 3 to 4 minutes, stirring frequently.
3. Add the forest floor and California bay leaf and mix with the meat. Pour in the beer, cover, and place in the oven. Cook for approximately 3 hours, turning the meat chunks every hour throughout the cooking time. When done, remove from the oven, taste, and add honey and salt or pepper if necessary. Let cool and place in the refrigerator overnight.
4. Reheat for 30 minutes prior to serving. When you plate, you have the option of removing the forest ingredients, leaving a few, or letting the guests pick the meat out of the mix.

* See Making Primitive Wild Beers on page 58. You could also use a nice fruity Belgian beer such as a gueuze.

BEEF STONE-COOKED IN FOREST FLOOR

This is a dish that we sometimes create in my foraging classes. It's based on a primitive cooking method, whereby we simply place the meat with a forest blend on a very hot flat stone heated by a wood fire below. We carefully choose the ingredients for flavors. In February, we used grass, forest floor leaves (willow, cottonwood), oyster mushrooms, sagebrush, sweet white clover, and a couple of mugwort leaves. There is a bit of an art to choosing the right quantity of each ingredient, but this will come with practice. Actually, it's hard for this dish to taste bad.

Ingredients

15 beef chunks (approximately)

Salt and pepper to taste

Spice blend—I often use our chaparral blend (see Creating Wild Spice Blends on page 157) but you can also use regular blends such as Italian or French spice blends

2–3 tablespoons oil or rendered fat

A handful forest floor mix

1 garlic clove

1 small onion, roughly chopped

Procedure

1. Place your meat in a large bowl and season generously with salt, pepper, and spices. Add oil (rendered fat works as well) and mix everything thoroughly with your hands for 20 seconds. Add your forest ingredients and the chopped garlic and onion, then massage the meat vigorously again for a minute or so.

2. Place everything on the hot flat stone. Move the ingredients around from time to time with kitchen tongs (or sticks) to make sure the meat is cooked on all sides. Depending on the stone's temperature, this usually takes around 10 minutes. Once done, rest the meat in a bowl for 3 to 5 minutes with fresh grass on top. The end result is quite delicious, smoky and loaded with forest flavors. If you can forage them, mushrooms are a bonus in this recipe.

In February, when this photo was taken, we used grass, forest floor leaves (willow, cottonwood), oyster mushrooms, sagebrush, sweet white clover, and a couple of mugwort leaves.

The Musky Flavor of Mushrooms

Southern California is not a fantastic place for mushrooms, so I must admit that I'm really not an expert in that field. I stick to a few edible mushrooms that I know well, such as oyster (*Pleurotus ostreatus*), chanterelle (*Cantharellus cibarius*), and inky caps (*Coprinus* spp.), and leave the rest to experts.

Due to this lack of delectable fungi, I became interested in exploring what I could forage in decent amounts. During the winter we get a quite a few mushrooms growing on fallen trees. Although not edible per se because they are really too tough, I was truly intrigued and fell in love with the woody and musky smell of our most abundant one: turkey tail mushroom (*Trametes versicolor*).

Thorough research found that they are extremely medicinal (as with some other fungi, they strengthen the immune system) and no side effects have ever been reported in historical uses or in modern research, so they seemed ideal for foraging.

I made quite a few culinary experiments with the turkey tail and currently use the mushroom in some of my wild beers and infusions. It's really great for hints of earthy and musky flavors when used fresh, but there is also some definite bitterness, which is intensified if they are dehydrated (making them good for beer). For culinary uses, I like to freeze them to preserve as much flavor as possible.

TURKEY TAIL MUSHROOM VINEGAR OR VODKA

My favorite application is to infuse fresh turkey tail mushrooms in vinegar or vodka.

Ingredients

Turkey tail mushrooms (10–20 depending on the size), cut to fit into half-pint jars

Enough vinegar or vodka to fill the jar (I like to use a good-quality apple cider)

2 teaspoons (14 g) honey or (8 g) sugar

Procedure

1. Clean the turkey tail mushrooms. Cut the mushrooms if necessary to fit into the jars.
2. Pack half-pint jars with the mushrooms. Fill the jars with vinegar or vodka and close the lids. Let the mushrooms infuse for a couple of months (or more) in the refrigerator.
3. At the end of the infusion period, strain the vinegar or vodka using a coffee filter. Each half-pint jar renders about ½ cup (118 ml) of infused liquid. While you end up with good mushroom flavors, the taste is also quite bitter, so I usually add 2 teaspoons (14 g) of honey or (8 g) sugar. If I intend to serve the vinegar to guests, I like to pasteurize it at a low temperature once it's bottled. (See Pasteurizing Your Vinegar on page 252.) Infused vodka does not need to be pasteurized.

CLAY COOKING WITH FORAGED AROMATICS

This method of cooking is inspired by primitive cooking; it works very nicely with foraged ingredients. It's pretty much something I can put together on location while fishing in the local mountains.

Think of the clay as a primitive oven. The clay keeps trout or other fish tender and moist while the flavors from the aromatic herbs, which can't escape, really impregnate the flesh. Although it requires a decent amount of work to put it together, it's hard to go wrong with this type of cooking.

I like to cook fish and game meat with ingredients foraged from the environment they live in: Somehow the flavors seem to complement each other. This works perfectly for preparing trout, as I often find delicious and complementary aromatics such as sweet white clover, watercress, and white fir on the banks of the river where I'm fishing.

Procedure

Forage or purchase your clay. In Southern California, finding good clay isn't easy, but I have found some great clay deposits in the Malibu area. You can also purchase clay from the local art store. (Tell them what it's for so they will give you suitable clay.) My other method is to mix the local sandy clay with egg whites until I achieve the right consistency for shaping—but this is not my favorite option.

Gather your aromatic herbs and place them inside and on both sides of the trout. The last time I did this type of cooking I used sweet white clover, white fir needles, and a bit of sagebrush. I also added some salt, pepper, lemon, butter, and garlic (½ clove chopped roughly). On other occasions I've used other wild spices such as fennel, white sage (in moderation), California bay leaves, chervil, watercress, crushed juniper berries, epazote, wild onions, and oxalis (instead of lemon). Of course you can also use regular culinary herbs such as dill, parsley, cilantro, or thyme.

You'll need to find some large leaves to wrap your fish with. Where I live, I have several choices such as fig, sycamore, or maple leaves. Curly dock leaves work very well too. While attending primitive skills classes I have seen people just wrapping a bunch of grass around the fish and using mud to cover everything. The idea with the large leaves is mostly to separate the fish from the clay; the clay container is really just a primitive oven, which will keep the contents tender and moist. Make sure you know what you're foraging: Some large leaves—such as castor oil plant (*Ricinus communis*) or, in California, tree tobacco (*Nicotiana glauca*)—can be highly poisonous. Use a string to tie the leaves around the fish. I often use some local yucca fibers. Long grass stems work too.

Your next step is to wrap the fish with clay. You can unleash your inner Michelangelo if you want, but it's not necessary to create an art piece. You just want your fish to be wrapped inside a clay cocoon around ¼ inch (6 mm) thick.

If you're cooking outdoors, place your creation in the middle of your campfire. Cook for 15 minutes on one side, then turn over and cook for another 15 minutes. If you are using a conventional oven, you can cook the fish for 35 minutes at 450°F (232°C).

When finished, crack the clay using a stone or hammer, remove the trout, and enjoy!

This process is really not complicated and it's a lot of fun to cook this way with guests. Recently we hosted a private dinner and cooked small pieces of trout in clay. Each guest was given a stone to break the clay. It was a fun and highly interactive (and quite noisy) experience that everyone enjoyed very much!

Making Wild Cheeses

A few years back I began experimenting with using plants to curdle milk and create various wild cheeses, basically an interesting take on what we call farmer cheese. They are extremely simple to make.

Farmer cheese is made with milk curdled using an acidic solution such as vinegar or lemon juice. The solution coagulates the milk, which separates into curds and liquid whey. Using a sieve or cheesecloth, the whey is drained off and you are left with the cheese (solid curds). Farmer cheese is usually eaten somewhat dry and crumbly; it is often added to salads or spread on toast.

This type of cheese can be made from the milk of sheep, goats, or cows. I like to use mostly raw goat milk from my friend's farm, but milk purchased at the local store is fine too as long as it isn't ultra-pasteurized milk (which won't curdle).

To make the wild cheeses, out of necessity I came up with an interesting technique to make the curds stick together to form a somewhat cohesive and hard cheese.

Aside from the actual procedure of making the cheeses, there are no specific rules or precise recipes for making them. It's pretty much open to your own creativity and the flavors you want to create. Although I use the cheeses to feature local wild edible and aromatic plants, you can use regular spices as well with excellent results.

You can use dry, fresh, or cooked ingredients, and even mix them. The real fun is in experimentation. Some examples of ingredients to incorporate into wild cheeses include the following:

Fresh garlic and dry chaparral spices (white sage, sagebrush, California bay, black sage, garlic, peppercorns, and sea salt). Italian or French spice mixes can be good substitutes.

All dried ingredients: garlic powder, homemade sea salt, and chaparral spice blend.

All fresh ingredients: chopped sweet white clover with garlic and salt. Other fresh foraged ingredients that could be used include watercress, fennel, mints, nasturtium, and so forth.

Cooked ingredients: nettles sautéed in garlic, white wine, salt, and pepper. You can also use lamb's quarters, spinach, or any other appropriate plants.

Fresh garlic and dry spices, dehydrated ingredients and spices, fresh and cooked ingredients.

Step 1

Step 2

Step 3

Step 4

Step 5

Step 6

Step 7

Step 8

Step 9

Step 10

BASIC WILD CHEESE

It's extremely easy to make this very basic cottage cheese. When you add wild ingredients and aromatics, the number of interesting flavorful combinations is pretty much infinite.

Ingredients

½ gallon (1.9 l) milk (not ultra-pasteurized)
¼ cup (59 ml) vinegar or lemon juice
1 teaspoon (6 g) sea salt (optional if salt is included in the spice blend)
A mix of 1 or 2 cloves garlic, 1 teaspoon spices (around 4 g), and any wild ingredients you want to use
Fresh flowers, leaves, spices, and herbs for decoration

Procedure

1. Pour the milk into a large pot with a heavy bottom and bring to a boil over medium heat. Stir it from time to time so the milk doesn't scorch on the bottom. Make sure your pot is made of non-reactive metal (no copper, tin, or aluminum). Stainless steel is okay.
2. When the milk begins to boil, add the vinegar or lemon juice and stir for a few seconds. Turn off the heat. The milk should separate into curds and whey extremely fast.
3. Let the milk rest for 5 minutes. While you're waiting, line a colander with cheesecloth or a clean cheese towel.
4. Pour the curds and whey through the cheesecloth. The whey will pass through and the curds will accumulate in the cloth.
5. Wait 5 to 10 minutes to let the cheese curds cool off a bit, then tie up the cheesecloth and press it with your hands to remove the excess whey.
6. Now open the cheesecloth carefully, making sure the cheese does not stick to the fabric. Using a spatula or spoon, remove the cheese and place it in a bowl.
7. Add the sea salt and the garlic, spices, and/or wild ingredients to the cheese. Use a fork to mix everything thoroughly.
8. Now, using both hands, create a compact ball. It's not always easy, as the cheese has a tendency to crumble. Just make it as round and smooth as possible; don't stress too much about it.
9. Finally, set the cheese ball on a plate and decorate it. I usually add flavorful spices, leaves, and flowers. Wrap the cheese ball in plastic and twist the wrap to compress the cheese. You want to make it very tight so the curds will stick together as the cheese is cooling down in the refrigerator.
10. Store the balls in the fridge overnight and for up to a week. I like to use the cheeses within a day or two to keep the flavors of the herbs fresh. When it's ready to use, remove the wrap and plate the cheese ball. You may want to add fresh herbs as decoration. Serve and enjoy!

Wild sweet white clover farmer-style cheese.

TINY CHEESY WILD SNACKS

While it's quite enjoyable to make a sizable wild cheese, I think it's much more fun to make little cheese ball snacks. With a half gallon (1.9 l) of milk you can make 15 or more small cheese balls. You can create countless combinations with various spices and foraged ingredients. And don't feel limited to using just spices; I've made some cheese balls with foraged seeds such as fennel, chia, mustard, and other seeds that native peoples used to eat.

Herb powders are great too for their aesthetic quality, and some are really delicious. You can try experimenting with sweet white clover or watercress powder, for example. Cattail pollen is just fantastic to feature some bright yellow colors. Have fun—there are truly no limits to what you can make, from crunchy to spicy, with foraged ingredients or ingredients sourced at a farmer's market or elsewhere.

Ingredients

1 recipe Basic Wild Cheese
Seeds, spices, aromatic herbs, herb
    powders, fresh leaves

Procedure

1. Follow the recipe for Basic Wild Cheese on page 27 through step 6.
2. Now, instead of making a large ball with the curds, create 15 or so smaller cheese balls. You can mix herbs, spices, or other ingredients into the curds before making the balls, but very often I just leave the cheese as is. The real fun comes later.
3. Wrap the cheese balls tightly and leave them overnight in the refrigerator. This should give you enough time to dream up all kinds of wild spices and concoctions to bring flavors and colors to your tiny cheeses.
4. When you unwrap the cheeses, they're usually a bit wet, so you simply need to dip them into the spice mixes you've created. You can also wrap the cheese balls in leaves. Wild mints are perfect for this—my favorite mint wrap is made with water mint (*Mentha aquatica*). It's even better if you wrap the leaves around the cheese overnight to let the flavors infuse.

Tiny Cheesy Wild Snacks
with wild aromatics,
seeds, and herb powders.

Plant Rennet

Aside from making cheese with acidic solutions (lemons, vinegar) or using animal rennet, you can also use specific plants to curdle milk and make cheese.

I'm still researching and experimenting with the use of specific plants to curdle milk. Recently I've had good success with nettles and fig sap.

In the past I've also used silverleaf nightshade berries (*Solanum elaeagnifolium*), which are considered poisonous but have been used to curdle cheese in South America. They worked extremely well as far as curdling the milk, but, not having an actual experienced person to show me the process, I decided to skip eating the cheese. When dealing with potentially poisonous plants, you're always better safe than sorry.

Although I've not used them all, from my research the following plants have been used traditionally to curdle milk to make cheese:

Nettles
Our lady's bedstraw (*Galium verum*)
Butterwort (*Pinguicula vulgaris*)
Ground ivy (creeping Charlie)
Teasel
Mallow
Knapweed
Bark and leaves of the common fig tree (*Ficus carica*)
Milk thistle flowers
Thistle/artichoke

Cheese curdled in fig sap.

GOAT CHEESE WITH FIG SAP

I don't have fig trees in my garden, but I find plenty in the local forests. I usually bring a small jar of fresh, cold goat milk with me into the forest; collect my sap on location, adding it directly into the cold milk; and bring it home. Hopefully you have a tree in your garden so you don't have to wander through the forest with a cooler bag. It does make for some great funny conversations, though, when you have to explain to someone why you're in the middle of the forest dropping sap into a jar of cold milk.

Ingredients

5 drops fig sap, plus one branch to use
  for stirring
1 quart (scant 1 l) cold goat milk
White sugar to taste

Procedure

1. Cut the top of young fig branches and place 5 drops of sap into the cold goat milk jar. Reserve one fresh branch to be used as a stirring stick. Don't use more sap or your cheese will be too bitter. Once back home, add the milk with the sap to 1 quart of goat milk (not ultra-pasteurized or it will not curdle).
2. Pour the milk in a non-reactive pot and start heating. Stir with your branch. When curds form, which happens before the milk is actually boiling, continue with the instructions at step 3 for Basic Wild Cheese on page 27. Depending on the time of the year, the milk may have a tad of bitterness; because of this, I like to add sugar to this cheese instead of salt.

Preserving—
A Forager's Perspective

When I tell people that I'm a forager, most of them think that I spend the majority of my time in the local wilderness.

Nothing could be further from the truth. Foraging is actually the least time consuming of my activities. I would say that I spend roughly 25 percent of my time foraging, 25 percent exploring new locations, and 50 percent preparing and preserving the bounty.

There is good reason for that those time allocations: Many plants, fruits, nuts, and berries have a very limited life span. For example, I may have a two- to three-week window of time to gather yucca buds before they become too hard and unpalatable. If I don't pick ripe elderberries right away, they'll be eaten by birds within a week or two. Where I live, a similarly short window of time exists for wild currant berries, pineapple weed, chia seeds, and wild onions in the desert, to name just a few examples.

So it's the ages-old survival battle of harvesting the food while it is available and preserving it so you can enjoy it in the future.

Currently I'm not living in a world where the preservation of wild food is vital to my survival, but if I want to work as a professional forager, preserving is a crucial activity for my vocation. Without it, when the summer comes in Southern California and the terrain turns into a desert, I would have a very hard time finding enough variety or quantity of wild edibles. This becomes a real issue if I'm working with chefs or when we have private dinners scheduled.

But if we were just looking at preserving food from a survival perspective, I think we would be missing the point. What started as a necessity through human ingenuity and creativity has been transformed into gourmet practice. Through the magic of preservation, a simple ingredient such as milk can be made into countless delightful cheeses and other delicacies, such as butter or ice cream. Plants, fruits, sugar, and water become beers, liqueurs, or wines. Meat can be magically transformed through curing into ham, bacon, salami, prosciutto, and sausage. Even fish guts and salt can be metamorphosed into a golden, umami-rich liquid called fish sauce, an essential ingredient in some Asian cuisines.

The possibilities and types of products that can be created through preserving are virtually endless. Factually, the vast majority of what you buy at the store are preserved products. In my local supermarket, out of the 16 aisles for food products, 14 are dedicated to preserves, with 3 aisles alone reserved just for frozen products.

With foraging, preserving is really where the fun is at. Not only can you take some of your foraged ingredients and turn them into unique and delicious products, but, through research and experimentation, you can also create brand-new products such as mugwort beer vinegar, sweet white clover salt, coffee berry jam, wild spice blends, insect-flavored beers, and so on.

Many of the products I create are a compound of various preservation methods. For example, my last wild "Dijon" mustard was ground by hand using my *molcajete* (primitive stone grinder) and was composed of elderberry wine, mugwort beer vinegar, homemade sea salt from dehydrated seawater, raw mountain honey, and foraged black mustard seeds. The flavors are truly unique (several chefs have told me it was the best mustard they'd ever had) but, if you take into account the number of hours to create it, it's nearly priceless. If I valued my time at $25 an hour, creating all the sub-products (wine, beer, and so forth) and gathering in the wilderness the elderberries, the seawater, the mustard seeds, and the plants to make the beer, the true cost of a half-pint jar would be in the range of $250.

While a chef or restaurant would have a hard time justifying buying such an expensive product, that calculus accurately reflects the quality of ingredients we provide when Mia and I host private dinners.

To be honest, I've provided such products to some of the chefs I've worked with at much lower cost, mostly because I'm driven by passion rather than economics (and that's not always a good thing), but I don't think most chefs had any idea of the labor involved in making them.

All the various preservation methods can be applied to wild edibles. Thus, as a forager, you have the ability

to create an infinite number of products. It doesn't matter if you are located in California, New York, or France: There are enough plants and other edibles out there to fulfill your wildest dreams in terms of creating ingredients. The only exception may be in extreme climate conditions such as Antarctica or the Sahara Desert—choosing to become a forager there may not be the smartest career choice.

If you don't know basic preservation techniques, you are seriously limiting yourself. I could not have made a living working with chefs for over four years without the ability to create products using wild plants. My "wild" preserves such as vinegars, sodas, spice, and blends were more sought after by some chefs than the actual wild ingredients themselves.

Preserving food has also allowed me to provide products during the lean times (summer in California) and continue making a living despite a harsh, desert-like environment.

Due to my warm-climate location, cellaring (preserving fresh food by storing in a cold cellar) is not a method I've experimented with very much.

SOME OF THE PRESERVATION TECHNIQUES I USE WITH MY WILD EDIBLES INCLUDE:

Dehydration
Lacto-fermentation
Alcoholic fermentation
Pickling
Dry salting
Canning (both water bath
    and high-pressure canning)
Preserving in fat
Preserving in sugar
Preserving in water
Preserving in alcohol
Freezing
Curing
Smoking
Vacuum packing

Food Safety

You cannot talk or write about food preservation without touching on the subject of food safety. Most of the preservation methods, such as dehydration, fermentation, salting, freezing, and so forth, are very safe. It becomes a little bit more complex once you get into canning.

If you are interested in pickling or making jams and jelly, understanding the basics of food safety such as pasteurization and low-acid versus high-acid foods is a must.

It's even more crucial for wild foods. Why? Because very often you are in uncharted territory. When I took the Master Food Preserver program a few years ago we learned about food safety, and our job was to demonstrate and promote the various methods of food preservation using USDA-approved recipes. Having recipes that were tested in a laboratory made it simpler and safer for people to get into canning.

Guess what? There are no approved recipes for preserved wild edibles. You won't find an approved recipe for pickled acorns, fermented black walnuts, dandelion kimchi, or canned goat meat cooked in forest floor in the USDA literature. So if you want to create your own gourmet wild food preserves and custom pickling solutions, the only thing you can do is to fully understand and apply the basic principles of food safety to make sure that what you do is 100 percent safe.

Even if you have some objections to the modern ways of preserving food, a good understanding of the concepts behind food safety can at least offer you an educated approach and practice. Armed with that knowledge you can decide if it's a good idea to preserve those mushrooms in oil, or if it would be safer to add acidity to the solution before canning it.

Unsafe preservation methods can make you very sick, or worse. This can range from becoming nauseous from ingesting harmful bacteria due to unsafe storage temperatures to potentially dying from botulism if you don't follow food-safety practices for canning high- and low-acid foods. If you share your preserved food with others, it would be highly irresponsible to neglect studying and understanding the subject.

If you are interested in food preservation, do some research to find whether there is a Master Food Preserver program available in your area. It's well worth your time.

You can also find all the basics of modern preservation at the National Center for Home Food Preservation (http://nchfp.uga.edu). Presently they offer online classes.

Canning: My Basic Water Bath Method

A few preserve recipes in this book require a technique called water bath canning, whereby food placed in a jar with a vinegar solution goes through a process of boiling to make it shelf-stable, which means you don't have to keep it refrigerated and can place it somewhere on a shelf for later consumption.

The principles and logic in preserving food in an acidic solution, such as vinegar, using water bath canning are simple. The heat (boiling) used in the process and the high acidity of the pickling solution destroy microorganisms that could harm you or spoil food, thus assuring the food's safety and keeping quality.

That said, nothing is eternal. Over time food will degrade and become unpalatable, but ingredients that are properly preserved through water bath canning can last for a decent amount of time—typically a year or two, and sometimes more depending on various conditions such as storage temperatures or exposure to sunlight.

The water bath method is used for high-acid preserves and for jams and jellies. Low-acid food preserves—such as meat, fish, poultry, or various vegetables not placed into highly acidic solution—use another method called high-pressure canning, whereby high-temperature processing kills all unwanted microorganisms and prevents dangerous toxins such as botulinum (which causes botulism) from forming in the preserve.

Because some recipes in this book will give you the option to use the water bath method, I want to explain the process I use so interested readers can readily do it. That said, there is much more to learn about water bath canning and the various techniques used in this process. I urge you to get yourself well educated on the subject. In addition to the resources cited above, the canning jar manufacturer Ball also has a great book titled *Ball Blue Book: The Guide to Home Canning and Freezing* that is usually available wherever canning supplies are sold. It can also be purchased online.

For most of my pickled wild preserves, such as wild radish pods, yucca buds and flowers, thistle stems, ash keys, and so forth, I use a "raw packing" water bath method very similar to approved recipes for pickling green beans or carrots. It's very easy to do. You place your fresh ingredients in clean jars with spices, bring your vinegar-based solution to a boil, and pour it into each jar, leaving a half-inch of headspace. Close the jars, place them in hot water—140°F (60°C)—bring the water to boiling for a specific amount of time, and voilà! It's really that simple. You don't always have to use pure vinegar; for flavoring I sometimes add spices and even wine, beer, or regular water to the mix, but if I do so I will verify that the acidity level is adequate for water bath canning.

Because I deal with wild food and no USDA-approved recipes, I often err on the side of caution when boiling the jars—I probably boil them for longer than necessary, but my guiding mantra is better safe than sorry. Of course, if I find an appropriate "approved" recipe then I would use that one. For example, if I want to can my mountain sauerkraut (cabbage fermented with white fir, pine, and California juniper) or wild kimchi, I'll use the approved recipe for canning sauerkraut. It's important to use common sense and do your research.

I have done my best to apply everything I know about basic food-safety principles and correct preservation techniques in my recipes, such as ensuring the correct acidity level of my pickling solutions and even my ingredients by using specific tools, such as digital pH meters. Because I started foraging many years ago, most of my recipes have also been through empirical testing.

BASIC WATER BATH CANNING

Here is the step-by-step basic water bath raw-packing method I use. You will need some basic canning equipment to do it at home. I usually use a boiling-water canner, although for small batches I sometimes use a regular pot and a specifically designed mesh at the bottom so the jars don't touch the hot surface. Most of the time, however, I use my canner, and I very strongly suggest you purchase one if you are interested in canning.

Basic equipment

Boiling-water canner
Canning jars, lids, and bands
Thermometer
Jar lifter
Jar funnel
Various regular kitchen utensils, such as funnel,
   measuring cups, ladle, wooden spoon

Procedure

1. Fill your canner with warm water, depending on the size of the jars you will be using. Adjust the amount of water so you will end up a couple of inches over the top of the filled jars later on. Heat the water to 140°F (60°C).
2. Place your raw ingredients into the jar, including spices if the recipe calls for them.
3. In a separate pot, bring your pickling solution to a boil, then remove from the heat.
4. Fill the jars with the hot pickling solution while the water in the canner is heating up.
5. Remove any air bubbles using a non-metallic spatula by inserting it inside the jar and pressing gently on the food to release any trapped air.
6. Wipe the rims of the jars using a clean cloth or paper towel.
7. Place the lid on each jar and screw the band until fingertip-tight. It should be tight and firm, but obviously not as firm as if you were using the full force of your hands to screw it. I call it "finger strength."

8. Using your jar lifter, load the filled jars into the canner (with the wire rack already in the water). (You can also load the jars into the wire rack first and then use the rack handles to lower it into the water.) Add boiling water so that the water level is a couple of inches above the jars.
9. Turn the heat up, cover the canner with the lid, and bring the water to a vigorous boil for the amount of time called for in the recipe. It's okay to lower the heat if the boiling is excessive, but you want to keep the water at a vigorous boil. The processing time starts when your water is boiling vigorously (not when you place the jars in the hot water).

   When the jars have been processed in the boiling water for the recommended time, turn off the heat and remove the canner's lid.
10. Using the jar lifter, remove the jars one by one and set them aside. It's a good idea to place a towel on the counter for the jars to sit on. Let them cool off undisturbed for at least a day.

   As the jars are cooling a vacuum is created by the contents inside. After a while you should hear a "pop" sound and the lid should become slightly concave in the center. Once the jars have been cooling for 12 hours, you can remove the screw band and verify that they are sealed properly by inspecting each one visually. You can also gently press the middle of the lid with your finger—if the lid springs back up when you release your finger, it is an improper seal. If the jar is improperly sealed, place it into the refrigerator and consume the food within the next few days.

Creative Canning

Before you can start to experiment with incorporating and mixing foraged aromatics, wild blends, and all kinds of interesting and unusual ingredients, it is extremely important that you understand the basics of canning and how acidity plays a role in food safety. You also need to invest in a good electronic pH tester to measure acidity.

Every wild preserve I make for the first time is pH tested before canning and again when I open it before serving. Food acidity can change over time and can make the food unsafe to consume.

I spent a long time using regular canning recipes before moving to more adventurous ones. Like any art form, once you have gained a good understanding of the subject and mastered the skills, it is wide open for creativity.

As with regular food recipes and dishes, the number of flavors you can create in preserves by incorporating wild ingredients is infinite. In the beginning you'll probably make a few mistakes in terms of flavors, but very quickly you'll learn how to use each ingredient. Start by adding a small amount and go from there. When I use new ingredients, it's not unusual for me to make three or four different jars, each with a specific amount. You may waste a bit of food in the beginning but it's part of learning.

The flavors you can find in your local wilderness can be quite amazing: Keep your mind open and don't just look for berries, seeds, and aromatic leaves. Dehydrated stems can have

fantastic flavors, and various smoked barks or woods can infuse some subtle smoky accents to your pickling solution. (See Cooking with Dirt, Sticks, Bark, Leaves, Sap, and Stones on page 83 for a discussion of smoked woods.) Aromatic flowers such as elderflower will impart floral qualities to your preserves.

HERE ARE SOME EXAMPLES OF LOCAL WILD INGREDIENTS I'VE USED SO FAR IN MY PRESERVE MAKING:

Seeds (wild fennel, mustard, epazote, coriander)
Herbs and plants (burr-chervil, wild fennel, mints, sages, kelp, sweet clover, California sagebrush
Dehydrated stems (mugwort, yarrow, epazote, fennel, various sages, California sagebrush)
Flowers (elderflower, oxalis, black mustard)
Berries (California juniper, manzanita, toyon, elderberries, currants)
Leaves and needles (white fir, pine, California juniper, eucalyptus, various sages, some aromatic wild currant leaves)
Barks and woods (oak, mesquite, fig, juniper, olive, alder)
Mushrooms (candy cap, turkey tail)

Three variations on preserved nasturtium capers are shown in the photograph on page 40. Each jar was filled with hot apple cider vinegar (5 percent acidity). I also added 1 teaspoon (6 g) of salt (true capers are supposed to be salty), and processed the jars for 15 minutes using the water bath canning method.

Three variations on preserved nasturtium "capers" (*top to bottom*): with elderflowers and wild fennel seeds; with white fir, crushed California juniper berries, and turkey tail mushrooms; with roasted oak bark, white fir, crushed California juniper berries, and a small yarrow stem.

Foraging and Preserving with Sea Salt

For as far back in history as we can track humanity's survival practices, salt has been used to preserve food. If you're a food history buff, you will find records of such methods used in ancient Egypt. (The Egyptian mummification process itself was accomplished by drying the body in salt.)

The discovery of America and other territories would not have been possible without the knowledge of food preserving through salt. Not so long ago the American settlers survived bitter winters by using root cellars for extended storage and salt-curing foods such as salt pork and ham.

Salt is used in several specific food preservation methods:

Fermentation: A small quantity of salt encourages specific salt-tolerant bacteria (*Lactobacillus*) and inhibits potentially harmful others. Very often the bacteria are already present on the plants themselves, and the addition of salt and water is enough to start the fermentation process. This is how sauerkraut and kimchi are made.

Dehydration: Salt draws water out of food and dehydrates it. Water being necessary to all living things, harmful bacteria cannot survive without it. It is why so many of the preserved dry foods you buy at the supermarket—such as potato chips, soup cubes, and beef jerky—are so salty.

Elimination of microbial activity through saturation: Microorganisms cannot survive in food above a certain salt concentration. Through a process called osmosis, when a solution with greater concentration of salt exists outside of microbial cells, the microbes will break down. Thus, preservation is assured through killing the bacteria that would initiate food spoiling.

Brining or salting: The latest method requires either a very highly concentrated brine (over 10 percent salt) or a large quantity of salt mixed with your organic material. To make such a concentrated brine, you need the equivalent of ¼ cup of salt dissolved in 2 cups of water. The brine is made by boiling the salt-and-water solution. Boiling is necessary to get all the salt to dissolve in the water.

THE ADVANTAGES OF PRESERVING FOOD IN SATURATED BRINE ARE:

1. You can preserve food without the need for refrigeration or freezing for a long period. (I've preserved food in saturated brine for over a year in Southern California.) In a cold and dark place such as a basement, people in rural areas have been able to store vegetables in brine for up to three years.
2. Salt is still cheap and it's easy to work with. You don't need any special equipment. You can also forage your own salt by dehydrating seawater.

DISADVANTAGES OF SALT BRINING:

1. The salt must be removed from the vegetables or wild plants before consumption. This requires lengthy soaking and repeated rinsing.
2. It is generally considered to be a good health practice to eat salt in moderation, making this a good option for preserving condiments more than foods that would be eaten in larger portions.
3. Flavors can be altered over time.

SEA SALT

I don't know why but originally I thought making my own sea salt would be a complex process. My logic was that if it were extremely simple a lot of people would already be doing it. Well, I was wrong! This is probably the easiest procedure in this book. I don't know why more people are not making their own sea salt, aside from the inconvenience of having to source the seawater.

The only ingredient you need is seawater. How simple is that?

The sole problem I've encountered is pollution. I'm highly suspicious of the water quality near Los Angeles, and for good reason. So sourcing my seawater is always a great excuse for a trip outside of the city. I usually drive 2 to 3 hours north to a bit beyond Santa Barbara, where I load up.

You'll be amazed at how much salt you can get from just a couple of gallons of seawater. One gallon (3.75 l) should provide you with a bit more than ½–¾ cup (around 300 g) of salt. The process is simple evaporation.

Procedure

The first step in making sea salt is filtering the water. There is likely some sand, floating particles, and tiny critters in the harvested water. A regular coffee filter and funnel work nicely, or you can also filter the seawater through cheesecloth.

Once you've filtered the water, the next step is to boil it until almost all of it is gone. You end up with some sort of damp salt mush at the bottom of your pot. Place that damp salt in a bowl or plate and set it in the sun or a dehydrator to complete the evaporation.

I use a dehydrator and I like to supervise the process a bit. Every 2 to 3 hours I inspect the salt; using a fork, I mix and crush it a bit to make sure I don't end up with a solid mass. At the end of the process, when the salt is nearly ready, I may have to do that every 20 minutes or so. If you don't have time, another option is to simply grind the final product.

This salt is a bit different than what you buy at the store, in a good way; it is crisp, quite light, and does not linger on the palate.

Damp salt mush.

Harvesting sea water. *Photo courtesy of Mia Wasilevich.*

PRESERVING IN SATURATED BRINE

This method works well with foraged ingredients such as cattail shoots, bulbous plants, wild radish pods, and roots. For herbs such as chervil, watercress, clover, wood sorrel, and so forth, see Salted (Wild) Herbs on page 46. Clean your plants thoroughly. If you use large wild plants, similar in size to tomatoes or chilies, you will need to cut them in such a way that the brine can penetrate to the inside; otherwise they may rot.

I suggest using spring or store-bought water for brining; tap water contains chlorine, which will affect the taste of your food. If you are using coarse salt, weigh it to make sure you have the same quantity as fine sea salt. Don't use regular table salt, which contains iodine and other added chemical agents.

Inspect the jars for any defects and ensure the jars are clean before you begin. (Wash them with soap or place in boiling water for 10 minutes.) Always use good hygiene, and wash your hands often in the process.

Ingredients and equipment

Sea salt

Measuring cup(s)

Springwater

Fresh foraged ingredients (cattail, field garlic, acorns, groundnuts, etc.)

Jars

Olive oil

You also may need a weight that is non-reactive to salt to keep the vegetables down in the brine, although in most cases this isn't necessary, since most vegetables have a tendency to rest at the bottom of the jar once saturated with salt. I often use a small stone (cleaned and pasteurized in boiling water).

Procedure

Make a brine using a ratio of ¼ cup (68 g) of salt to 2 cups (514 ml) of water. Boil the brine and let the brine cool.

Wash and prepare your foraged ingredients. Cut the ingredients if necessary so the brine can penetrate. Blanch the vegetables in boiling water (approximately 3 minutes) and place them in jars. (I usually boil tubers and roots until they are fully cooked.)

Fill the jars with brine, leaving ½ inch (1.25 cm) of headspace. Finish with a capful of olive oil and close the jar. The oil is an added protection and is used as a buffer against oxygen, thus reducing the risk of spoilage.

Foods preserved in this manner will keep for up to a year in a cold, dark place. When you are ready to enjoy, soak the vegetables in water to remove the salt before cooking them. You may need several soaking and rinsing steps. I usually place my vegetables in fresh water and put them into the refrigerator for 8 hours, then I taste and change the water to repeat the soaking if necessary. I do this every 2 hours after the initial 8 hours of soaking.

I've used an alternative method with acorns.

Place the leached and cooked acorns in a clean jar and make the brine. Pour the hot brine into the jar, leaving ½ inch (1.25 cm) of headspace. Finish with a capful of olive oil and immediately seal the jars tightly. When the brine cools off it will create a vacuum, which will seal the jars.

I have preserved acorns for up to 9 months at room temperature using this method. In a cool and dark place, I'm sure they would preserve well for over a year. Salted acorns require extensive soaking and water changes before use.

SALTED (WILD) HERBS

This is a traditional European method for making soup stock preserved by salt. This preserved stock will keep for a couple of years when stored in a cool, dark place. I still enjoy stock I made two years ago, so I know it will keep for a long time.

It's extremely easy to make. You can use the finished product as a salt substitute and to flavor soups or sauces—usually 1 or 2 tablespoons (15 ml) will do.

I give this stock recipe a little twist by using wild food, but you can use this method with any vegetables.

The first step is to gather and clean all your plants/herbs. To make this soup stock preserved in salt, I used burr-chervil and onions as the main base and added nasturtium, dandelion, miner's lettuce, nettles, wild celery, and chickweed. You could use ramps (wild leeks) instead of onions.

Note that in my experience and after doing some extensive research, I have not found soup stock preserved in salt that included garlic. It's a bit odd, but for right now I am sticking with the traditional method and don't use garlic.

The principle of this preservation method is really very simple. You just need salt and vegetables. In enough quantity, salt makes it impossible for microorganisms to grow, which allows you to preserve the food.

So what is the ratio of salt to vegetables?

Traditional recipes ask for a ratio of anywhere between 30% salt and 70% vegetables to 14% salt and 86% vegetables. I like to play it safe and use a ratio of 1 part (20%) salt to 4 parts (80%) herbs/vegetables. The best salt to use is sea salt or kosher salt. Regular salt may have unnecessary additives, which could alter traditional recipes.

Hygiene is extremely important, so make sure you wash your hands for at least 20 seconds with soap and water before handling.

Procedure

Clean and chop roughly your herbs and vegetables, then weigh them to determine how much salt is needed. Mix the vegetables and salt thoroughly.

Using an electric or manual blender, grind all the elements. I like my salted soup stock a bit thick, so I use one of my meat grinders. (I have several grinders; I use this one just for vegetables and other wild foods such as acorns and nuts.) If you are using a manual grinder, do *not* discard the juice; you will need it when placing the soup stock in a jar.

Place everything in a bowl and add the juice, cover it with a clean kitchen towel or plastic wrap, and let the mixture stand for 8 hours in the refrigerator.

Remove from the fridge, clean your hands, and mix all the ingredients one more time for 20 seconds or so.

The next step is to sterilize the jars in which you will place the soup stock. I use regular canning jars. To sterilize, place the jars in boiling water for at least 10 minutes.

Place the ingredients in your sterilized container, using a clean spoon to push the ingredients down. The idea is to remove any air bubbles (as much as possible). This is why keeping the juice from grinding is important—the liquid is a big help in discouraging air bubbles.

Add one more thin layer of salt on top of the soup stock. Clean the edge of the jar so you have a proper seal. Close the lid tightly.

That's it! You've just made a traditional soup stock—or, if you foraged your ingredients, a traditional wild food soup stock. You will need to store it in a cool, dark place, such as a cellar or refrigerator.

I also added a small layer of salt at the bottom of the jar in the photo; it's not a must, but some recipes recommend doing so.

Wait at least 3 to 4 weeks before using. If you want to test (and taste) your concoction, boil some water and add some of your salted herbs. If you made a great aromatic mix you will be amazed by the flavor.

You can also lightly brush your salted herbs on eggs, potatoes, steaks, and other foods with amazingly tasty results.

MAKING GARUM (FISH SAUCE)

I love Asian cuisine and I'm completely addicted to fish sauce. For those who don't know, fish sauce is made from fermented fish, and for the longest time I was really repulsed by the idea of actually making it. I was somehow associating fermenting fish with rotting meat.

I changed my way of thinking when a friend gave me a bunch of fresh local sardines and asked me to make some fish sauce for him. I thought, "Why not?" and decided to give it a try. I'm really glad I did—it was a fascinating process.

There is a long history behind fish sauce. Presently it is mostly made in Southeast Asia and used widely in their cuisine. Go to any Thai restaurant and you'll usually see it on your table. But if you study history you find that fish sauce was extensively used by the Romans and was a major industry for them. The Romans called their fish sauce *garum*. In Asia you will find it under other names, such as *nước mắm* (Vietnam), *nam pla* (Thailand), and *jeotgal* (Korea).

What is so special about fish sauce? Think of it as a flavor enhancer. Fish sauce can enhance and harmonize the flavors of a dish, turning something good into a spectacular culinary experience.

I plan to experiment much more with making fish sauces in the future, but I started with the simplest recipe—garum. You really just need two ingredients: fish and salt. How simple is that?

To make garum you will need some *fresh* fatty fish, such as sardines or mackerel, and sea salt (you can also use kosher salt). The idea is to mix the fish and salt together. Enzymes already present in the fish entrails will start digesting and dissolving the proteins, turning the whole thing into a liquid brown mush, which you will then filter to obtain a clear liquid.

The ratio between salt and fish is important—your fish could spoil without enough salt. The amount of salt also dictates the amount of time you will be fermenting the fish. Asian fish sauces have a ratio (by weight) ranging from 1 part salt for 3 parts fish to 1 part salt for 1 part fish. The extra salt in the Asian fish sauce slows the fermentation process considerably—sometimes it is fermented for up to 18 months. Studies of Roman fish sauces, which were found in old shipwrecks preserved in amphorae, indicated a ratio of 1 part salt to 7 parts fish, suggesting a sauce that would be ready to use after only a few weeks of fermentation.

From a food-safety perspective I was a bit nervous with the 1 to 7 ratio, so I opted for the middle range and used a ratio of 1 to 5.

Procedure

My first step was to cut the fish in small pieces and mix it with the salt. Everything goes in: entrails, heads, and every other part. I placed the mixture of salt and fish in a food-grade bucket with the lid loosely secured (to protect from insects but not fully airtight).

For the first 4 weeks, I churned the mixture twice a week. After 4 weeks the flesh started to dissolve. After 2 months, it turned into a brown mush but the fish wasn't fully dissolved yet. During that time, I churned the mixture once every couple of weeks.

Six months later, all the flesh had dissolved into a mush. Only bones and scales were left. (By the way, throughout the whole process the smell was really not that bad. It reminded me of the smell of salted anchovies.

The final steps were very simple. I took the mush and passed it through a thin sieve to remove the bones and scales. This worked very well, and I ended up with some sort of brown liquid, very similar to wet mud. The last step was to filter it through a coffee filter. This was quite a slow process; it took a whole day to filter drop by drop.

By that evening, though, I had my final product: a beautiful amber-colored fish sauce and a very thick paste (called *allec* by the Romans) remaining in the coffee filter. The paste is actually a delicious by-product and can be used as a condiment. My favorite use of allec is to spread it lightly on a hot piece of toast or pizza.

Interestingly enough, the paste is pretty much identical to a British condiment called Patum Peperium, which is basically made of anchovies, butter, herbs, and spices.

The sauce itself was also very good, although much stronger and salty than other fish sauces available at our local Asian markets, and thus it must be used sparingly. You can also dilute it with water.

If I do this experiment again, I'll probably add some wild spices, such as our Chaparral Wild Spice Blend (see page 158), during the fermentation process, to add some of the local flavors.

1. Fresh sardines. 2. Cut sardines mixed with salt. 3. Sardines fermented for 2 months. 4. Sardines fermented for 6 months. 5. Filter the fermented fish. 6. Filter the paste (*allec*) to obtain the fish sauce.

Discovering Acorns, a Delicious Native Staple

Acorns are one of my favorite wild foods. Acorns—the nuts of oak trees—can be foraged in the later months of the year, usually from November through January. I usually pick them off the ground, and my strategy is to make foraging trips to some of my "secret" acorn locations after a windy day. The ground is usually littered with acorns then and they're easy picking.

Some years are better than others, and while some oak species yield crops every year, many others only produce one crop every two or three years. One good tree can provide over two hundred pounds of acorns.

You can find acorns in most parts of the world. Worldwide there are over nine hundred species. They are very common throughout the United States; here in Southern California, it's not unusual for me to gather acorns from 10 different species of oak. Some acorns are more bitter than others, and their nutrition values fluctuate. Because I deal mostly with restaurants, I've learned to forage acorns based on their flavor.

As an aside, I find it interesting that many chefs have this (strange, to me) habit of biting into unknown ingredients to get an immediate flavor profile. While this approach may work in a farmer's market setting, it does not work well with quite a few wild ingredients, including acorns. Most of the acorns we find in Southern California are terribly bitter! It makes for a good laugh every time I see a chef chomp into an acorn, for the facial expression it produces.

Although they were one of the main food sources for local native peoples, acorns have pretty much disappeared from the local culinary scene. I always find it a bit baffling that "California cuisine"—supposedly a style of cuisine defined by fusion and fresh local ingredients—does not include acorns in its repertoire.

The only place where I can actually find acorn products in Los Angeles is at the local Korean markets, where they still sell acorn flour, jelly, and noodles. When I provided acorns to some of the chefs I was working with, they had no clue as to how to prepare and use them.

Acorns are naturally bitter, and they must be prepared to remove this bitterness, in order to make them palatable. The bitterness of acorns comes from tannins. All acorns will contains some bitter tannins to a lesser or greater degree, depending on the type of oak. Tannins are not something you want in your diet because they are not healthy in large quantities and could even damage your kidneys over time.

Tannins are removed through a process called leaching, whereby tannins are drained away from the acorns using water. We're not re-inventing the wheel with leaching. Squirrels bury acorns in the ground and leave them there for a long period of time to let rain and groundwater percolate through them and leach the tannins out.

You can leach acorns by either cold or hot leaching. Cold leaching involves removing the tannins using cold water, whereas hot leaching removes them through boiling. The method you want to use is determined by what you will be making with the acorn meats. If you want to make acorn flour or an acorn-meal mush, for example, you don't want to boil the acorns, since at the same time you will be cooking the starch. Once cooked, the starch cannot be used as a binder.

The techniques used for cold or hot leaching are varied. I've attended many classes and workshops over the years on leaching acorns and, although the principles were the same, every single person had a slightly different way of doing it.

I'll share my own techniques here, but feel free to explore the subject much more and learn about other ways of leaching acorns.

Foraging and Preparing Acorns

As mentioned earlier, I usually forage acorns from November to January. Historically, the season to forage began in September—native people used to harvest acorns by climbing the tree and knocking the acorns to the ground using long sticks. Being 54 years old, I tend to avoid climbing up large trees if I don't have to, and thus I pick them up off the ground. It's probably not optimal, so by all means, if you are up to it, start in autumn by climbing oak trees and knocking the acorns down!

The best time to gather acorns is after a windy day, when there is usually a large quantity of fresh acorns littering the ground. In the old days, people used to camp on location for several weeks, but presently I have the luxury to drive an hour or so, spend the morning in my secret location, and come home with 30 or 40 pounds of acorns. I can then do the basic preparation in the comfort of my home.

In my area, probably up to 30 percent of the acorns I forage are infested by grubs. The bad acorns are easy to spot: You usually will have one or more very visible little holes in the shell. Some people like to only pick the good ones on location, but I'd rather gather as many acorns as quickly as possible and head home. It's not that I'm lazy; it's part of a carefully planned culinary move. By the time I'm back home, the bottom of the bag will be crawling with grubs, which are a nice little delicacy in their own right—but we'll feature them later.

Other than visual inspection, there is also a faster way to sort out the bad acorns from the good ones. Because I pick them up from the ground, I like to clean my acorns. If you place them in water, you'll realize that the bad ones will float, but the good ones will drop to the bottom. This makes sorting them much faster and easier than a visual inspection done on location.

Don't leave the acorns in the water too long, as softening the shell makes them more difficult to prepare. Simply remove the bad acorns and then get the good ones out of the water as quickly as possible and place them somewhere to dry. What you do next is influenced by what you want to make with the acorns.

If you want to make acorn flour or mush (called *wiwish* by native peoples), you need to use the cold-leaching method.

For making acorn flour, you should think about drying the acorns first. You have two choices for a drying process. You can take your whole acorns and leave them to dry in the sun for a few days, then store them in paper bags or baskets. Local Cahuilla Indians used to grind and process some of the acorns on location and carry the rest to the village. They were then stored in aboveground granaries, designed to let fresh air circulate through the acorns.

You can also make a small incision in the husk, crack it with a rock, and remove the acorn meat, which you then lay out to dry. The acorn meat dries faster outside of the husk and is less prone to rotting. For my part, I like to cut the husk with a knife and remove the acorn meat. You definitely need working gloves to do this, but with practice I've found that I can process 20 acorns or more per minute. You also have the option of chopping the acorns into smaller pieces, which are then faster to dry and leach than whole acorns.

Please note that, due to their high oil content, acorns can go rancid over time. Store them in a cool, dark place.

If I intend to process the acorns by hot leaching, I usually don't dry them; I undertake the hot-leaching process while they're fresh, but you can still use dried acorns if you want. Once the leaching process is completed and the tannins have been removed, I freeze them or preserve them in brine. Sometimes I also pickle them.

COLD LEACHING ACORNS

For cold leaching you can work with fresh or dried acorns; I generally find dehydrated acorns easier to work with. Either way, it makes the leaching go much faster if you blend or crush the acorns into small bits. When I use fresh acorns, I usually remove the shells and process the acorns through a sausage grinder, but you can also chop them finely with a knife. The dry acorns can be crushed into small pieces or coarse flour with primitive tools, such as stones. Make sure to remove the brown skin surrounding the acorn meat before blending or grinding, as it is quite bitter.

Procedure

Place a clean towel or cheesecloth folded several times over a colander or basket. Place your acorn coarse flour in the towel and pour water over it. The water will leach out the tannins. Lukewarm water works faster than cold water.

This can be a somewhat lengthy process depending on the type of acorns you use and their bitterness. When I attended a native cooking class a few years ago, it took over an hour of continuous leaching to remove the tannins, and the acorn flour was still a bit bitter.

Another method that works well is to simply mix the coarse acorn flour with cold water and place everything into a large jar or food-grade bucket. I use around 30% acorn flour and 70% water, and I change the water several times a day. The leaching can take anywhere from 1 day to a week, depending on the type of acorns and the number of water changes. Be sure to change the water carefully, so as not to lose any of your precious nut meat.

Take a small spoon and taste the flour when you think it may be done. If it's still too bitter, just continue the leaching process.

When the leaching is completed, separate the flour by slowly pouring the contents onto a clean towel or cheesecloth (folded three or four times) that is placed over a colander. (For a small quantity you can also use a large coffee filter.) Let the acorn meat rest there for 30 minutes.

The last step is to remove the filtered coarse flour, spread it over parchment paper on a baking sheet or on a large dish, and dehydrate it. If you use a dehydrator, make sure the temperature is not too high; around 120°F (50°C) would be fine. In California, I usually place it outside; by the end of the day it is usually dry.

You want a nice and smooth flour, so the final step is to grind it using a coffee grinder or a stone grinder (I use my *molcajete* for that final step, too). The end result should be very similar to flours you purchase at the store—thick and powdery.

You can store the acorn flour in mason jars or paper bags. Because of the fat content in acorns, it is best to place the jars or bags of acorn flour in a cool place, or else it may go rancid over time.

HOT LEACHING ACORNS

Hot leaching is a method I use for many culinary applications, such as making acorn burger patties, pickling, or stews. There are tons of other uses, as well: At Melisse restaurant in Santa Monica, they sometimes leach acorns in sugar water, caramelize them, and sprinkle little bits on desserts.

You can easily leach whole acorns or large chunks of acorn meat in a relatively short time. The only problem with this method is the fact that the starch will be cooked and thus can no longer act as a binder (the way gluten does).

Most the time I use fresh acorns for hot leaching, which I then preserve through freezing, dehydrating, or brining.

Procedure

Shell the acorns. I know, it's easier said than done. I usually hold the acorn with my thumb and index finger and cut the shell in two using a knife. Please, always wear work gloves on the hand holding the acorns and proceed carefully. Shake the acorns a bit and the nut will fall out of the shell. It works better if you let the acorns dehydrate for a week or so before attempting shelling them.

Once you have shelled all your acorns, place them in a large pot with cold water (one-third acorns and two-thirds water by volume). I like to add 1 teaspoon (6 g) of salt.

Bring the water to a boil and simmer for 30 minutes. The acorn skins will detach and float. You can remove them using a skimmer.

Pour the water and acorns into a colander. Fill the pot with hot water, add 1 teaspoon (6 g) of salt, and place the acorns in the pot. (Note that it is important to fill the pot with hot instead of cold water. If you use cold water when changing it, you will bind the tannins and the acorns will remain bitter.) Bring the water to a boil, and then simmer for another 30 minutes.

Continue draining, changing the water, and simmering until your acorns no longer taste bitter. The flavor should be nutty and creamy. This may take two to four changes of water (or more), depending on the type of acorns you are using.

Once completed, you can use the acorns right away in various recipes. You can also dehydrate or freeze them for future uses. Sometimes I also preserve them in strong salted brine.

Dehydration works especially well—when making a stew I just drop my dehydrated leached acorns early on into the pot.

ACORN PANCAKES

Ingredients

¾ cup (96 g) acorn flour (cold leached)
¾ cup (96 g) white flour
2 teaspoons (5 g) baking soda
½ teaspoon (6 g) salt
3 tablespoons sugar (40 g) or honey (60 g)
1¼ cups (300 ml) milk (I like to use goat milk)
3 tablespoons (44 ml) olive oil
1 egg, beaten

Procedure

1. Combine the flours, baking soda, and salt. If you use sugar, add it at this step.
2. Combine the milk, oil, and egg in a separate container. If you use honey, add it at this step.
3. Place all the ingredients into a bowl and mix thoroughly to achieve a smooth batter.
4. Drop the batter onto a heated skillet.
5. Cook until golden (I usually do a test first to determine the right amount of time) and flip.
6. Serve hot. You can top your pancakes with syrups and fruits. In the photo I topped them with mugwort beer syrup, blueberries, lerp sugar, and fennel pollen.

Acorn pancakes topped with mugwort beer syrup, blueberries, lerp sugar, and fennel pollen.

PICKLED ACORNS

This is a recipe that's still in progress; each year I seem to improve it a bit. It's not a quick process but when done properly, they're a nice addition to wild food salads or cold dishes. There are more traditional and simple recipes that can be found online (search for pickled acorns) but I think the brining step, while adding a few days, makes the final product shine.

Ingredients

1 pound (453 g) leached and halved acorns (hot leached)
½ cup (136 g) sea salt
2 cups (472 ml) water
2 cups (472 ml) apple cider vinegar or red wine vinegar
¼ cup (59 ml) balsamic vinegar
½ cup (118 ml) water or white wine
1½ cups (330 g) brown sugar
½ teaspoon (1.5 g) peppercorns
½ teaspoon (1.5 g) ground allspice (I sometimes use Italian or French spice mix)
2 teaspoons (10 g) fresh-grated ginger
1 teaspoon (3 g) garlic powder
½ teaspoon (3 g) ground cloves
1 dry chili pod per jar (optional)

Procedure

1. Place the freshly leached acorns in a salt-saturated brine: ½ cup (136 g) of sea salt to 2 cups (472 ml) of water. Let stand for 2 to 3 days. Remove the acorns and let them dry for half a day.

2. Combine the vinegar and all remaining ingredients (except the acorns) in a pot. Bring the solution to a boil, then reduce to a simmer for 15 minutes. Meanwhile, place the acorns in clean half-pint jars (a larger jar is okay if you don't intend to can them but simply want to store them in the refrigerator).

3. Pour the hot solution over the acorns in the jars. I like to include the boiled spices. Divide the solution equally among the jars. Seal tightly.

4. Place the jars into your refrigerator or use the water bath method of canning (see Basic Water Bath Canning on page 38) and process the jars for 15 minutes in boiling water. Wait at least 1 month before tasting.

Making Primitive Wild Beers

There is something primal and almost magical about making beers using locally foraged ingredients. In some strange ways, it makes me feel connected to long-lost times when things were done more simply and people had a deeper connection with nature and understood how to work with it.

The magical aspect is being able to take a walk in the local forest or mountain and pick up ingredients as you go along. As you learn more about wild plants you are able to create more intricate and complex brews.

For me, the process of making wild beers usually starts in the environment itself. Each location has a unique flora with countless scents and flavors. In winter, the forest offers musky fragrances from rotten leaves, decomposing wood, and various mushrooms, but it also imparts some grassy and earthy qualities. I like to visit the mountains in spring or summer, when the California sun releases the pine and juniper essences.

Whatever location you may choose, the inspiration is always right there. I often tell people to think of the environment as a giant gourmet store that nature has gifted to you. At first, when you explore the shelves, many of the ingredients may be unknown to you, but as you read their "labels" you will gain more and more knowledge of what they are and what you can do with them.

You don't need to know a lot to get started with primitive brewing. In the old days, many primitive beers were made with common and easily identifiable herbs such as nettle, elderflower, ginger, dandelion, and horehound. Some beers were medicinal (nettle beer is high in vitamin C), while others were brewed for their psychotropic effects.

From a culinary perspective, wild beers have numerous uses. While you can enjoy them as is, they also provide a wide array of flavors for cocktails, cooking, or even pickling. Once you know how to make wild beers, you can also create interesting ingredients such as wild vinegars.

Wild vinegars, in turn, can be used to create other condiments such as mustards, sauces, marinades, and so forth. Being able to create truly unique and interesting wild-sourced products is another exciting aspect of primitive brewing. For example, my wild mustard is made with foraged black mustard seeds, mugwort beer vinegar, homemade salt from seawater, and elderberry wine. Try to buy something like that at the store!

The condiments you create become a true reflection of your local terroir and the seasons. And, from my perspective, that's what local drinks and food should be.

My journey into making wild beers started many years ago, when I learned about the very aromatic plant called mugwort. I was researching the potential culinary and medicinal properties of that herb when an article mentioned its use long ago as a main flavoring ingredient in brewing.

Interestingly enough, the implication is right there in its common name:

Wort: *A plant or herb used medicinally.*
The sweet infusion of ground malt or other grain before fermentation, used to produce beer and distilled malt liquors.
Mug: *A large cup, typically cylindrical and with a handle.*

So we are talking about a plant infused for a mug.

The more I researched mugwort, the more I became completely fascinated with the possibility of making my own brews with wild plants.

There are numerous websites and books on this subject, but if you want to venture into creating wild beers, the book *Sacred and Herbal Healing Beers* by Stephen Harrod Buhner is your best reference. I consider this the bible of wild brewing.

While I started with recipes from that book and from other sources, over the years and through experimentation I created my own formulas or refined existing recipes to fit the local flavors. A plant growing in California under specific growing conditions and soil will have different flavors than it would if it were grown in New York State. Like wine, the taste of primitive beers will reflect the plants' terroir. Our local mugwort, whose botanical name is *Artemisia douglasiana*, has a different aroma and flavors than its relative *Artemisia vulgaris*.

Presently my favorite approach is to create my beers using seasonal ingredients or the whole ecosystem—it's a very dynamic process. A winter beer made with forest components will taste completely different than a summer beer because I'm dealing with very distinct plants. And that's the whole point: being able to capture the essence of each season, the true flavors of the moment.

Unlike commercial beers, which are designed for very specific uniform criteria (carbonation, flavors, alcohol content, and so forth), primitive beers are much more wild and alive. Like the plants they come from, they continue to evolve and mature. A young beer, which is great for cooking, will be more sugary with lower alcohol content; an aged beer may be more sour and alcoholic. With experience, you learn to play with these parameters to achieve the result you want.

Debunking the Myth—Making Beer Is Very Easy!

Primitive beers are . . . well . . . primitive, and that's a good thing.

Beers have been made for millennia. Early brews were made before people had any concept of hygiene or knew what bacteria and yeast were. If you are a novice and seek information online, such as on brewing forums, beermaking will seem at first to be a confusing and daunting task. Basic brewing kits are usually composed of over 15 items, and you'll need to familiarize yourself with all kinds of exotic equipment and terms, like *hydrometer*, *specific gravity*, *mash pH*, *oxygen wash*, *iodine sanitizer*, *priming*, *cappers*, and so on.

Forget all that for now and let's go back to the basics, the way beers were originally made in the Western world and are still made in the deep jungle of the Amazon or in Africa. The biggest surprise that people have when they attend my workshops on making primitive beer is how easy it is to do. The second surprise is how delicious some of the beers are.

All you *really* need to make primitive beers is plant(s) + water + sugar + yeast.

That's it! And all the equipment you need is already in your kitchen. The only special equipment I advise people to purchase are an airlock, to monitor the fermentation process, and swing-top bottles for storing the beer. I'll explain their functions in the basic beermaking procedure, below.

Each of the ingredients necessary for beermaking already exists in the environment. Our job is simply to combine them properly so nature can do its magical work. Sugar can be found in various natural sources, such as sugarcane, sugar beets, fruit molasses, tree sap (maples, birch, box elder, sycamore, etc.), and even insect excretions (honey, lerp sugar). Yeast is present everywhere, including in the air you're breathing right now, but can be found in larger quantity on various plants, flowers, and berries. (See the section on harvesting wild yeast on page 79.)

So, now that the preliminaries are over, let's make some beer!

BREWING WILD BEERS: THE BASIC PROCEDURE

The simplicity of this process is what surprises people the most. You basically combine plants, sugar, and water and then add yeast. It's not very different from making tea.

Ingredients and equipment

Plants/ingredients as indicated in the recipe

1 gallon (3.75 l) springwater or distilled water (not tap water)

Brown sugar or other type of sugar, as specified in the recipe

Yeast

Large pot with lid

1-gallon (3.75 l) bottle with airlock

Sieve

Funnels (one small and one large)

Swing-top bottles (at least seven 16-ounce bottles [375 ml total capacity] for a 1-gallon batch of beer)

Measuring spoon

Scale

Small quantity of white or brown sugar

Procedure

1. Gather the ingredients you will use to make the beer. Weigh the ingredients according to the recipe you're using.
2. Place the ingredients into a pot and bring to a boil for the length of time indicated in the recipe.
3. Place the pot into a pan of cold water to cool the solution to a lukewarm temperature, around 70°F (21°C). Keep the lid on the pot to make sure airborne bacteria or insects such as flies don't infect your brew. Placing ice in the cooling water will speed up the cooling process. Change the water as necessary to cool down the liquid faster.
4. Once the solution has cooled, pour the liquid through a sieve and funnel into your main fermenter (bottle or fermenting bucket).
5. Add the yeast. Note that you can also add the yeast into the cooled solution before you pour it into the fermenter.
6. Place a clean airlock into a rubber or plastic stopper on top of the fermenter. Fill the airlock with water up to the lines indicated on the airlock. (Some people use vodka to fill the airlock.)
7. Within 24 hours the fermentation should be active—you will see froth forming on top of the liquid and bubbles moving up in the airlock.
8. Let the beer ferment for the amount of time indicated in the recipe. Then, using a funnel, pour the contents into swing-top bottles. Both the bottles and the funnel should be thoroughly cleaned before use.
9. Fill the bottles until the liquid reaches the base of the neck. When done, prime each bottle with ½ teaspoon (2 g) of regular white or brown sugar. Close the top and wait 5 to 6 weeks, then enjoy!

Step 1

Step 2

Step 3

Step 4

Step 5

Step 6

Step 7

Step 8

Step 9

ARE THOSE REAL BEERS?

In his book *Eating Your Words*, William Grimes gives this straightforward definition of beer: "An alcoholic drink made from yeast-fermented malt flavored with hops." So if you are a purist, you may have other names for my wild fermented beverages, such as herbal brews or gruits. But if you study the history of beer you'll realize that this narrow and culturally accepted definition of beer has more to do with monopolies, profits, and taxes than a respect for tradition.

Historically, a brew fermented with hops and malt was just one of the countless combinations that could be made with plants.

Call me an anarchist brewer if you want, but I define beer in terms of practicality. If it tastes like a beer, I call it a beer. If the flavor is more similar to a cider, I will call it a cider. I like the simplicity of this, and so far my descriptions have been favorably accepted by people who have tasted my fermented concoctions.

DO I NEED AN AIRLOCK?

An airlock is a practical little device that you place on your fermenter and fill with water (some people use vodka because it is antibacterial). It allows the carbon dioxide (CO_2) produced by the fermentation to escape, without allowing airborne bacteria or insects to enter the fermenter and infect your brew.

Using an airlock isn't a must, however; you can use a clean paper towel or cheesecloth tied up on top of your fermenter instead.

I like to watch the CO_2 bubbles going through the liquid in the airlock, though; it tells me how active the fermentation is, which can be useful when making wild sodas.

WHY SWING-TOP BOTTLES?

Wild brews can have higher carbonation than regular beers. If the pressure is too intense, a regular capped beer bottle can explode. Swing-top bottles are designed to release the pressure if it becomes excessive. Based on experience and broken bottles, I strongly advise people to use swing-top bottles for wild fermented beverages.

NATURAL CARBONATION

Even after the initial fermentation, your beer is still alive and fermenting once you bottle it. The natural carbonation of your beer or cider is achieved by the CO_2 pressure released by the yeast eating the sugar. With enough pressure, the CO_2 is absorbed into the liquid. That's why we add a bit of sugar before sealing the bottle: It's to ensure the fermentation process kicks off again with just enough sugar so that we get a nice carbonation inside the bottle.

With wild beers, the carbonation inside the bottles will vary depending on several factors, such as the plants used, storage temperature, the type of sugar, and even the seasons. As with champagne, never point the bottles toward people when you open them. I usually place my left hand on top of the bottle, push down, and open the swing top slowly. If there is excessive pressure and carbonation, you can release it bit by bit with your hand.

YEAST

You can use either commercial yeasts or wild yeasts.

To start with, I would advise you use commercial yeast, which can either be bought online or at your local homebrewing supply store. I usually use basic ale yeast such as Lallemand Nottingham Ale Yeast. However, there are numerous types of yeasts and each one can impart some slightly different flavors.

As you gain experience with making your own wild beers, you can begin experimenting with wild yeasts (see The Quest for Wild Yeasts on page 79).

Do not use bread yeast unless you want your beer to taste like bread.

BROWN SUGAR VERSUS WHITE SUGAR AND MOLASSES

In general, for beermaking I use brown sugar, molasses, and various wild syrups such as maple and birch; I use white sugar for making cider, champagne, and wine. Honey is used to make mead.

I also brew with all kinds of other sugars, such as cactus pear syrup, fruit molasses, and lerp sugar; for some recipes I may use several types of sugar for flavoring. I don't categorize these brews as either beer or wine. They're simply fermented drinks—but if a certain brew tastes like a beer, I may call it a beer.

HYGIENE

Hygiene is very important when you are making fermented drinks of any kind. You don't want unwanted bacteria or insects to infect your brew. I used to buy all kinds of products to sterilize my utensils as I was making the beer. These days I simply use dish soap and hot water. In the last five years I've never had a beer go bad.

I like to clean and sterilize my bottles when I reuse them by placing them in a bleach solution for a couple of minutes (use 1 tablespoon [20 g] of bleach per gallon) and rinsing them several times (at least three times) with very hot water. Some people like to let the empty bottles or fermenter sit for at least an hour after rinsing out the bleach and rinse water.

Which Plants Can I Use?

As you learn about plants and their potential brewing uses, you will be able to create countless wild fermented beverages. Some, such as nettle beer, can be made for medicinal purposes (nettle beer contains a high concentration of vitamin C and was once used as a remedy for scurvy); others can be made specifically for their high alcohol content or for their delightful flavors. Many of the beers I make are intended for culinary uses only, as I incorporate the beer into cooking and into making jams, vinegars, and sauces.

And I keep discovering new plants each year.

SOME OF THE PLANTS AND INGREDIENTS TRADITIONALLY USED IN BEERS INCLUDE:

Myrica gale	Nettle
Yarrow	Dandelion
Wild rosemary	Ginger
Wormwood	Horehound
Yarrow	Coriander
Sages (I use many local wild sages)	Mugwort
	Saint-John's-wort
Juniper	Borage
Birch	Elder (elderflower
Maple	and elderberry)
Pine	Caraway
Fir	Dock
Oak	Mint

BASED ON MY FORAGING EXPERIENCE AND RESEARCH IN THE LOCAL TERROIR, I HAVE ADDED THESE LOCAL PLANTS TO MY BREWING REPERTOIRE:

Local sages (white, purple, and black sage)	California fan palm fruits
	Wild cherry
California sagebrush	Mexican elder (elderflower
Kelp	and elderberry)
Various oak barks	Passion fruit
Yerba santa	Toyon
Prickly pear cactus	Currants
Tree leaves (willow, cottonwood, etc.)	White fir
	Various local pines
Mushrooms (turkey tail and candy cap)	Mormon tea
	Rose hips
Manzanita berries	Wild grass
Lemonade berries	Several types of
Figs	local mints

MUGWORT-LEMON BEER

This is a very basic recipe that I've used for many years—in fact, it was the first beer I made, and it hooked me to experiment much more with wild brews. The flavor is between a beer and a cider. I use this recipe all the time in my brewing workshop as it is the perfect example of how tasty and delicious a wild brew can be.

Ingredients

1 gallon (3.75 l) springwater or distilled water

0.3 ounce (around 8 g) dried mugwort leaves

1¼ pounds (577 g) dark brown sugar

3 large lemons

Yeast (beer yeast or wild yeast)

Procedure

1. Mix the water, mugwort, and brown sugar in a large pot. Cut and squeeze the lemons into the pot. Bring the solution to a boil; let it boil for 30 minutes.
2. Place the pot into a pan of cold water; cool to 70°F (21°C), then add the yeast. One bag of commercial yeast is usually enough for 5 gallons, so you don't need to use the entire contents of the bag. Just use around one-fifth of the bag.
3. Strain the brew into your fermenter. Position the airlock or cover your fermenter with a paper towel or cheesecloth. Let the brew ferment for 10 days.
4. Siphon into beer bottles and prime the bottles with ½ teaspoon (2 g) of brown sugar for carbonation. Close the bottles and store somewhere not too hot. The beer will be ready to drink in 3 to 4 weeks. I usually wait at least 7 or 8 weeks, however, for better taste and carbonation.

WHITE SAGE–LIME CIDER

This is one of my favorite recipes; the taste is akin to a nice light cider with some sage flavors. It's great to drink but also a fantastic brew to cook seafood, such as mussels and clams.

For cooking, I usually substitute lemons for limes in the recipe.

Ingredients

1 gallon (3.75 l) springwater or distilled water
0.15 ounce (around 4 g) dried white sage leaves
1¼ pounds (577 g) light brown sugar
3 large limes
Yeast (beer yeast or wild yeast)

Procedure

1. Mix the water, sage, and brown sugar in a large pot. Cut and squeeze the limes into the pot. Bring the solution to a boil; let it boil for 30 minutes.
2. Place the pot into a pan of cold water; cool to 70°F (21°C), then add the yeast. One bag of commercial yeast is usually enough for 5 gallons, so you don't need to use the entire contents of the bag. Just use around one-fifth of the bag.
3. Strain the brew into the fermenter. Position the airlock or cover your fermenter with a paper towel or cheesecloth. Let the brew ferment for 10 days. (See note below.)
4. Siphon into beer bottles and prime the bottles with ½ teaspoon (2 g) brown sugar for carbonation. Close the bottles and store somewhere not too hot. The cider will be ready to drink in 3 to 4 weeks. I usually wait at least 7 or 8 weeks, however, for better taste and carbonation.

Note: The fermentation speed will vary quite considerably depending on the season, soil composition where your ingredients grew, and other factors. Wild sages are quite peculiar sometimes. It's a bit of an advanced fermentation; it takes some experience to determine when exactly to bottle the brew and the length of fermentation after bottling. I've had cases of above-average carbonation in the bottles, and have experienced below-average carbonation as well, despite following the same exact recipe.

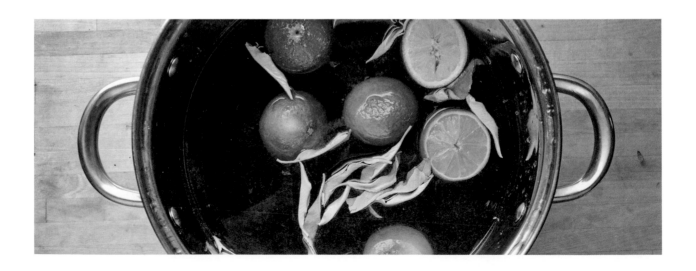

CANDY CAP MUSHROOM BEER

This is a strong-tasting brew suited for drinking in small amounts or creating cocktails. You can cut the amount of candy cap mushrooms to ½ ounce (21 g) or even less in order to make a more mild-tasting beer.

Ingredients

1 gallon (3.75 l) springwater or distilled water

1 ounce (42 g) candy cap mushrooms

¼ cup (55 g) dried elderberries

0.3 ounce (around 8 g) dried mugwort leaves

¾ pound (340 g) dark brown sugar

4 ounces (120 ml) molasses

4 ounces (120 ml) maple syrup

2 sweet lemons

Yeast (beer yeast or wild yeast)

Procedure

1. Mix the water, mushrooms, elderberries, mugwort, brown sugar, molasses, and maple syrup in a large pot. Cut and squeeze the lemons into the solution. Bring the solution to a boil; let it boil for 30 minutes.

2. Place the pot into a pan of cold water; cool to 70°F (21°C), then add the yeast. One bag of commercial yeast is usually enough for 5 gallons, so you don't need to use the entire contents of the bag. Just use around one-fifth of the bag.

3. Strain the brew into the fermenter. Position the airlock or cover your fermenter with a paper towel or cheesecloth. Let the brew ferment for 12 days.

4. Siphon into beer bottles and prime the bottles with ½ teaspoon (2 g) brown sugar for carbonation. Close the bottles and store somewhere not too hot. The beer will be ready to drink in 3 to 4 weeks. I usually wait at least 7 or 8 weeks, however, for better taste and carbonation.

BASIC MUGWORT BEER

This basic recipe uses molasses or maple syrup and doesn't include lemons. It creates a darker beer with less fruity accents than the mugwort-lemon beer. It is loosely based on a recipe found in the book *Sacred and Herbal Healing Beers* by Stephen Harrod Buhner; I adapted the proportions to the flavors of my native mugwort.

Ingredients

1 gallon (3.75 l) springwater or distilled water
0.3 ounce (around 8 g) dried mugwort leaves
¾ pound (340 g) dark brown sugar
4 ounces (120 ml) molasses or maple syrup
Yeast (beer yeast or wild yeast)

Procedure

Use the same procedure as for Mugwort-Lemon Beer (page 65).

HOREHOUND AND CALIFORNIA SAGEBRUSH BEER (BITTER BEER)

This is quite a bitter beer; feel free to tweak the ingredients in future recipes after tasting it.

Ingredients

1 gallon (3.75 l) springwater or distilled water
0.1 ounce (3 g) dried horehound
1¼ pounds (577 g) dark brown sugar
0.05 ounce (around 2 g) dried
    California sagebrush
3 lemons
Yeast (beer yeast or wild yeast)

Procedure

Use the same procedure as for Mugwort-Lemon Beer (page 65).

STINGING NETTLE BEER

This is mostly a medicinal beer meant to give you a nice boost of vitamin C.

Ingredients

1 gallon (3.75 l) springwater or distilled water
1 pound (450 g) young stinging nettles
¼ ounce (7 g) gingerroot, chopped roughly
1 ounce (28 g) cream of tartar
1 pound (450 g) light brown sugar
3–4 lemons
Yeast (beer yeast or wild yeast)

Procedure

Use the same procedure as for Mugwort-Lemon Beer (page 65), but ferment for only 3 to 4 days in a warm place before bottling. Drink after 7 to 10 days.

Drink the Forest

What does the forest taste like?

A couple of years ago I started experimenting with creating wild primitive brews using foraged ingredients from the forest.

As I explained in the beginning of this chapter, my inspiration came while foraging after a couple of rainy days. The whole forest had this incredible winter "perfume" emanating from the countless plants, trees, mushrooms, and leaves decomposing on the ground. It was like smelling the wilderness itself, and I was inspired to try recreating the experience from a culinary perspective.

I started introducing forest ingredients into my cooking and I really liked some of the results. But as I was exploring native and primitive brews, I became fascinated with using some of the same ingredients in my fermentations.

Forests—and even other whole environments or biomes, such as the mountains or the local chaparral—are really an endless source of flavors. Sometimes it takes a lot of research to make sure you can use the various elements safely, but as you have more and more ingredients to play with, it is truly a worthwhile activity. Originally I started with less than ten ingredients; today I'm probably able to combine over one hundred various ingredients ranging from grass, leaves, and mushrooms to bark, berries, aromatic plants, seeds, and even insects.

Do these brews really taste like the forest?

Yes and no. If you smell some of my concoctions you'll know where they come from. It's much easier with the mountains, where you have very distinctive aromas, such as pine. In my opinion a regular forest is a much more complex environment. Through fermentation flavors are often altered, sometimes for better and sometimes for worse. You'll have to discover that for yourself through experimentation.

Presently my "forest brews" are more closely related to Belgian sour beers; very often they end up tasting somewhere between a beer and a cider. They're not something you want to drink in quantity, like regular beers; still, based on the feedback I've received, they're quite enjoyable. Some of them are fantastic for cooking.

The recipes and flavors are always changing with the seasons too. Some plants, such as mugwort, will have a stronger flavor once the plant has set seeds. In summer the dry mugwort leaves that are foraged in the shade will have tons of character, even though those same leaves are pretty much tasteless if foraged in the sun. The last beer I made with seasonal forest ingredients had interesting accents of grapefruit, although none was present in the recipe. There are always surprises, and as I continue experimenting and tweaking recipes I'm able to have more good ones instead of failed attempts.

It's really a work in progress and you could probably spend your whole life experimenting with wild brews. Who knows? Maybe one day I'll open a bottle and, amid the esters and alcohol aromas, I'll get a hint of the forest that inspired me that long-ago winter.

WINTER IN THE FOREST BEER

This recipe is ever changing with the season, but is a good example of a winter forest beer I made. The end result was somewhere between a beer and a cider, a bit sour like some wild-yeast-fermented Belgian beers, but delicious.

Ingredients

1 gallon (3.75 l) springwater or
   distilled water
0.2 ounce (around 3 g) mixed fall leaves
   (cottonwood, alder, and willow)
0.2 ounce (around 3 g) forest grass (basic
   grass growing in the forest)
1 ounce (28 g) manzanita berries
0.1 ounce (1.5 g) California sagebrush
0.2 ounce (around 3 g) dried
   mugwort leaves
0.3 ounce (around 8.5 g) turkey
   tail mushrooms
1¼ pounds (680 g) dark brown sugar
3 lemons
Yeast

Procedure

1. Mix the water with all of your foraged ingredients and brown sugar in a large pot. Cut and squeeze three lemons into the pot. Bring the solution to a boil; let it boil for 30 minutes.
2. Place the pot into a pan of cold water; cool to 70°F (21°C), then add the yeast. One bag of commercial yeast is usually enough for 5 gallons, so you don't need to use the entire contents of the bag. Just use around one-fifth of the bag.
3. Strain into the fermenter. Position the airlock or cover your fermenter with a paper towel or cheesecloth and let the brew ferment for 10 days.
4. Siphon into swing-top bottles and prime the bottles with ½ teaspoon (2 g) of brown sugar. Close the bottles and store somewhere not too hot. The beer will be ready to drink in 3 to 4 weeks.

Creating Other Wild Blends for Beers

Forests, mountains, chaparrals, and deserts are infinite resources for creating unique blends.

I have created some very interesting and flavorful local mountain beers using various combination of ingredients such as white fir, roasted white oak bark, pine needles, mugwort, juniper berries, giant nettles, yarrow, sagebrush, currant leaves, mushrooms, and manzanita berries.

Our local chaparral has numerous aromatic plants, such as white sage, black sage, sagebrush, purple sage, and yerba santa, and interesting berries such as toyon, various currants, wild cherries, and lemonade berries.

I have yet to play with the local desert and plants from the coastal area, but I know there are beers currently on the market that include seaweed as one of the ingredients. One, appropriately named Kelpie, is brewed in Scotland by the Williams Brothers Brewing Company.

I don't really follow brewing recipes anymore but instead I create as the seasons change. My last beer was made with mugwort, lemons, and elderflowers. The next one will feature mugwort, elderberries, and maybe a tad of yarrow and mountain native currant leaves.

If I do very experimental blends and I'm not sure what the results might be, I use half-gallon bottles and economize on sugar and other ingredients.

Imagination is really the only limit to your creativity, but please be cautioned: *You must be certain about the identity and properties of the plants you are using.* Be sure to thoroughly research so you will understand all the various aspects of each plant—from culinary to medicinal.

For instance, while brewing with willow and cottonwood leaves is fine, before serving you may want to ask if anyone is allergic to aspirin (which was originally made from willow bark). Granted, there is likely to be a negligible amount of willow in a glass of the brew, but you're always better safe than sorry. Don't just think you will incorporate any leaves or other plant matter if you don't know what it is—that beautiful red leaf could be poison oak. You need certainty and knowledge.

As a general rule, I also don't serve wild beers to anyone who is pregnant (and, needless to say, anyone who is underage). Within these parameters, you can create and have fun with an infinite variety of flavors!

Wild brew using foraged ants for flavor.

INSECT INGREDIENTS IN BEERS

There are no exact boundaries if you arc on a quest to capture the true flavors of a local terroir, and you would be limiting yourself if you only research and use herbs.

As I mentioned earlier, barks and leaves can become very tasty ingredients. So can insects and their offerings. For example, honey is a product created by bees, and each batch of honey can be vastly different based on the local flora.

If I make a shrub (a vinegar-based drink) with plants from the local mountains, I always try to use honey that comes from the same location so the shrub is a true representation of that environment.

Insects themselves can have very interesting flavors. We have served local ants in many of our dishes; some actually taste like lemons and others even have floral qualities.

For a long time, I have been intrigued with the idea of actually using insects in some of the wild drinks I create. Last year I started experimenting with the concept by using crushed ants, with excellent results.

Then I decided to take it a bit further—I tried brewing my first beer using ants for flavors and some local lerp sugar for the fermentation. It's not something I intend to make often, mainly because the amount of time necessary to forage the ingredients makes it impractical. Foraging enough ants (2,000 or so) and enough lerp sugar takes the better part of 2 days!

On the other hand, there was something deeply satisfying about the concept that, in theory, a person could simply forage the wilderness and find all the ingredients necessary to create a tasty brew from scratch, including the yeast. This is a true wild beer!

Procedure

This recipe continues to be a work in progress, but essentially I went out on a foraging hike in mid-June and collected seasonal ingredients suitable for a good simple brew. I ended up with a decent amount of mugwort and an abundance of elderflowers.

First I made an elderflower cordial (see the Elderflower Cordial recipe on page 208) using the following ingredients:

¾ pound (340 g) brown sugar (less than a traditional cordial recipe)
1 gallon (3.75 l) springwater or distilled water
2 lemons, juiced
80 Mexican elderflower heads (use 30 flower heads with regular elders—Mexican elders have smaller flowers)
⅓ cup (55 g) citric acid

I let the solution sit in the garage (where the temperature wasn't too hot) for a couple of days, then I filtered everything.

My next step was to add the following ingredients:

2 cups (160 g) lerp sugar
2,000 crushed lemon ants (foraged from local eucalyptus trees)
0.2 ounce (around 3 g) mugwort and a tiny bit of yarrow leaves (3–5 leaves)

I brought the solution to a boil for 20 to 30 minutes. Then I followed with the usual procedure (cool down the liquid, add yeast, ferment for 10 days, and bottle).

The result was a floral and sour beer that was quite delicious. And, yes, the insect ingredients did make a difference in taste as compared with a regular elderflower and mugwort beer.

Next time I'll follow this same recipe but will add ½ pound (240 g) of brown sugar or an additional 2 cups (160 g) of lerp sugar to make it less sour.

This "ants" beer was used by renowned mixologist Matthew Biancaniello as the basis for a cocktail he created recently.

Primitive Herbal Meads

Mead is basically a kind of wine that is fermented using honey. Due to its simplicity, it's probably one of the oldest drinks known to mankind. It goes back to the fundamentals; all you need is raw honey, water, and plants. Raw honey contains the wild yeast necessary to get fermentation going. It's easy to imagine that the first brew could have been made by accident: just a bit of honey left in a pot, a bit of rain, and within a couple of weeks you could have a delicious boozy beverage.

As with beermaking, though, making mead can be more complex and elaborate. Again, whole books have been written on this subject, and maybe one day I'll delve much deeper into mead-making myself. But for now, I'm very happy with my simple recipes (which are a good start if you want to learn more).

For making my primitive meads, I don't use purchased yeast but rely upon the wild yeast present in the raw honey. This type of yeast usually won't allow for a higher alcohol percentage than 4 to 5 percent. This is important to know if you want to make a drier or sweeter style of mead.

Before going into details about making a primitive mead, let's first do some rough calculations. If we assume that you will be using the wild yeasts from the honey itself and letting the fermentation of your mead go all the way to completion (which can take months), roughly 1 pound of honey (a bit more than 1½ cups or 355 ml) mixed with 1 gallon of water (3.75 l) will give you around 4 to 5 percent alcohol. If you make mead using 1 gallon (3.75 l) of water and 2 cups (473 g) of honey, the yeast will convert most of the sugar and your mead will end up somewhat dry. Following the same principle, if you use 3 cups of honey (710 ml), your mead will end up somewhat sweet, and if you use 4 cups (946 ml) it will be very sweet. It's important to know this if, like me, you enjoy your mead a bit on the sweeter side.

In terms of how long you should ferment your mead, from my perspective there are no hard-and-fast rules. You can enjoy your mead quite young or fully fermented; it's all about having the flavors you like. Some of my meads were fantastic after only 1 to 3 weeks of fermentation, but ended up being rather tasteless after a year. One of my favorite meads, which I only aged for 2 weeks, was made was using lemon balm; it was still quite sweet, and the flavors were outstanding. Presently I mostly brew young meads, although I have a couple that have been aging for more than a year.

Mint and lemon herbal mead.

FRESH MINT AND LEMON HERBAL MEAD

If you've never made mead, let's start with a simple concoction using mint and lemons. I usually use local wild mints (we have at least seven species of mint in Southern California), but you can also purchase some mint at your local store or grow your own. We'll look at a couple of methods to make it. This mead is best enjoyed young and, as such, it is pleasantly sweet, but you might experiment with aging it as well. You need to use raw honey for this recipe; pasteurized honey does not contain live yeast.

Ingredients

13 cups (around 3 l) springwater or distilled water (don't use tap water)
2–3 cups (0.45–0.7 l) raw honey
2–3 large bunches mint
4 lemons

Procedure

1. Thoroughly clean the lemons, mint, and every utensil and jar you are going to use to make your mead. Mix the water and raw honey in a large jar or plastic food-grade container. Stir until the honey is dissolved.
2. Roughly chop the mint and slice the lemons. Place everything in the water-and-honey solution. Stir one more time to make sure everything is well mixed, then cover with a clean paper towel or cloth and wrap tightly with a rubber band or string.
3. Stir the mead three or four times a day: Remove the cover and use a clean spoon to mix everything for 10 to 20 seconds. This helps activate the wild yeast in the solution and, from my experience, speeds up fermentation and avoids potential spoiling. (Each time I mix I clean the spoon with regular soap and water to remove any bacteria.) Cover the jar after stirring.
4. Depending on the temperature and the willingness of the local fermentation gods, in 3 to 5 days you should see some bubbling. This means fermentation is active. Smell the brew as an added assurance—a healthy fermentation does not smell bad. Another indication that fermentation is active is the fact that your ingredients (mint and lemon rings) will float on the surface because of the large amount of bubbles in the mix.
5. Using a clean sieve and funnel, strain the solution into a 1-gallon (3.75 l) jug. Again, make sure you clean your sieve and funnel properly so you don't introduce unwanted bacteria into your mead. I use regular dish soap with hot water and so far have never experienced any problems.
6. Position the airlock (see the procedure for making beer on page 60) or cover the jug with a paper towel or cheesecloth wrapped tightly with a rubber band or string. Wait 2 to 3 weeks before enjoying.

Step 2

Step 3

Step 4

Step 5

Step 6

Boiling to Extract Flavors

Some wild ingredients such as mugwort, yarrow, and mushrooms may require boiling to extract the flavors for brewing. The procedure is very similar to the steps used in beermaking:

Procedure

1. Boil the water and plant ingredients in a pot for 15 to 20 minutes. Place the hot pot in a pan of cold water to cool (adding ice to the pan helps to speed this process). To protect the brew from unwanted bacteria, keep the lid on while cooling the pot.
2. Once the solution is lukewarm, pour it into a glass or plastic food-grade container, add raw honey (which contains wild yeast), and stir until the honey is dissolved. Then cover with a clean paper towel, kitchen towel, or cheesecloth. Use a string to tie it up nicely so insects or unwanted bacteria don't get in.
3. Remove the cover three or four times a day and stir the mixture with a clean spoon for 10 to 20 seconds. Depending on the temperature, after 3 to 5 days you should see some bubbling, indicating that fermentation is active.
4. Using a sieve and funnel, strain the solution into a 1-gallon (3.75 l) jug. Position an airlock or cover the jug with a clean paper towel or a cloth wrapped tightly with a rubber band or string. Wait 3 weeks before enjoying.

Once you've played around with these simple primitive meads and built up your brewing confidence, do some research, look at various recipes, and start experimenting with creating more elaborate concoctions and aging meads.

Mugwort (*Artemisia douglasiana*).

The Quest for Wild Yeasts

Many people don't realize it, but yeast spores are present everywhere. We find them in the air we breathe; in plants, flowers, fruits, and soil; and even on our own skin. There are over 1,500 types recorded so far, but probably thousands more can be found in the wild waiting to be discovered and recorded.

The fascinating thing about these microscopic fungi is the fact that they have the wonderful capability of converting sugar into alcohol and carbon dioxide. In fact the origin of the word *yeast* comes from the Old English *gist* and Old High German *jesen* or *gesen*, meaning "to ferment."

Since the dawn of humanity, people have enjoyed a deep relationship with yeasts. The first evidence of beer-making was found in present-day Iran on jug fragments that were at least five thousand years old. And based on hieroglyphs we know the Egyptians made leavened breads using wild yeasts (sourdough) around 1000 B.C.E.

Considering that the simple action of mixing raw honey (which contains a lot of wild yeasts) with water can create a natural fermentation within 3 or 4 days, it is highly probable that fermented drinks existed in prehistoric times.

Until the articulation of modern scientific concepts, the wonder of a liquid transforming itself into a magical solution capable of altering your senses was seen as divine intervention, often the domain of shamans and priests. In many cultures alcohol was a gift of the gods: Songs were written praising its virtues, and divinities such as Dionysus and Bacchus, gods of the grape harvest and winemaking, were worshipped.

Primitive societies had many rituals revolving around this miraculous transformation. Some had rites that called for dances, chants, and noisemaking to attract the spirits so they could inoculate the brew, while in other cultures calm and silence were the norms so as to not scare the spirits away

The creation of wild brews could often be unpredictable. Such is the nature of wild yeasts, which are invisible, mysterious, and feral. At the same time the fermentations they create can be full of often delicious surprises.

Primitive beers or wines made with wild yeasts can have ever-changing qualities due to complex factors such as the seasons, location, and yeast sources (plants, berries, and so forth). While some people are nervous or disturbed by this lack of control, culinary adventurers see that same unpredictability as a blessing. Alcohol content, acidity, brightness, smoothness, and many other factors influencing the flavors will fluctuate in the same way nature does—sometimes unpredictably. It is a true reflection of a wild, untamed terroir.

The modern trend in making beers or wines is to use specific commercial yeast strains that provide desirable and predictable effects and results. For example, champagne yeast will allow you to make fermented beverages with a high alcohol content. Some yeast strains can also be chosen for the flavors they impart, their speed of fermentation, or their ability to withstand low temperatures.

The old trend (which, by the way, is becoming popular again) is to experiment with what nature has to offer.

Having grown up in Belgium, I've had the chance to experience the funky flavors of local farmhouse-type beers, which were made originally with wild yeasts. While you can now purchase commercially some more civilized versions of these beers, their origin was pretty wild.

Original farmhouse beers were humble brews designed to quench the thirst of farmworkers during the busy hot summer months. They were simply made with whatever grain was at hand (usually wheat or barley) and various spices (juniper berries, ginger, licorice, or coriander seeds, for example). Often these beers had a relatively low alcohol level so as to not inebriate the workers. Wild yeasts could be obtained from the environment—and, over time, from the actual location where the beer was being made, as the yeast naturalized in the brew room. And yeasts could also be sourced from the brewing ingredients themselves— for example, juniper berries and ginger are both good sources of wild yeasts.

Presently about 50 percent of my brews are made with wild yeasts. Late spring and summer are the best times to forage these microorganisms, as they are attracted to sugars and we have a lot of berries

Wild yeast starter made with juniper berries.

ripening in California during those seasons: elderberries, wild grapes, and juniper berries, to name a few.

As you experiment with wild yeasts, you'll realize that you may have to tweak your regular recipes. For example, my usual mugwort beer recipe uses 1¼ to 1½ pounds (567 to 680 g) of brown sugar per gallon. However, when I use wild yeasts I change the recipe and only use 1 pound (454 g) of sugar, because wild yeast does not survive in high alcohol concentrations; it usually dies off once the beer reaches 4 to 5 percent alcohol. Using my standard recipe, my wild-yeast brews tended to be too sugary because the yeasts died, and thus much of the sugar was not processed into alcohol.

The key to foraging wild yeast is to find it in enough quantity to make a good starter. A few times I've tried to make wild beers by placing some of my cooled herbal solution outside, in the hope that yeast spores present in the air would somehow decide to make a home in the solution. But I didn't experience any success with that method. After a few days, mold would form on the surface of the solution, and the smell became unpleasant enough that you would not want to risk drinking any of it.

Like anywhere in this world, it's a competition out there: All kinds of microorganisms are competing for survival. Even if a few yeast spores land in your brew, it may not be enough for them to win the battle against other organisms that would spoil it. The key is to find yeasts in enough quantity to actually give the yeasts an edge and help them take over.

If you decide to forage yeasts, you'll have the best chances with berries and fruits. They are usually loaded with sugar and often you will find a white bloom on the skin, similar to the bloom you see on organic grapes at the farmer's market. This bloom is mostly composed of yeasts. My local elderberries and juniper berries have a substantial amount of bloom, which helps a lot in making some good starter for my wild brews.

A lot of unwashed *organic* fruits (grapes, plums, apples, and peaches, for example) are also excellent sources of yeast.

HERE ARE SOME EXCELLENT SOURCES OF WILD YEASTS:

Juniper berries	Figs
Elderberries	Prickly cactus pears
Wild grapes	Tree barks, especially birch (*Betula* spp.)
Elderflowers	and aspen (*Populus tremuloides*)
Blueberries	Wildflowers
Blackberries	Raw honey

Wild yeast starter made with elderberries.

MAKING A STARTER

The idea with making a yeast starter is to create a solution where you increase dramatically the cell count of the yeast by feeding it with sugar before "pitching it" (placing it) into your brew. The large quantity of yeast pretty much insures a successful fermentation.

The method I presently use is almost 100 percent effective. Here are the steps:

Procedure

1. Make a sweet solution composed of 30% sugar and 70% springwater or distilled water. Don't use tap water, which may contain chlorine.
2. Place the solution into a clean bottle. Washing the bottle with soap and water before using works well, but pasteurizing the bottle by placing it in boiling water for 10 minutes or more will increase your chances of success. I can tell you from experience, though, this isn't a must.
3. Place your berries (or other foraged yeast sources) in the bottle with the sugar solution. I don't have a precise quantity, but it's usually around 20 percent of the solution or more.
4. You don't want insects or unwanted bacteria to contaminate your starter, but you need to let fermentation gases escape, so position an airlock on top of the bottle or tightly wrap a clean kitchen towel, paper towel, or cheesecloth around the top of the bottle.
5. Shake the bottle three or four times a day. In 4 to 5 days you will notice some bubbling in the solution. Congratulations, your fermentation is active. Just in case, I like to smell it too as added assurance. If it smells really bad, don't use it.
6. If you are making beer or wine, drop some of the fermenting starter into your cooled solution. I use around ⅓ cup (70 ml) of starter for 1 gallon of brew. From there, follow the beer- or winemaking recipe. If I see that fermentation starts more slowly, I may keep the brew in the main fermentation vessel for 12 to 14 days (instead of the usual 10 days) before bottling.

Cooking with Dirt, Sticks, Bark, Leaves, Sap, and Stones

In my world, opportunities for innovation abound and no good wild ingredient is deemed unusable. During my foraging trips I like to look for the unusual. Sometimes I even stop, sit for a little while, and, as an exercise, look around and try to find a new plant to research or a new element that I could explore as a food. The idea is to come up with something new to play with. For example, one weekend I picked up some oak twigs. I sat down for 20 minutes and started dreaming up what could be done with them . . . skewers? ice cube holders? tannic powder? primitive forks?

Often these musings go nowhere, but sometimes you can get some interesting ideas. This is how I came up with the concept of candying tree leaves and other interesting culinary applications for foraged foods.

Foragers should not feel limited to just picking up edible or aromatic leaves and tender plants; there are so many other interesting possibilities. For example, one easily overlooked wild food ingredient is stems. In the past, I just foraged the leaves of aromatic plants such as mugwort or California sagebrush for my spice blends; then one day I realized that the dried stems would make awesome skewers and infuse flavors into meat and vegetables when grilling meat pops and kebabs.

Now I use stems regularly for this purpose. I usually place the stem/skewer in my meats or vegetables, wrap the container with plastic food wrap, and leave it in the refrigerator overnight to let the stems' flavors infuse into the food. This method works well with tough stems and with small branches from California bay trees and mugwort. (Here's a tip: If you don't want to burn your stem, grill the meat with the stem pointing upward.)

Tender stems such as epazote or California sagebrush are usually inserted into the food just before grilling, as they would become too soft and limp if placed overnight into the meats or vegetables. I still have a lot of experimentation to do with this concept, but so far I've used stems from:

Mugwort
California sagebrush
White sage
Black sage
Epazote
California bay (small branches)
Yarrow
Wright's cudweed

Some stems or branches that do not have strong aromatic properties are nevertheless great for making chopsticks or Popsicle sticks. Cattail, oak, willow, and mulefat (*Baccharis salicifolia*) fall into this category.

White fir ice cream, fir sugar powder, coffee berries, candied willow, and cottonwood leaves.

CRUNCHY CANDIED TREE LEAVES

I always wanted to do something with tree leaves, but very often they're not palatable—they're either too bitter or too tough to eat. With this method you can turn many types of non-poisonous tree leaves into crunchy, sugary, and tasty dessert decorations. You must think ahead, though: This procedure takes 5 days from start to finish.

Ingredients

A few non-toxic tree leaves (willow, cottonwood, and others)
Water
½ teaspoon (3 g) salt
1¾ cups (350 g) sugar
Flavoring ingredients: lemon slices, a couple of fresh ginger chunks, wild aromatic herbs

Procedure

1. Wash the leaves and place them in a pot with the water. Add the salt and bring to a boil. Reduce the heat and simmer the leaves for 15 minutes. Change the water and repeat the procedure for another 15 minutes. This will remove most of the bitter taste in the leaves.
2. Drain the leaves. Add 3 cups (750 ml) water and the sugar to the pot. Heat the syrup solution to a boil, add the leaves, and bring to a light simmer. Cook for 20 minutes. Remove from the heat and let stand overnight.
3. Day 2: Bring the leaves and syrup to a boil. Turn the heat down and simmer lightly for 20 minutes. Remove from the heat and let stand overnight.
4. Day 3: Bring the leaves and syrup to a boil again. Turn the heat down and simmer lightly for 20 minutes. Remove from the heat and let stand overnight.
5. Day 4: This is the time to add ingredients such as lemon slices, ginger, and wild aromatic herbs to flavor the leaves. I usually add 3 to 4 lemon slices, a couple of ginger chunks, and a couple of white sage leaves to the syrup and then repeat the previous instructions: Bring the concoction to a boil, then simmer lightly for 20 minutes. Remove from the heat and let stand overnight.
6. Day 5: Preheat the oven to 340°F (171°C). Bring the leaves and syrup to a simmer and cook until the temperature reads 240°F (115°C).
7. Using a fork or spoon, carefully remove the leaves from the syrup, placing the leaves on a plate. Using a rubber spatula, remove excess syrup from the leaves and lay them carefully on a piece of parchment paper or a silicone baking pad.
8. Bake the leaves for 2 to 3 minutes, then remove them from the oven and place them on a fresh sheet of parchment paper. Let dry for 30 minutes. I usually use them the same day, but they should keep for days in dry conditions. Humidity will make them softer (not a good thing).

Foraging Wood, Bark, Twigs, and Aromatics for Grilling

If you love grilling, you are certain to know that various woods impart delicious smoky flavors to grilled meat, fish, and vegetables. Strong-tasting woods such as oak, mesquite, and hickory are traditionally used to grill meats such as bison, lamb, pork, and beef, while woods with more subtle profiles such as apple, maple, or cherry are used with game birds, fish, and poultry.

I've foraged specific woods and barks that I reduce into chips for local chefs and also for our own cooking, but my favorite application is to create custom "wild" grilling/smoking blends. When making the blends I'm not stuck with just using various woods and barks—I also like to add some local aromatic ingredients such as California juniper berries or twigs, dehydrated black sage, fennel seeds, and bay leaves.

In addition to the woody and aromatic ingredients, you can add another layer of flavors by infusing the wood chips or barks with beers, wines, or juices. Oak chips infused with elderberry wine add a nice fruity quality to the grill. Manzanita chips infused with mugwort beer impart intense aromatics and a hint of bitterness, a combination that I love with strong-flavored meats such as goat or lamb.

Woods, barks, aromatics (leaves, plants, and seeds), and the additional infusing step with wild brews have the potential to create so many subtle flavors for grilling and smoking that a whole book could be written on this subject alone.

THE LOCALLY FORAGED WOODS I USE FOR GRILLING AND SMOKING, ALONG WITH THEIR TASTE PROFILES:

Alder—sweet and musky
Ash—light flavor; good as a base with more flavorful woods
California bay—medium flavor, with a hint of bay
Cottonwood—neutral, good to use with more aromatic woods
Eucalyptus—strong flavor; I use it sparingly, since it can be overwhelming
Fig—mild and fruity
Manzanita—mild and fruity
Maple—medium-sweet flavors
Mesquite—strong and somewhat sweet flavors; use sparingly
Oak (wood and bark)—medium; good base for blending with other woods
Olive—medium flavor, with a hint of mesquite
Walnut—medium; a bit bitter
Willow—mild; a bit bitter

THE LOCAL WILD AROMATICS I USE INCLUDE:

Sages (black sage, white sage, purple sage, etc.) and some sagebrush
Epazote
Eucalyptus leaves
California juniper twigs and berries
Wright's cudweed
Sweet clover
California bay
Mugwort
Fennel seeds

USING A GRILLING/SMOKING BLEND

I'm not an experienced pit master; I have a simple and cheap charcoal grill, so I tend to keep my cooking quite primitive. However, this procedure works well on gas grills too, and you don't have to go through lighting the charcoal.

Procedure

First I prepare the smoking mix. Creating a good mix is a bit of an art form that you need to learn from experience. Some woods, such as mesquite or hickory, may have overwhelming flavors, so it's best to mix them with other woods. Spices include California juniper twigs and berries, Wright's cudweed, and fennel seeds.

I like to soak the chips in water for around 30 minutes before use. That way they won't burn right away on the hot coals. If I plan to soak some of my chips in wine or beers instead of water, I usually do so overnight.

When it comes time for grilling, I make the fire. At the bottom of the grill I place a few pinecones with dry materials, such as leaves, pine needles, and grass. Then I put good layer of store-bought hardwood charcoal over them. Cooking or smoking with pinecones is not a good idea because of their strong and acrid flavors, but by the time the charcoal is going nicely, the pinecones have been reduced to ashes and won't influence the flavors. I use pinecones at the base because they burn very nicely and are a good starter for the charcoal. Feel free to use other materials.

Once the fire is going, I usually wait around 20 to 30 minutes for the coals to turn white-hot. When the coals are ready, I either place the smoking mix directly on the white-hot coals or wrap the mix in aluminum foil, poke some holes into the package, and place it over the hot coals. The smoking lasts a bit longer using this method. This is also a great method for cooking on a gas grill.

As a rule of thumb I like to throw my blend onto the hot coals around 3 to 5 minutes before I place my food on the grill. If there is too much smoke, I may wait longer. It's a bit of an art and there are countless opinions about the right way to do it—too much smoke or the wrong blend and the flavors can easily become overpowering.

I like to lightly oil the food I plan to use so it doesn't stick to the grill. The cooking time will obviously depend on what you are grilling.

When starting to create with your own wild blends, don't use too much material to begin with and experiment a bit until you get it right and it's just the way you like it. Remember, it's all about flavors. If it tastes awesome, your blend was a success.

Choosing the Right Woods

Here are some of the common woods you can forage to use in grilling and smoking. Opinions vary on what constitutes a strong, medium, or mild wood, but this list will give you a good start.

STRONG WOODS:

Traditionally, strong-flavored woods such as mesquite, oak, maple, and hickory are mostly used in grilling lamb, beef, and pork. Personally, I consider oak a good medium-flavored base for blending with other highly aromatic woods (such as mesquite and hickory) and for grilling game birds or fish.

MEDIUM WOODS:

These woods don't have overwhelming flavors, like mesquite or hickory, but they still have a lot of character and specific flavor accents. Note that there are no real rules about what wood works best with what meat, fish, or poultry. Experiment and form your own opinion.

Acacia (a bit similar to mesquite)—good for meats and vegetables

Apple, pear, crab apple, manzanita (sweet and fruity)—good for everything, including curing meats

California bay (spicy)—good for meats (I have not tried it with fish or poultry yet)

Beech (like oak, a good base)—good for meats, fish, game birds, poultry, and vegetables

Birch (slight similarities to maple)—good for meat, fish, and poultry; try it with bacon too

Grape (fruity)—good with game birds and strong-flavored meats, such as lamb and goat

Juniper—medium strong, so mix with other woods; I love it with seafood

Maple (sweet and fruity)—I like this wood with everything; great for curing bacon, ham, and other meats

Mulberry—I haven't experimented with it yet, but it seems to have similarities to manzanita or apple wood

Olive—hints of mesquite; a fantastic wood in my opinion, good for everything

Walnut—somewhat strong and bitter, use sparingly with other woods; great with game meats

MILD WOODS:

These woods have mild and often subtle flavors. When creating a blend, any of these woods can provide a good base, and you can add some stronger woods for added flavors.

Alder—good for meats, fish, game birds, poultry, and vegetables

Almond (a bit sweet)—good for meats, fish, game birds, poultry, and vegetables

Avocado—good for meats, fish, game birds, poultry, and vegetables

Cherry (fruity and good for blending)—good for meats, fish, game birds, poultry, and vegetables

Cottonwood—quite a neutral flavor, in my opinion; use with other woods for flavors

Fig (mild and fruity)—I use fig often and for cooking everything; it makes a great base to combine with other woods

Lilac (mild, fruity, and spicy)—great with fish, poultry, and vegetables

Pecan/chestnut (mild, fruity)—good for meats, fish, game birds, poultry, and vegetables

Willow (mild and a tad bitter)—a great base to combine with stronger woods

OTHER WOODS THAT CAN BE USED:

Ash, orange, lemon, grapefruit, apricot, plum, peach, nectarine. Washed seaweed has been traditionally used in Europe for cooking/grilling shellfish.

NOT TO BE USED:

Fir, pine, spruce, cedar, redwood, cypress, elm, sycamore, sweet gum.

Although eucalyptus wood is not recommended in the United States, it is used in Australia for its distinctive flavors. I use it very sparingly.

Also note that, in France, a traditional dish called *éclade* features mussels cooked and smoked in pine needles. It's quite delicious.

Foraging Stones

There is so much that can be said about stones and rocks. Our skilled ancestors fashioned stones into countless tools and weapons. The most enduring and beautiful art pieces are made of stone, and even entire civilizations were built with them. Even today we're still in awe of the Great Pyramid of Cheops, the Great Wall of China, and the Acropolis in Greece. You could say that stone is the solid foundation upon which our world was built.

Stones are easily overlooked today, but as a forager I've learned to appreciate the deep connection they offer to nature and our own history. Although my kitchen has a lot of modern equipment, when dealing with wild food I often find myself going back to stones, and there are good reasons for it. Try breaking the shell of black walnuts or grinding dry acorns and wild spices into fine powder and you'll find out why a couple of high-end restaurants I work with bought primitive *molcajetes* (stone grinders). Sometimes modern equipment is not up to the task.

I'm not very good at carving rocks and I don't have the tools for it. Instead, during my foraging hikes, I'm always on the lookout for what nature already made for me, and I'm always extremely thankful for the gift. Here are some of the specific rocks I look for and their applications.

GRINDERS, MORTARS, AND PESTLES

It takes a bit of patience and luck, but with persistence you can find some perfect stones to create beautiful grinders and mortars. I probably have 12 of them at home that I use for my workshop on creating wild spice blends. Matchmaking is fun—I believe that for each grinder somewhere there is the perfect grinding stone, and part of the fun is creating a perfect set. You want the stones to be rough enough so you can crush and powder your spices or your dehydrated berries. I also have a dedicated black walnut and acorn shell stone-cracking setup. Don't be surprised if sometimes it looks like your chosen stone has been used before: I suspect that a couple of my grinders were actually used as such long ago by a fellow forager.

COOKING STONES

The best stones for cooking are somewhat large and very flat; they are usually no more than 1 inch (2.55 cm) thick. These are great for primitive cooking over coals or firewood. These kinds of stones are pretty rare where I live—I've only found a couple of perfect ones in the last two years.

WEIGHT STONES

I do a lot of fermenting in jars, and I'm always eager to find the perfect round stones that will fit nicely through the jar tops. These can be used to keep the fermenting ingredients under the brine and thus reduce the possibilities of spoiling. I pasteurize the stones before use by cleaning and boiling them for at least 15 minutes or placing them in a very hot oven (usually around 350°F/ 177°C) for the same amount of time. Once they have gone through a successful fermentation, a lot of *Lactobacillus* bacteria will be present on the surface of the stones, making them perfect starters for the next batch.

PLATING STONES

Small, flat stones make perfect wild food plates. Recently, a local sushi restaurant asked me to provide them with over 50 flat stones to plate some of their dishes. We often use some of my stone plates in our private dinners.

HEATING ROCKS

Cooking with heated rocks was practiced by local natives for the simple reason that clay or wood pots could not be heated over flames. The solution was to throw stones in the fire and use the heated stones to cook the food inside pots, bowls, or earthen pits.

As a nod to native cooking, we sometimes heat wild food soups using stones from a wood fire or heated in the oven at the highest temperature. Do not use river rocks; they may contain water and so can break or explode and possibly injure someone.

Roasted or Smoked Bark Vinegars

I love vinegars, and there are so many culinary uses for them. You can infuse them with fruits, berries, herbs, and even aromatic leaves or needles. My favorite is mountain vinegar, which is composed of infused white fir, pine needles, manzanita, and California juniper berries. Depending on the season I may add some aromatic currant leaves too.

Another favorite is smoked vinegar. I often sprinkle some smoked vinegar on fish to add interesting flavors. It also makes delicious salad dressings; or you can use it in sauces. The technique is very simple—you just add some roasted or torched wood or barks from specific trees to infuse flavors.

I still have a lot of experimenting to do with various foraged woods, barks, and herbs, but so far the one I like the most is a blend made of oak bark, California sycamore bark, and California juniper berries.

Some woods that aren't suitable for grilling are great when roasted. Sycamore wood falls into this category. Sycamore is usually not recommended for smoking or grilling. I tried it and was really not fond of the flavors. However,

sycamore bark was used by natives to make a medicinal tea as a cold and flu remedy.

The trick with the sycamore bark is that you want to roast it, but you don't burn it or torch it. When I tried torching it, the overwhelming smoky flavor it imparted was irritating to the throat. The technique I use is to make a bark tea in an old pot. I put in just a bit of water, boil it for a while, and then let the water evaporate. When it is nearly evaporated, I place the lid on the pot. After a while the bark will start smoking; I allow the bark to smoke for around 3 minutes with the lid on. At this point the bark is roasted but not burned. I'm sure the same technique could be done in the oven, but so far this is the way I've done it.

I use a different technique for roasting oak bark. First I forage a nice chunk of bark from a fallen tree in the forest. It should not be too old or rotting. I take it home, clean it if necessary, and place it in the oven at 200°F (93°C) for 20 minutes or so for a rough pasteurization. Then, using a torch, I roast it on all sides before placing it into my vinegar.

SMOKED OAK BARK AND SYCAMORE VINEGAR

I use Neanderthal measurement units for this recipe (hand sizes), which seems to work pretty well. If you don't have sycamore trees in your area, you can just use oak bark. Most of the flavors will come from the oak bark and juniper berries.

Ingredients

1 gallon (3.75 l) vinegar

A chunk of torched oak bark three-quarters the size of your hand and approximately ¾ inch (2 cm) thick

A chunk of roasted sycamore bark three-quarters the size of your hand (optional)

30 California juniper berries, crushed (you can substitute regular juniper berries, but the flavor will be different)

Procedure

1. Place the barks and berries in the vinegar. Cover the container so you don't attract unwanted flies, bugs, and other critters. I use plastic wrap, but you could also store the vinegar in a large jar and close the lid.

2. Age the vinegar for a couple of months in a cool, dark place. The end result is vinegar with nice smooth, smoky flavors as if it had been aged in a toasted oak barrel. The California juniper adds some nice lemon and pine accents. I use a coffee filter to strain the vinegar. Pasteurizing the vinegar after bottling is a good idea. See Pasteurizing Your Vinegar on page 252 for the procedure.

Natural Wraps

Cooking food in wraps is a good method for keeping the food moist and tender. Wrapping also allows spice flavors to better penetrate the food. Wrapping your food also keeps it clean—a good thing if you are cooking a fish in hot ashes. As a forager you have quite a large palette of materials you can use as wraps. I usually use large leaves from non-poisonous plants, but when necessary I've also used grasses or barks.

Some of the leaves I've used to wrap food in Southern California include:

Sycamore	Wild grapes
Maple	Large black
Fig	mustard leaves
Curly dock	Mallow
Giant reed (*Arundo donax*)	Grass (tightly wrapped)

Strings can be made using yucca leaves, grass stems, cattail leaves, or rushes (sedgelike herbs of the Juncaceae family). If you know the method (which usually requires soaking) and have the time, the inner bark of various trees such as cottonwood, willow, juniper, aspen, moosewood, maple, and basswood can be twined into strings.

> **CAUTION:** *Never* use the leaves of a plant you can't identify. For example, the large leaves from the castor bean plant (*Ricinus* spp.) are highly poisonous.

The Flavors of Dirt

A couple of years ago, while foraging after a decent rainfall in the forest, I became completely enamored with the smell emanating from the soil. The rotten leaves and decomposing organic matters had this fulsome forest aroma that reminded me of fresh grass, mushrooms, rain, fall leaves, and countless

other essences. I usually express that smell by telling people that it "reeks" like a forest in fall, in a good way. If you like to hike, you probably know the scent experience I'm writing of.

As a simple experiment, I foraged some of that forest dirt, placed carrots in the middle of it, and wrapped the whole thing with sycamore leaves. I baked the packet in the oven at 300°F (149°C) for 30 minutes. The end result was fantastic. The carrots had a very nice forest "topsoil" flavor. I also tasted a hint of unexpected bitterness, but it was not overwhelming at all. Since that time I've used this technique in our private dinners to cook carrots, onions, and potatoes. You can add your favorite aromatics to the forest dirt.

Soon I plan to experiment with creating my own blends of wild plants and herbs mixed with local clay or topsoil to create "culinary composts."

CAUTION: As with cooking with forest floor, foraging dirt is advanced foraging. You just can't grab some forest topsoil and call it a day without observing and knowing the whole environment. Decomposing poison oak, poison ivy, or white snakeroot (*Ageratina altissima*) leaves, datura seeds, or the fruiting body of some deadly mushroom mixed in with your dirt could have disastrous effects. This type of foraging requires knowing with absolute certainty which poisonous and toxic plants or mushrooms may grow in the environment, and inspecting your foraged dirt carefully for traces of these.

Topsoil is loaded with microorganisms helping to decompose the organic ingredients; botulism bacteria can be present too. To destroy any unwanted bacteria or botulism toxins when cooking with dirt, make sure your cooking temperature reaches at least 250°F (121°C) inside the wrap. Don't estimate it or chance it—use an oven thermometer to check.

Cooking in Tree Bark

In my quest to use as much as my wild environment can provide in terms of culinary uses, I started to experiment with the uses of barks in various baking methods.

Like wrapping food in clay or leaves, baking in bark has several advantages: preserving moisture in the food, allowing the flavors from added aromatics to infuse slowly (or rapidly) into the food being baked inside, and, if the bark is aromatic, adding flavors.

During my research, so far I found very little evidence of barks being used for baking aside from Australia, where the local natives used the bark of a specific tree called broad-leaved paperbark (*Melaleuca quinquenervia*). Appropriately, Attica restaurant in Melbourne, Australia offers a dish featuring a local fish cooked in paperbark. The tree is found presently in Florida and considered invasive.

The use of the bark from the broad-leaved paperbark makes sense—the bark is aromatic and reportedly adds a smoky aroma when food is baked in it. However, my local trees don't really infuse specific flavors so it's really a matter of adding aromatic plants and spices to the ingredients being baked and the only use of the bark is to preserve moisture and lock in the flavors. I like the primal aesthetic of it, though, and I've managed to get some smoky accents by using toasted oak barks when baking trout.

So far, I've experimented with oak, alder, cottonwood, and sycamore bark. The sycamore bark works better: The tree sheds its bark every year, you can get large chunks, and it is thin enough to be wrapped easily around the ingredients. I'm sure other barks can be used for baking, such as birch; it's a matter of doing some research about your own foraging territory. Again, you would need to make sure that the bark is not toxic.

I don't have precise recipes; this is part of experimenting with the seasons and your terroir's offering. Last year I used oak bark placed around a trout and aromatic forest herbs (mugwort, sweet white clover, grass, wood mint, black sage, and California sagebrush). This year, I experimented with baking large shrimps in sycamore bark with excellent results. I usually brine the shrimp in salted water with California juniper berries for an hour or so. Then I wrap them in bark with white fir, crushed manzanita berries, California juniper berries, and lemon rings, and bake for 10 minutes at 350°F (177°C). The end result is quite delicious, lemony with hints of pine.

Trout cooked in bark with herbs and plants from the river bank, including grass, black sage, sweet white clover, willow leaves, mugwort, and yerba santa. The bark was soaked in mugwort beer. Cooked in a 350° F (175° C) oven for 30 minutes.

SPRING
The Greens Time

Photo courtesy of Mia Wasilevich.

Spring Recipes

I call spring the "greens time" because the forest and mountains turn completely green in Southern California in these months, although in my immediate locale the mountains actually turn yellow on account of the flowering mustard.

In the spring most of the winter plants are still available, and we have a host of new ones as well. It's a good time to forage beautiful edible flowers, such as wild radish, mustard, yerba santa (*Eriodictyon californicum*), and so on, that chefs love to use for plating. Some are quite delicious—my favorite are the black mustard flowers, which have a very pronounced wasabi-like flavor and make incredibly tasty mustard.

If you're into creating wild food salads, early spring is just an incredible time, with plentiful edible greens and flavors.

You can pretty much forage anywhere at this time of year, but my preferred location is the chaparral. I think there is a lot of misunderstanding about chaparral. It's usually defined as semi-desert environment consisting mostly of shrubs and thorny bushes, but this couldn't be further from the truth once you become familiar with it. Sure, there are shrubs and thorns, but there is also so much more!

The chaparral is a great place to look for aromatic plants—such as white sage, black sage, California sagebrush, some fragrant currant leaves, yerba santa, wild fennel, and many more—which can be used to create quite interesting spice blends.

You'll also find a lot of unripe berries and nuts, such as currants, black walnuts, elderberries, and manzanita berries, that can be turned into tasty pickled treats.

In Southern California, spring also means it's time to get busy preserving food. Slowly but surely, the environment will get more and more dry due to the lack of rain and will eventually turn into a semi-desert. The high temperatures of the summer will make it much more difficult to forage.

Many herbs and flowers, such as watercress, chickweed, wild radish, and mustard flowers or leaves, are collected in this season, dehydrated carefully, and turned into savory or colorful powders. Of course, you can't overlook some pollens, such as those from fennel or cattail plants.

Pickling also goes into high gear in the spring. I make a lot of pickled radish pods, yucca flowers, unripe figs, and much more.

Spring is also a great time to make various beers and primitive brews. Our local mugwort is available in large quantities in the local forest or near streams and water bodies, but you can also find many other plants that have been used traditionally to make herbal or medicinal beers, such as stinging nettles, horehound, or yarrow.

As a forager, spring really means it's time to work hard and preserve, taking full advantage of the abundance before the hardship of the upcoming summer.

Emerging Buds and Greens

You can really take advantage of the young buds and greens appearing in early spring. It may take some experience to identify plants and berries in the early growing stages but once you're able to do it, a new culinary universe opens up, allowing you to create interesting as well as unusual ingredients and condiments.

CACTUS FLOWER BUDS

After the winter rainy season, the cactuses look nice and plump; their flower buds are emerging at this time, and they are a true delicacy if collected and prepared properly. Locally, they usually show up around March or April and will be available in large quantities for a couple of months or more. One year I was able to forage a few in October, but this is quite unusual.

Let's just say that so far I have not found this very common and plentiful ingredient in the local stores or the farmer's market. Even the nearby Hispanic grocery store does not carry it, although you will find cactus pads and cactus pears.

I don't think it's the flavor that keeps them out of the markets, because the flower buds have a nice lemony accent, so I assume the fact that they're not there simply reflects how time consuming it is to forage and prepare them properly. Do it the wrong way and you end up with tiny cactus needles in your fingers and other places. I get better every year at collecting them, but I remember the first year I did it was extremely painful, with tiny needles pricking every part of my body.

Foraging cactus flower buds can be a game of patience, but over time I've learned to welcome the yearly challenge offered by this true native food, and to even find pleasure in doing it. Although you can cook them right way, traditionally the buds are boiled and dehydrated in the sun to be used later on. Properly stored, they will stay viable all year long.

You can forage flower buds from a variety of cactuses, such a buckthorn or staghorn cholla. I've even used the emerging buds of prickly pear cactus. Depending on the species, some buds may have many more needles than others. The hair-like needles, known as glochids, are the ones to be very careful of; they're quite tough to remove from your skin. My local cholla flower buds can be quite challenging and smaller in size, while the prickly pear cactus flower buds are much easier to collect. The flavors are pretty much the same, but I like to forage both types nevertheless. Every year I seem to get better at preparing them, but so far I've not been able to avoid getting pricked. At this point I just understand it comes with the job.

As always, think in terms of sustainability and don't pick too much from any one cactus. I never take more than 10 to 20 percent. Depending on the state you live in, some cactuses may be protected, so be aware of the local laws.

Don't rush when you harvest and prepare the cactus buds, for if you do a sloppy job and leave behind needles or glochids you won't be able to eat them. Also, I've found that removing needles when the buds are dehydrated is an impossible task.

Always wear gloves and use kitchen tongs when foraging cactus flower buds! Unless you are a really skilled forager, you'll probably end up with a few needles in your finger.

Here is the method I use for preparing and preserving cactus flower buds:

Procedure

1. Choose the right buds. You want the petals to still be cone-shaped and tight. If the flower is already formed, it will create a mess when you boil them later on.
2. The first thing you want to do is to make some sort of primitive bundle with whatever nature provides

you at that location: sagebrush, dry grass, twigs, and so forth. Slap and brush the buds with the bundle while they are still attached to the cactus to remove most of the glochids. This works very well, but make sure you do it upwind of the cactus so they don't end up on your clothes. Sometimes I think the needles have some sort of sophisticated internal guidance system and will find a way through the clothing fibers to get to your skin.

3. Next, remove the buds by twisting them off— using your fingers if you did a good job removing the needles, though most people use kitchen tongs. Place them in your bucket or paper bag. I usually make a layer of buds and top that layer with dry grass or leaves, such as sycamore, then add another layer of buds. I may end up with three layers of buds in my bag. Placing paper towels between layers works fine too. The idea is to try to prevent any remaining needles on one bud from pricking the other buds. I wasn't too careful the first year I harvested cholla buds, and there were so many needles stuck in the buds (they pricked each other) that I could not remove them properly and had to throw away my entire morning's forage.

4. Once home, you can place the buds onto a ¼-inch (6 mm) mesh screen and brush with a dedicated whisk broom to remove any remaining needles. There are other methods, too—some people choose to burn the remaining needles in a stove or place the buds in cold water for an hour and scrub the (now) soft needles away with a dedicated kitchen scrub sponge. It's recommended that you wear gloves during that process.

The final step is to inspect the buds one more time and remove any remaining needles with tweezers if necessary. The goal is perfection. Take your time; you will be rewarded by delicious and nutrition-rich food later on.

5. Before use, your buds should be boiled for at least 20 to 30 minutes. After that they can be stir-fried, used in salads and stews, or even pickled.

6. Traditionally, after boiling them, the buds were dehydrated and stored for use in the winter. You can dehydrate them in your dehydrator or oven (set at the lowest temperature). Living in Southern California, I usually place them outside for 2 or 3 days to dry in the sun. You can also freeze them.

7. Before using your dehydrated buds you will need to reconstitute them by pre-soaking them in water overnight. The ratio is 1 part dry buds to 5 parts water. In the morning, transfer the buds to another pot with water and simmer them until they are soft, which can take anywhere from 30 minutes to a couple of hours, depending on their size. The dried buds should triple in size once reconstituted.

By the way, dehydrated buds can also be ground into a powder. The flavor is quite lemony and the powder is great for thickening sauces or soups.

Cactus pads are a delicacy on their own, and a quick search online can provide you with lots of information related to preparation and recipes. Because the information is so easy to find, it would be redundant to repeat in this book. But by all means, do some research and have fun with this delicious native food.

Soft-Shelled Walnuts

Around May is the time to forage the local native unripe walnuts. It may sound unusual but unripe walnuts can be used to create a very unique and tasty condiment. I didn't come up with anything new but simply adapted an old British recipe for pickled unripe walnuts. In England they use the regular Persian walnut (*Juglans regia*)—it's the one you usually buy at the store. Of course, being a forager and living in Southern California I adapted the recipe to use my native walnuts (*Juglans californica* and *Juglans hindsii*) and my local wild spices.

PICKLED UNRIPE BLACK WALNUTS

I've been working on this recipe for the last few years. It has become quite popular among my students and the local chefs.

The flavor is something between a Worcestershire and an A1 Steak Sauce with a little wild kick and a *je ne sais quoi* aftertaste that only walnuts can provide. The native walnuts are also said to be more flavorful than commercial Persian or English walnuts. They're much smaller too, usually one-third of the size, and, when ripe, the shell is probably twice as thick.

Ingredients

Unripe walnuts
Salt
Water
1 cup (236 ml) white wine
2 cups (472 ml) red wine vinegar
4 ounces (120 ml) balsamic vinegar
1 cup (200 g) brown sugar
¼–1 teaspoon (1–4 g) peppercorns
1–2½ teaspoons (3–7 g) garlic powder
½–1 teaspoon (2–4 g) Italian or French
   herb mix
¼–1 California bay or regular bay leaves
½–1 teaspoon (2–6 g) grated fresh ginger
2–6 cloves, whole
Dried chilies (optional)

Procedure

1. Forage the walnuts (early May in Southern California) while the shell is still soft inside. If the shell is already hard, it's too late. Use a knife to test a couple of walnuts from the tree and evaluate if they're good for pickling; it should slice through the shell easily and you should see the unripe walnut inside. It's a good idea to wear gloves while doing this, as the walnut juice can stain your skin.

2. For this recipe, you will need to poke holes in the unripe walnuts. You do this so that the brine and the pickling solution can permeate the inside of the nut. It also allows the walnuts to release their "juice." I usually use a little wooden board with a nail, place a walnut between my fingers, and make around 8 to 10 holes in each. I can process around 10 to 12 walnuts a minute that way. Again, wear gloves as it a messy business and you can end up with stained fingers. Yes, you'll probably poke your fingers from time to time . . . sorry.

3. Place the walnuts in a brine solution. The ratio for the brine is ½ cup (137 g) salt to 5 cups (1.2 l) of water. Boil the brine first so it is well saturated with the salt, then cool it down. Now it's ready to use.

   Make sure that the walnuts are under the surface of brine. I used a clean plate and a boiled (pasteurized) rock to keep them down. Once the walnuts are saturated with salt they will not float, but this can take days.

4. Leave the walnuts in the brine for around 10 days. Shake once a day.

   After a couple of days, the surface of the brine will look a bit like the surface of some sort of toxic waste and, well, it really doesn't appear very appetizing. Don't worry, you're doing fine. Nothing bad is happening underneath the surface scum.

5. Remove the brine, rinse the walnuts very briefly, and replace the old brine with a new solution.

6. Wait 10 more days, shaking once a day.

7. Remove the walnuts from the brine. I rinse them briefly with regular water and place them in the sun. Living in California, by the end of

the day they have turned jet black. In another region, where the sun isn't as strong, this may take a couple of days. Once they're jet black, they're ready for pickling.

8. To make a basic pickling solution (my favorite after some trials and errors over the last couple of years), combine wine, vinegars, and brown sugar in a medium pan. Bring the solution to a boil.

9. Gather the jars you will use. There's no need to sterilize the jars, since you will be placing them in a boiling-water bath for more than 10 minutes. Just clean them with soap and water.

10. In each jar place the following spices:

	½ pint (250 ml)	1 pint (500 ml)	1 quart (1 l)
Peppercorns	¼ teaspoon (1 g)	½ teaspoon (2 g)	1 teaspoon (4 g)
Garlic powder	1 teaspoon (3 g)	1½ teaspoons (4.5 g)	2–2½ teaspoon (7 g)
Italian or French herb mix	½ teaspoon (2 g)	¾ teaspoon (3 g)	1 teaspoon (4 g)
California bay or regular bay leaves*	¼ leaf	½ leaf	1 leaf
Grated ginger	½ teaspoon (2–3 g)	¾ teaspoon (4 g)	1 teaspoon (5–6 g)
Whole cloves	2	4	6

* Double the amount if you are using regular bay leaves.

You can add some dehydrated chili if you want some spicy kick.

11. Fill the jars with your black walnuts. Pour the hot pickling solution inside the jar, leaving ½ inch (1.25 cm) of headspace (measuring from the surface of the pickling solution inside to the top of the jar) and tighten the lid to "finger strength."

12. Process using the water-bath method: Place the jars in hot water and bring the water to a boil for the time specified below (see Basic Water Bath Canning on page 38).

½ pint jar (250 ml): 15 minutes
1 pint jar (500ml): 25 minutes
1 quart jar (1 l): 35 minutes

13. Remove the jars from the water and set on a towel on the counter. Verify that you have achieved a proper vacuum inside; the lid should make a popping sound as the jars cool. Let the jars cool completely. Check the seal the next day by pressing on the center of the lids; they shouldn't bounce back. Store in a cool, dark place. The walnuts should be preserved in good condition for a year or more.

Pickled black walnuts get better with aging. The minimum amount of time you should allow them to sit before consuming them is 3 weeks, but they taste much better after 2 or 3 months, when all the flavors have blended together.

Don't feel the need to stick with this recipe—there are many creations you can make with unripe walnuts and the pickling solution. Enjoy!

Note: If you don't want to use the water bath method you can simply place the jars in your refrigerator. Just let the jar cool down after you've poured in the hot pickling solution and closed the lid. Then store the jars in the fridge and wait at least 3 weeks before sampling them. The walnuts should store well this way for many months.

If you do use the refrigerator method, pasteurize your jars beforehand by placing them in boiling water for at least 10 minutes.

Note: Some people who tried my pickled unripe walnuts recipe on the east coast told me that their native walnuts ended up mushy. If this is the case, you could use a blender to make an A1-type sauce instead of using whole walnuts as a condiment.

LOCAL MOUNTAIN NOCINO

Nocino is an Italian liqueur made with unripe walnuts steeped in vodka. It's quite delicious on desserts or as a digestive after a large meal. The flavor is quite aromatic and somewhat bitter, although the bitterness is balanced by sugar used in the recipe.

For the last couple of years I've made a traditional recipe using local unripe black walnuts, until I realized that I should really make a nocino that is a reflection of my terroir instead of the Italian version. So I began to alter the ingredients to add local flavors.

A basic traditional recipe follows. To reflect my terroir, I removed the vanilla bean from the ingredients and used only one cinnamon stick. I then placed 20 local California juniper berries and three small branches of white fir (cutting the needles so the flavors would be extracted more easily). Both the white fir and juniper berries added a lovely pine/lemon undertone. In the future I'll add some roasted oak bark to the concoction as well.

It's a good idea to make a somewhat traditional recipe to start with, but don't be afraid to experiment.

Ingredients

30 green English walnuts (I use 60–80
    smaller unripe black walnuts)
4¼ cups (1 l) vodka
5–8 cloves
2 cinnamon sticks
1–2 inches vanilla bean
Zest of 1 lemon or orange, cut into strips
2½ cups (500 g) granulated sugar

Procedure

1. Cut the unripe black walnuts in two and place in a container with the vodka. (Be careful when handling walnuts: The juice can leave a heavy stain, so it's a good idea to wear gloves when cutting them.)
2. Add the cloves, cinnamon, vanilla, lemon or orange, and sugar. (This is the step where I add my white fir and California juniper berries instead of the vanilla bean.)
3. Cover with a clean towel. Stir the mixture with a wooden spoon daily for the first 7 days. Then cap with a regular lid so you don't get too much evaporation over time. Stir two or three times a week for a couple of months. During this time the liquid will turn jet black and the bitterness will mellow considerably.
4. Strain the liquid into bottles and age it for at least 6 months. Then decant and enjoy.

Mountain nocino with white fir and California juniper berries.

Tender Ash Seedpods

I had no idea that ash seedpods (ash "keys") were edible until one day, while doing research on possible medicinal properties of ash tree leaves, I found an old English recipe from the seventeenth century for pickled ash keys.

To be honest, it didn't seem like fantastic food, as ash keys can be quite bitter and tough. I remember chewing on a few as a kid and my first instinct was to spit them out right away. Timing is important if you intend to forage them and try this recipe. You need to pick the ash keys when they're still quite tender and the seed inside is not yet fully formed. Where I live, that can be anytime between April and June.

With the proper pickling solution, they're quite okay to eat, and in fact they were originally used as condiments with fish or cheese. And ash keys are really quite plentiful at the right time of the year, so it would be a shame for a forager not to try them.

Here are a couple of simple recipes for you to try. Each recipe makes six half-pint (250 ml) jars—each recipe calls for around 1½ cups (375 ml by volume) of ash keys.

ASH KEYS AND GINGER

By themselves ash keys are pretty much tasteless, so you really depend on the pickling solution for flavors. In this recipe, the ginger imparts some nice accents and the mild rice vinegar is not too overwhelming. I would not say it's delicious, but it's a nice light garnish addition.

Ingredients

1½ cups (375 ml) ash seedpods
Water
Fresh gingerroot
3 cups (750 ml) rice vinegar
2 tablespoons (30 g) salt
6 tablespoons (90 g) sugar

Procedure

1. Remove the stems and wash the ash keys, then place in a pot filled with enough water to cover the keys (use 1 part keys and 2 parts water). Bring to a boil, then simmer for 5 to 10 minutes.
2. Strain off the water and replace it with hot water. Bring to a boil and simmer again for 5 to 10 minutes.
3. Drain off the water and pack the ash keys loosely into clean half-pint (250 ml) jars, filling each jar about three-fourths full of keys.
4. Add a small piece of fresh ginger to each jar.
5. In a medium pan, bring the vinegar, salt, and sugar to a boil. Let the solution simmer for a couple of minutes, then pour into each jar, leaving ½ inch (1.25 cm) headspace. Screw the top down fingertip-tight.
6. Place the jars in the refrigerator and wait at least a couple of months before tasting, or use the water bath method (see Basic Water Bath Canning on page 38) to preserve the jars (boil for 15 minutes). I like to enjoy the preserved ash keys after storing them 4 to 5 months.

SALTED ASH KEYS

This simple recipe is basically my approach to making ash key capers. It's quite salty but packed with flavors. Nice as a garnish in salads or with fish.

Ingredients

1½ cups (375 ml) ash seedpods

Water

2 lemons, cut into rings

Chili pods (fresh or dehydrated)—you can use any type of chili pepper and any size you want based on the flavors and level of heat you like

6 small thyme branches

3 cups (750 ml) apple cider vinegar

3 tablespoons (45 g) salt

Procedure

1. Remove the stems and wash the ash keys, then place in a pot filled with enough water to cover the keys (use 1 part keys and 2 parts water). Bring to a boil, then simmer for 5 to 10 minutes.
2. Strain off the water and replace it with hot water. Bring back to a boil and simmer again for 5 to 10 minutes.
3. Drain off the water and pack the keys loosely into clean half-pint (250 ml) jars, filling each jar about three-fourths full of keys.
4. Add 1 lemon ring, 1 chili, and 1 small thyme branch to each jar.
5. In a medium pan, bring the vinegar and salt to a boil. Let the solution simmer for a couple of minutes, then pour into each jar, leaving ½ inch (1.25 cm) headspace. Screw the top down fingertip-tight.
6. Place the jars in the refrigerator and wait at least a couple of months before tasting, or use the water bath method (see Basic Water Bath Canning on page 38) to preserve the jars (boil for 15 minutes). I like to enjoy the preserved ash keys after storing them 4 to 5 months.

Young Broadleaf Plantain

Edible does not necessarily mean "palatable"— for the longest time I didn't know what to do with broadleaf plantain, a highly nutritious and medicinal wild food. The leaves are quite tough and the taste is quite bitter, so I never understood why this plant was considered edible raw, and I thought that it surely would be unremarkable cooked. However, I spent some time doing various culinary experiments with it and came out with this interesting recipe.

The key to cooking plantain leaves is timing. Boil them too long and they fall apart; if you don't boil them long enough, they're too tough. I found that the sweet spot is around 3½ minutes for younger leaves and around 4½ minutes for older leaves. Personally I like to forage younger leaves only.

Boiled properly in slightly salted water, you end up with a leaf that has very much of an algae look and texture. The algae characteristic makes it perfect for creating Asian-style dishes. The leaves won't taste like algae, but if you add the right condiments you could fool many people into thinking that they're actually eating seaweed.

BROADLEAF PLANTAIN "SEAWEED"

This is a recipe using a basic "Asian" sauce, but by all means if you're a fan of Asian cooking, feel free to create your own version.

Ingredients

Young broadleaf plantain leaves
Water
Ice water
1 tablespoon (15 ml) sesame oil
1 tablespoon (15 ml) soy sauce
1 garlic clove, chopped
1 teaspoon (5 g) roasted sesame seeds
Salt to taste

Procedure

1. Clean the young leaves and place in boiling water for 3½ minutes. Remove quickly and place in ice water. Remove the leaves after a couple of minutes and place the leaves into a bowl.
2. Mix the sesame oil, soy sauce, garlic, and sesame seeds. Taste and add salt if necessary. Toss carefully with the leaves and let rest for 5 minutes before serving. (I have also served the leaves with roasted white sage seeds and some of my local walnuts.)

PICKLED WILD RADISH PODS (AND OTHER PRESERVES)

During the year, I pickle a wide variety of wild edibles that we use as condiments for our private dinners. I've tried a wide variety of pickling solutions—there is one basic and simple recipe that I really like to use for many of my foraged ingredients, including wild radish pods, purslane, curly dock stems, cactus flower buds, and yucca shoots, flowers, and seedpods.

Ingredients

3 cups (700 ml) apple cider vinegar
2 cups (475 ml) dry white wine
4 teaspoons (24 g) white sugar
2 teaspoons (12 g) sea salt
2 pounds (1 scant kilo) wild radish pods
To each jar I usually add 1 crushed garlic clove, 1 dried chili pod (if I want to add some spice), a dash of an Italian or French herb mix, or wild herbs such as dehydrated sweet white clover. Fresh sweet clover or fennel works well too. For some recipes, such as pickled yucca shoots, I'll add ginger instead of the herbs, garlic, and chili pod. Feel free to experiment with this very basic pickling solution.

Procedure

1. Mix the vinegar, wine, sugar, and salt in a nonreactive pot. Bring to a boil and decrease the heat to a simmer for 5 minutes. Meanwhile, fill your clean jars with the radish pods, spices, and aromatic herbs.
2. Pour the hot vinegar solution into each half-pint (250 ml) jar, leaving ½ inch (1.25 cm) of headspace, and close the lid fingertip-tight. If you just want to preserve the jars in the refrigerator, let them cool first, then store in the fridge for 2 to 3 weeks before enjoying. They should keep for around 3 months.
3. For canning, follow the procedures for water bath canning (see Basic Water Bath Canning on page 38) and boil for 15 minutes, then cool and store. I like to use them within a year.

Wild Food Kimchi

Kimchi is one of my favorite condiments. I live in an area with a sizable Asian population and several Korean markets, where it's not unusual to have a whole aisle featuring various kimchis.

Kimchi is a traditional fermented dish made of various combinations of vegetables, such as cabbage, garlic, cucumber, onions, radishes, and chilies. There are hundreds of variations, and some recipes include such ingredients as shrimp paste, fermented anchovies, fish sauce, and so forth.

Needless to say, kimchi is a bit of an acquired taste, and its pungent smell is not always appreciated by everyone, but for me it was love at first taste.

Kimchi has been made for well over two thousand years. Like many preserved products, it was created to ensure a plentiful and nutritious food supply during the winter. Before modern refrigeration, kimchi was usually made in late fall and early winter, when the ingredients were available, and stored in large pots that were often buried in the ground, where the temperature was optimal for long-term storage. Depending on the recipe, some kimchis could be fermented for weeks, months, or even years. If you ever travel to Korea, you can still find some two- or three-year-old kimchi eaten as a special and valued delicacy.

These days, many Korean families opt to purchase special kimchi refrigerators with exact temperature control, which allows them to make specific traditional recipes if they wish. In places like Southern California where the climate is quite hot, such refrigerators are a necessity for long-term fermentation.

On the plus side, it really does not take weeks or months to make a very basic kimchi at home. In just a few days you can be rewarded with a tasty and nutritious fermented concoction. The process is very similar to making sauerkraut; you just need to add salt, as the microorganisms necessary for the fermentation (*Lactobacillus* bacteria) are already present in the ingredients themselves.

Of course, being a forager, I quickly became interested by the idea of making my own kimchi using locally foraged ingredients. After a few experiments over the years, I came up with this simple recipe, which works well with a lot of very common edible wild plants, such as curly dock, watercress, dandelion leaves, mustard leaves, wild radish pods, ramps, and so on.

Some kimchi purists may tell you that fish sauce is an essential ingredient for flavor or that you can't use any other chilies than the traditional Korean chili powder. However, based on my own experience and feedback from people who have eaten my wild kimchis, I beg to differ. I've made vegan kimchis with a wide variety of chilies, from mild to super hot, with excellent flavorful results. So let's get started!

BASIC WILD KIMCHI

This is the basic kimchi recipe I use. The ingredients and ratio change all the time depending on the time of the year. During the winter I will use mostly curly dock, dandelion, and watercress; while in spring I'll use mostly mustard and radish leaves. Where you live you may have ramps and other delicious wild greens. Experiment with what you have, anything from the mustard family will work extremely well. This recipe should yield a quart of kimchi depending on the wild greens you use. Feel free to add or subtract if necessary so everything fits in your jar.

Ingredients

3 cups (750 ml by volume) finely shredded wild greens, such as dandelion leaves, black mustard leaves, ramps, watercress, or curly dock (feel free to experiment with what you forage)

1½ cups (375 ml by volume) cabbage (*Brassica oleracea*), or variants such as napa, bok choy, or brussels sprouts

5–8 garlic cloves

1 onion

¾ cup (200 ml by volume) chili powder (either mild or insanely hot, if you like it that way)

2 cups (475 ml) springwater or distilled water

1 tablespoon (15 g) sea salt (with no additives or anticaking agents)

3 large cabbage leaves (large curly dock or mustard leaves would work as well)

Equipment

Cutting board and knife

1-quart or 1-liter canning jar

Mixing bowl

Canning funnel (optional)

Clean stone (used to keep the ingredients under the brine)

Canning jar lid and band

Procedure

1. Clean all the wild food and vegetables you will be using. Cut the cabbage into quarters and trim out the core. Slice each quarter into ¼-inch (.6 cm) ribbons, enough to fill 1 cup (236 ml by volume). Slice your wild edibles into thin ribbons as well—you can mix different plants such as dandelion, watercress, and curly dock. You will need around 2½ to 3 cups (600 to 700 ml by volume).

2. Using a blender or a *molcajete* (stone grinder), make a paste with the garlic, onion, and chili powder. I like to use my stone grinder because it gives the paste a rougher texture, but it's not terribly important. A nice smooth paste is fine too.

3. Wash your hands, scrubbing them with water and soap for at least 20 seconds. Then mix all the ingredients together with your hands for a couple of minutes.

4. Pasteurize or clean your jar thoroughly. Pack the jar tightly with the mixed ingredients; the jar should be about three-quarters full, but no more. A canning funnel is helpful for filling the jar, but it's not a must.

5. Prepare a brine with the water and sea salt. Make sure the salt is dissolved. Pour into the jar, leaving 1 to 1½ inches (3 to 4 cm) headspace.

6. With clean hands, fold the large cabbage leaves (or other large leaves) to fit the jar's mouth and push down. The idea is to create a seal so your shredded ingredients stay under the surface of the brine. (This is important to avoid a fermentation going bad.)

7. You will need to weigh down all the ingredients to make sure they stay under the brine. I usually use a stone that I have thoroughly cleaned and pasteurized by boiling it for 15 minutes. Some people use other methods, such as a clean drinking glass that fits nicely inside the jar's mouth, to push the ingredients down. Whatever you use, the idea is to keep everything under the brine. Use a spoon to remove any small floating bits as much as possible. Try to leave around ½ inch (1.25 cm) headspace and remove any excess brine.

Step 1

Step 2

Step 3

Step 4

Step 5

Step 6

Step 7

Step 8

Step 9

I also like to push down the stone a few times and let any air bubbles in the liquid escape. As much as possible, you want to remove air pockets and make sure that the ingredients are saturated with brine.

8. Place the lid and band onto the canning jar, but make sure it isn't too tight. The idea is to prevent any potential bacteria or flies from getting into your kimchi but at the same time allowing fermentation gases to escape. If you screw the lid down too tight, your jar may explode due to the pressure inside and you will end up with a big mess. If you've used another type of container, you can place a paper towel with a rubber band over the top, or simply cover with a clean kitchen towel.

It's also a good idea to place the jar onto a plate. During the fermentation process, gas bubbles will form inside your ingredients and the contents may expand a little, causing excess liquid to escape.

Once or twice a day I like to remove the lid and push the stone down again (using clean fingers) to let gas bubbles inside the jar escape. You'll see that there are a lot of them!

9. After 3 or 4 days, open the lid, smell, and use a spoon to taste the brine. It should be pleasant, spicy, and pungent. If it is to your liking, you can place the jar in the refrigerator, which will slow down the fermentation considerably. I like to eat my kimchi within a week or two.

Black mustard leaves, one of my favorites for making kimchi.

Cooking with Unripe Ingredients

"Unripe" is an interesting concept. For many people it just means that a fruit or vegetable is not ready, so you have to wait for a while and eat it when ripe.

In fact, even dictionaries such as the *Merriam-Webster Dictionary* define "unripe" this way:

> *of food : not fully grown or developed : not yet ready to eat : not ripe*

I still remember vividly the times when, as a kid, I tried biting into unripe apples or pears. Of course I would experience the puckering effect, spit it out right away, and vow never to try it again.

During my first few years as a forager, I never touched anything unripe. I simply waited to pick a plant, berry, or nut at the appropriate ripe time and never thought twice about it.

This all changed a few years ago when I tried to pickle unripe walnuts for the first time. I mean, let's face it, unripe walnuts are truly disgusting if you try to bite into one, and yet through exact preparations I was able to create something delicious out of them. I didn't think much of it for a couple of years, but once I started working with local chefs and restaurants I had much more pressure and drive to find a wide variety of ingredients for them to play with. Happy chefs make happy foragers.

So I started asking myself: What else is there to work with? And what can I do with it?

In retrospect, it should have been more obvious that unripe foraged foods are viable, but it was deeply ingrained in me that unripe is a no-go. But had I looked more carefully in the aisles of my local ethnic market, which shows the neighborhood's Hispanic and Middle Eastern influences, I would have seen unripe grapes, almonds, and papayas, green tomatoes, and sour green plums. I guess learning to work with unripe ingredients is a bit like learning plants: If you don't know them you won't see them, but once you've learned about them, you'll see them everywhere! Now I love to visit that market and search for unripe products or preserves for ideas.

The inspiration to make wild currant verjuice (or verjus) came from browsing the preserves aisles and finding unripe green grape juice, which was also labeled as verjuice ("green juice" in French).

Learning to appreciate unripe ingredients has been quite rewarding and has opened up a whole new vista of flavors for me. It also extended the foraging seasons considerably. For example, I'm now able to forage wild currants from spring to summer, starting with the unripe currants in March. I've also created many new preserves and interesting food items, such as unripe figs in syrups, wild currant and elderberry "capers," infused green California juniper berries, and unripe manzanita berry cider.

If I had to define *unripe* from my current perspective, I would express it as follows:

> *of food: not fully grown or developed—often tart and sour but capable of a wide range of flavors with the proper preparations or preserving techniques*
>
> *Unripe forager: Someone who is still too "green" at foraging to realize that unripe ingredients have tremendous culinary potential.*

Don't be an unripe forager! Look around and see what you can create with unripe wild ingredients.

Unripe wild currant berries.

Wild verjus could be of considerable interest to people who are into foraging or chefs interested in adding wild flavors to their culinary arsenal. It took me a great deal of research into books from medieval times and a couple of months of experimentation to get it right.

So what is verjus or verjuice?

The name says it all: *vert* in French means "green" and *jus* means "juice." So verjus is basically green juice—green not always in color, but in the sense of new fruit that isn't fully ripe.

Verjus was an extremely common ingredient for medieval cooks. It was used pretty much in the same way that we use vinegar and lemons today. In Europe, lemons were not cultivated until the middle of the 15th century, so most

Unripe currant verjus.

Europeans didn't have access to them due to local cold climate. From a modern perspective it's helpful to think of verjus as an alternative to vinegar or lemon juice. It is quite acidic, a bit tart, but also quite flavorful if made properly.

After being forgotten for centuries, verjus made from unripe green grapes is making a comeback. A company in Australia began producing it a few years ago, and some wineries in California and France are now producing it as well. Many chefs are now experimenting with it. Verjuice was never forgotten in the Middle East, though; in fact, I was able to find some at my local ethnic market under the name green grape juice or *hosrom*.

Verjus can be used in many ways, including as a dressing for salads, in sauces, and for marinating meat—you can simply use it as you would use vinegar or lemon juice.

So why is this interesting for foragers or chefs interested in something unique?

The reason is because wild edibles historically had an important place in the culinary arts, and, by studying very old books, as I have, you can rediscover some long-forgotten uses. Doing research on verjus proved quite fascinating. For instance, I learned that our ancestors didn't always have access to grapes, so they made verjus from all kinds of other fruits.

Aside from green grapes, verjus was also made from various unripe fruits (apples and pears), berries (currants, gooseberries), and tart or acidic plants (oxalis, dock, and rhubarb). Later, other fruits such as unripe oranges were also used. As a forager this opens the door to many culinary creations, and it means we don't have to wait for the "right" time to pick berries or fruits, because the right time may be when they're not quite ripe yet.

Currants

Having a large quantity of wild currants nearby, I decided to make verjus with them. I started my verjus experiment two years ago and probably made every possible mistake along the way. I'll share my experiences so you don't have to go through all the same errors.

The basic technique to make verjus is very simple:

1. Collect the unripe berries or grapes.
2. Juice them and pour the juice in a container. (I use a sterilized jar.)
3. Place the container in a cool, dark place or in a refrigerator for a week and let the sediment collect at the bottom.
4. Pour the juice into another sterilized jar, leaving the sediment behind.

Stored in the refrigerator, the verjus can last for weeks. I had fresh verjus in the fridge with a tad of olive oil on top to protect it from air, and I still enjoyed it 5 months later.

In the old days, when people didn't have refrigerators, they boiled the verjus, reduced it down to one-fourth of the original quantity, and added salt to it (2 tablespoons [30 g] per gallon [3.75 l]) to avoid fermentation. The verjus was then poured into a bottle and topped with a thin layer of olive oil to minimize the juice's contact with oxygen.

Presently we know how to preserve through canning, so salt isn't necessary; in fact, salt didn't taste good with wild currant verjus. (I tried it.) Because the unripe juice is very acidic and has a low pH, I like to can it using the water bath method (see page 38).

But back to green berries. The old books were not always very specific as to which types of fruit were used, or exactly when to pick them. In fact, they simply referred to green or unripe wild berries, gooseberries, and so forth. Often a good amount of time passes between when currant berries are extremely green and when they are nearly ripe—around 2 months, in fact.

My first attempt was with extremely young and green currant berries. That was a bad idea! The "verjus" from very green berries was so bitter and tart, it was impossible to use.

So every 2 weeks, I collected some unripe berries and went through the process of making verjus with them. It took me four attempts to get it right. That's a lot of man-hours to forage and process the berries, but I think it's well worth it and, heck, now you don't have to go through all of my trial-and-error experimentation.

The proper time to make verjus with wild currants (and probably other wild berries) is when they are *nearly* ripe. So if I want to make verjus with red currants, I'll wait until they're actually orange and then harvest them. It's a good idea to taste the berries before picking. They should be acidic, flavorful, and sour, a bit like lemon juice.

My first attempt at juicing unripe currant berries. They were too green!

WILD CURRANT VERJUS

Here is how I made my wild currant verjus.

Ingredients

4 cups nearly ripe currant berries (you'll need at least this amount to make it worthwhile)

Procedure

1. Forage the nearly ripe berries, discarding any green berries. It's actually important to not use the very green berries.
2. With currants, the best way I found to extract the juice is by using a wheatgrass juicer. If you were making verjus with unripe green apples or pears, a conventional electric juicer would likely work just as well.
3. Place the juice in a jar and leave it in the fridge for 3 to 4 days. The juice will clear and the sediments will deposit on the bottom. When the juice is clear, pour it gently into another jar, leaving the sediment behind. The verjus will easily keep for 2 to 3 weeks in the fridge.

That's it—you're done! It's that simple. If you will be storing for a longer period of time (months) in the fridge, you can also add some citric acid—approximately 2 teaspoons (7 g) per gallon (3.75 l) should work nicely.

Another option is to pasteurize the verjus by boiling it for at least 15 minutes, then place a fine layer of olive oil on top of the juice to minimize contact with oxygen. Note that boiling the juice will change the flavor somewhat.

To preserve it even longer (a year or more), you need to bottle it. Since the pH is quite low (around 3.5 for currant verjus), you can use the boiling method.

Boil your verjus for at least 15 minutes. While the juice is boiling, place your bottles in boiling water for at least 10 minutes to sterilize them. I don't like boiling the plastic caps, so I sterilize them using alcohol or a light bleach solution (1 tablespoon [15 ml] per gallon [3.75 l]) for a couple of minutes and then rinse them thoroughly (at least three times) in hot water. Some people do place the caps in boiling water as well. Check with the manufacturer if you have any doubts.

Use a clean funnel and a clean cheesecloth to remove more of the impurities and foam as you pour the hot juice into the bottle.

Immediately place the cap and briefly turn the bottle upside down (this helps sterilize the cap even more), then let it cool. Store in a cool, dark place. I've used my bottled verjus within 6 months, but it should last much longer. There are no "approved" USDA canning recipes for making verjus, so use your own judgment. If you see any mold forming or discover odd smells or flavors, discard the verjus. For added food safety, I check the pH again when opening the bottle or jars later on.

The same method can be applied to other wild berries and fruits: green apples, pears, gooseberries, grapes, and so on.

Perfect unripe currants to make verjus.

Unripe Currant Capers

March is the time of year when I forage unripe currant berries. The timing is somewhat important. You don't want them to be too small, but you also want to pick them up before the seeds are fully formed inside. Unlike the garden variety, the local wild currant has a lot of seeds. Once formed inside the unripe green berries, they add a lot of bitterness and a crunchy texture.

Picked up at the right time, they're much more tender, although still quite tannic. It's not really something you would eat raw, although at Melisse restaurant chef Josiah Citrin put them to a clever use. The very small berries were chopped up thinly and placed on top of fish. I did some experiments as well by roughly chopping some berries and letting them infuse in lemon juice with a tad of salt for a few hours in the fridge. That worked quite well. (Vinegar would work too, in place of the lemon juice.)

My main technique, though, is pickling them, basically making unripe currant berry "capers."

The pickling solution imparts the flavor, but the berries themselves have an interesting texture and lemony/tannic accents. These currant "capers" are used as condiments, so my goal is to create little "flavor bombs."

After foraging the currant berries, I rinse them thoroughly. I also usually remove the berries from the stems and the dry flowers. It's quite a tedious endeavor, but you can also skip removing the dry flowers—they're kind of cool looking on a dish, and cleaning the berries goes much faster that way. You still have the option of removing the dry flowers after they're been pickled.

After pickling, I usually wait at least four months before eating them. It takes quite a while for the pickling solution to penetrate the berries and mellow the flavors. If you eat them too soon, they're still too tannic and bitter. If you wait a few months, they will taste much better.

Use of thinly cut unripe currant berries at Melisse restaurant.

CURRANT CAPERS

There is a lot of room for creativity here, with different pickling solutions. This is the basic recipe I use for around five half-pint (250 ml) jars.

Ingredients

3 cups (700 ml) unripe currant berries, cleaned and prepped

Aromatic herbs, foraged or commercial

Garlic cloves (optional)

Lemon rind (optional)

Chilies (optional)

3 cups (700 ml) apple cider vinegar

2 tablespoons (30 g) sea salt

1 tablespoon (15 g) sugar or honey

Procedure

1. Place the unripe berries in half-pint (250 ml) jars, filling approximately 60 percent of the jar. Because they're quite tannic, you don't want to pack the berries too tightly into the jar—you're looking for a nice exchange of flavors between the berries and the pickling solution. Too many berries and the end result may still be too tannic.

2. In each jar, place aromatic herbs of your choice to add flavors. I like to use tarragon (it reminds me of some of the flavors that actual capers have) or our local sweet white clover and 1 small garlic clove (usually cut in half). But you could use thyme, Italian or French spice mixes (Herbes de Provence), or any other herbs that inspire you. You can also add a lemon rind, or even a chili, if you want them to have a spicy edge.

3. Bring the pickling solution to a boil, then pour it into the jars containing the berries and herbs.

4. Close the jars and process using the water bath method (see page 38). I use a boiling time of 15 minutes for half-pint jars.

5. Wait around 4 months before tasting. The currant capers get better with age. After opening the jar, store in the refrigerator.

FERMENTED UNRIPE ELDERBERRY CAPERS

A couple of years ago, while doing research on the use of unripe berries, I came across an interesting recipe used at the Nordic Food Lab in Denmark. As most foragers know, elderberries are supposed to be boiled or fermented before consuming to prevent potential mild cyanide poisoning. It's why some people get an upset stomach and possibly even vomit when they drink raw elderberry juice, but boiling the juice or fermenting it (making wine) solves the problem. Although some books will tell you that truly ripe berries are safe to consume, the difficulty is to evaluate when they are truly ripe.

Although I have not seen any actual lab testing results, the unripe elderberries are supposed to contain more cyanide than the ripe ones. The research from the food lab in Denmark indicates that, through fermentation, the unripe berries can be made safe to eat. It's not something you would want to eat in large quantities anyway—it's more like a garnish.

Procedure

The Nordic Food Lab's method is to ferment the unripe berries in 5% salt for 3 weeks and infuse them for 6 weeks in raw apple cider vinegar. I tried that method twice: The first time my fermentation went bad and the second time I wasn't too happy with the flavors. We deal with a different type of elder here in Southern California (Mexican elder), which may explain why.

To add flavors, I came up with the idea of fermenting the unripe berries in a kimchi. I basically used the same recipe as I would for Basic Wild Kimchi (see page 120), but instead of using 3 cups (700 ml volume) finely shredded wild green edibles, I used 2 cups (475 ml volume) of unripe green elderberries and 1 cup (235 ml volume) finely shredded wild greens. The rest of the procedure and ingredients was exactly the same.

I fermented it for 1 week in the kitchen, then placed the jar for 2 weeks in the refrigerator.

My next step was to strain the kimchi, reserving the fermented liquid and removing (with clean hands) the fermented unripe elderberries. I placed them in jars and made a pickling solution with the following ratio:

2 cups (475 ml) fermented brine
2 cups (475 ml) apple cider vinegar (or rice vinegar)
2 tablespoons (30 g) salt

The final steps are to bring the pickling solution to a boil and pour into the half-pint (250 ml) jars; then, using the water bath canning method (see page 38), boil the jars for 15 minutes. Another alternative to canning is to place the jars in the fridge and wait a few weeks before consuming.

Feel free to experiment with the pickling solution and add some spices too. In my version the flavors were tangy, sour, and salty. The capers make a very nice condiment for seafood dishes.

UNRIPE FIGS IN SYRUP

Sometimes it's a tough world for foragers: Some of the most delicious edible plants and fruits can be hard to forage because of the local competition with birds, animals, and even other foragers.

One particular year I had a terrible time foraging ripe figs. I probably managed to get only 30 figs that year. So the following year I decided to use another approach—I decided to forage them while they were not yet ripe.

The first thing to know when foraging unripe figs is that you must use gloves. The sap emanating from the stem can be quite irritating. I didn't know about this my first time out and used my bare hands. I usually have no problems with plants that can affect the skin, including poison oak, but after foraging the figs my hands were sticky and very itchy for a couple of hours. Not a huge deal, but definitely annoying.

I've seen conflicting information about the exact time to collect the figs. Some people advise you to forage them when they're very little, while others do it when they're nearly ripe. As far as I'm concerned, they are fair game at any stage when they're unripe, small or not.

After harvesting them, the next step is to cut off any excessive stem and clean them.

Once this is done, take a pointed object, such as a toothpick, and make four holes in each fig. Another method is to score the bottom of the figs. Both methods work well.

When you're done scoring or poking holes in your unripe figs, place them in hot water and bring the water to a boil. The goal is to remove the bitterness of the unripe figs, so take the following steps:

1. Boil for 15 minutes, then change the water.
2. Boil again for 15 minutes, and change the water again.

Taste one of the figs. If it is still bitter, boil again for 10 to 15 minutes, then strain the water out and place the figs in pint jars. For each jar, juice ½ lemon and pour the juice in it. Slice the other half of the lemon and place the slices in the jar. Also place 4 whole cloves into each jar.

Now make a syrup composed of 3 cups (600 g) sugar and 4 cups (approximately 1 l) water. Bring the syrup to a boil and pour it into the jars.

Close the jars, let them cool off a bit, and place in the refrigerator. Wait 3 weeks before consuming.

If you want to preserve them so they're shelf-stable, right after you pour the syrup into the jars, close the jars, then use the water bath method (see page 38) to boil the jars for 45 minutes (for quart jars) or 30 minutes (for pint jars). This timing is based on a USDA-approved recipe for canning ripe figs. I think it's excessive, but I like to play it safe.

Remove the jars and make sure they've sealed properly. Store in a cool location. They should be good for at least a year.

Preserving by Dehydrating

Dehydration is probably one of the easiest ways to preserve many types of food, from herbs, vegetables, and fruits to insects and meats.

The underlying principle is very simple: Most of our food contains a large amount of water, up to 95 percent for some fruits and vegetables and 50 to 75 percent for insects and meats. Like any living organism, the bacteria in our food need water to survive. If you remove the water, the bacteria that could spoil your food will be destroyed, thus ensuring a safe preservation.

If you walk around your local supermarket you will find a plentitude of dehydrated foods, including instant mashed potato powder, spices, pasta, tea, beans, and breakfast cereals, to name a few.

Dehydration is very often used with other methods of preservation, such as salting and sugaring, for added food safety, extended storage time, and enhanced flavor. Such is the case with potato chips, soup cubes, and beef jerky, which use salt, while other foodstuffs such as condensed milk, some power bars, and cookies will mostly use sugar.

Dehydration is also much more than just a method of preserving food. By using your imagination you can create countless interesting snacks, delicious infusions, and spice blends. It can be used to condense flavors, alter textures, and even add colors.

The real fun in experimenting with dehydration and wild foods is the potential for interesting and original creations.

Herb powders from nettles, dandelion, or watercress can be mixed into dough to create delicious and dazzling breads, pizzas, and flatbreads. Dehydrated aromatic leaves or pine needles can be ground with sugar or mixed with salts for colors and flavors. My favorite is a powdered sugar that I make using local white fir needles and regular white sugar, which we sprinkle on ice cream.

Dried fruits or berries can be infused in syrup or alcohol. I often infuse my local toyon berries in brandy, which we use on various desserts throughout the year.

You can also create countless infusions reflecting your terroir. I've put together all kinds of dried herbs and plant blends featuring the flavors of the local mountains, desert, forest, and chaparral.

With some experimentation and basic skills, you can also completely transform wild ingredients into something new. A few years ago I made yucca jerky with the young shoots of our local plant whose common name is Our Lord's candle (*Hesperoyucca whipplei*), and some people were convinced it was meat. Mallow leaves, with their mucilaginous qualities, were made into interesting "seaweed chips" by pressing leaves together with a layer of wet mallow powder and spices in between, then

Dehydrated wild figs soaked in syrup (mugwort beer syrup, lerp sugar).

Local mountain infusion blend
(white fir, pine, manzanita berries,
wild chamomile, and dehydrated lemon).

dehydrated. Even insects have awesome uses—I've made some intriguing spice blends using foraged crickets and ants.

Instead of considering dehydration as a food preservation practice, I like to think of it as an interesting method of food creation.

Drying Wild Herbs and Plants

It's a bit of an art to dehydrate wild plants properly. As you experiment with them you may find temperatures and methods that work better for you than what I suggest. When dealing with wild plants, I decide on the best way to dehydrate them based on their condition, time of the year, aroma, and so forth. For example, common stinging nettles (*Urtica dioica*) in January are very different from what we call giant nettles (*Urtica holosericea*), which are found in the forest in September. Young nettles in January are so fragile that I dry them carefully in paper bags, while the giant ones will dry just fine in a dehydrator.

As a general rule, I like to harvest plants that I plan to dry in the morning, and ideally at the stage where they are about to flower. Many plants and herbs have volatile aromatic oils that can somewhat evaporate after exposure to the direct sunlight during the day. If necessary, gently rinse them in cold water before drying. I never dry herbs in direct sunlight.

Although it requires some experimentation, to make it easier to start, I usually divide my plants and herbs into three categories: fragile,

Nettle bread made by wild food chef Mia Wasilevich. *Photo courtesy of Mia Wasilevich.*

medium, and tough. I will use slightly different methods of drying the plants in each category. Some plants that seem fragile but contain a lot of water, such as mint, watercress, or curly dock, must be dried in a dehydrator as they may rot if they are air-dried. Although during the summer here in Southern California rot is not a problem, it could be a problem in Florida, where it's much more humid.

FRAGILE HERBS AND PLANTS

This category consist of plants that are tender and often have somewhat delicate aromatic properties, such as fennel, chervil, epazote, yucca flowers, pineapple weed, chickweed, and yarrow.

Forage them in the morning if you can, rinse if necessary, and pat them dry using a clean towel (a paper towel is fine) or shake to remove excess water. I air-dry them by hanging in a paper bag in a well-ventilated area. Punch holes in the paper bag to facilitate evaporation. Once the leaves are dry and brittle, place them in a tightly closed jar or other container. Store out of light.

If you live in a very humid area, air-drying may not be possible. In this case, use a dehydrator at a temperature set as high as 125°F (52°C) and store in an airtight container as soon as the leaves become dry and brittle.

MEDIUM HERBS AND PLANTS

This category consists of plants that are less delicate and retain their aromas or flavors easily, such as nettles, wild celery, wild mints, lamb's quarters, sweet white clover, and mustard.

I forage the best specimens (usually in the shade) in the morning or early afternoon. Back home, I rinse them if necessary and pat dry using a clean towel, or shake to remove excess water. Place in a dehydrator at a low setting, around 100°F (38°C), and store in airtight container as soon as the leaves are dry and brittle. If you live in a very humid area, use a temperature as high as 125°F (52°C).

TOUGH HERBS AND PLANTS

This category consists of plants that are less delicate and retain their aromas or flavors easily, such as white sage, black sage, sagebrush, mugwort, California bay, white fir, and pine needles.

Forage, rinse, and shake off excess water. Place in a dehydrator at a somewhat low setting, around 135°F (57°C), and store in airtight containers as soon as the leaves are dry and brittle.

From experience, some "tough" herbs such as mugwort, eucalyptus, or bay leaves don't benefit from dehydrating rapidly and are much better air-dried on the stems in large paper bags with holes. I like to dry eucalyptus and California bay leaves for at least 2 to 3 months before using.

DEHYDRATED WILD KIMCHI SPICE

I really like dehydrating plants and herbs to create unusual spices. Aside from drying aromatics to make various spice blends, I like to experiment with creating more complex blends using fermented ingredients, aromatic woods, and sometimes even insects. Our local ants can add some fascinating peppery or lemony qualities.

Some of my best spices are made by dehydrating my fermented concoctions and grinding them into powder, which we then sprinkle on food. Depending on the ingredients used in the fermentation, the flavor range can be quite wide. For example, dehydrated sauerkraut that has been fermented with white fir branches and California juniper berries is still sour, but adds a definite "local mountains" touch with its pine and lemony flavors.

Maybe it's because I love kimchi, but my personal favorite blends are made from dehydrated wild kimchi powders. They're sweet, sour, spicy, and salty—perfect for fish and various dishes with an Asian influence. By changing the ingredients a bit, I can add some lemon hints (curly dock) or bitterness (dandelion, thistles, et cetera).

There is still so much experimenting to do, and the flavor combinations are really infinite. I haven't even yet touched upon other types of fermentations, such as with grains, beans, seeds, and starchy ingredients, which I'm sure can offer some interesting results as well. But for its simplicity, making kimchi powder is a great start.

Procedure

Make your kimchi (see Basic Wild Kimchi on page 120). If it is the first time making this recipe, simply use ingredients that you like and can find locally: Mustard greens, dandelion, dock, plantain, or sow thistle are good examples. A couple of them in the mix will do.

Once the fermentation is completed, place the kimchi on a silicone pad. You can also use a large plate or parchment paper on a tray.

Dehydrate the kimchi until it is thoroughly dry and crispy. This will take several hours or a whole day, depending on the temperature. I usually use a temperature setting around 135°F (57° C) in my dehydrator, but have gone as high as 170°F (77°C) in a regular oven. Dehydrating outside is not a good idea—flies seems to love kimchi.

The dried kimchi may not be a pretty sight, but trust me, the flavors are in there. Let it cool for a while. If you've made a large quantity, you can store what you won't use in tightly closed containers such as canning jars.

Using a *molcajete* (stone grinder) or a hand-crank or electric coffee grinder, grind the kimchi into powder.

If you plan to use an electric grinder such as one used to grind coffee, make sure to remove any pieces that are too hard, such as tough, dehydrated stems. Personally I think going primitive with a *molcajete* or using a hand-crank grinder is the way to go.

Herbs and Berries Powder

I often dehydrate various plants and berries and then reduce them to powder. We use these powders quite extensively and for various purposes during our private dinners. I currently have nearly 20 different kinds carefully preserved in jars. Here are some of the culinary uses we have for them:

Spices (or to be used as part of spice blends): various local sages (white sage, California sagebrush, black sage), sweet white clover, fennel, chervil, wild onions, mint, wild celery, epazote, California bay leaves, eucalyptus leaves, magnolia leaves and flower buds

Soup thickener: cactus pads (the pads are first boiled, then dehydrated), cattail roots, wild hyacinth bulbs (*Dichelostemma pulchellum*)

Sour flavors: curly dock, wild rhubarb, oxalis, boiled cactus pads, lemonade berries

Mixed with flour or in soup for flavors, color, added nutrition: nettles, curly dock, watercress, cattail shoots, various grasses, *Hesperoyucca whipplei* shoots (boiled first, then dehydrated), sweet alyssum, various mustard leaves, wild radish leaves, broadleaf plantain, lamb's quarters, chickweed, miner's lettuce, acorns, walnuts

Fruity and sugary powders often sprinkled over desserts, ice cream: elderberries, wild currants, manzanita, toyon berries, ripe black nightshade berries, yucca shoots, white fir needles

Powders for drinks: manzanita berries, elderberries, wild currant berries

Note that the flavors of some plants can be altered quite considerably through dehydration. A good example is black mustard—the fresh leaves are really spicy, but once dried, the "wasabi" quality will be gone.

Gouyères with sweet white clover powder by chef Mia Wasilevich. *Photo courtesy of Mia Wasilevich.*

Dehydrated lerp sugar: acorn and wheat flour cookies.

WILD FOOD SOUP CUBES

A few years ago I came up with the idea of making dehydrated wild food soup cubes instead of buying regular soup cubes from the store. It's a great way to preserve food and doesn't take much room in your backpack. These soup cubes also contain far fewer chemicals than the store-bought versions. Being able to drink some tasty organic soup after a long day exploring the outdoor induces a wonderful, comforting feeling. I use a wide variety of wild edibles when making my soups, but the procedure for making the dehydrated cubes is pretty much the same.

Procedure

Let's start with a very simple recipe, such as nettle soup. The typical ingredients are nettles, onions, garlic, potatoes, French or Italian spice blends, salt, and pepper. Some people add bacon as well, but we're making a vegetarian soup here. Usually I use 2 to 3 compacted cups (475 to 700 ml volume) of nettles (leaves or whole young nettles), 2 medium-sized onions, 2 potatoes, and around 6 cloves of garlic. Add spices to taste. It's not a set recipe; more nettles will make it even tastier.

The next step is taking all the ingredients and dehydrating them.

Wash your nettles (I used young nettles in my recipe, so I didn't remove the stems, which are still tender), slice the onions and potatoes, chop the garlic, and place everything in your dehydrator or oven at the lowest temperature.

For the nettles, usually around 3 or 4 hours in the dehydrator at 120°F (49°C) does the job. You can remove the nettles at that point. I then crank up the temperature a bit, to around 140°F (60°C), for the other ingredients. If you're using an old oven, your temperature will probably be higher than this, even on the lowest setting. If that's the case, place your ingredients in a single layer on a baking sheet and leave the oven door open 1 or 2 inches to improve air circulation. Some modern ovens have a dehydrate setting; if so, just follow the directions provided by the manufacturer.

Once your ingredients are dried, you need to reduce them into powders. I usually use my *molcajete* stone grinder to do this. It takes time, but it provides a good arm workout and it works very well too. If I

don't feel like having a workout I use my trusted hand-crank coffee grinder. If you want to use an electric coffee grinder, I would strongly advise you to crush the potatoes and garlic into small bits first (using a stone, hammer, or whatever does the job). Dehydrated garlic and potatoes can be very hard.

By the way, aside from the nettles, you can purchase all the dry ingredients instead of making them. Garlic, onions, and potatoes already exist in powdered form at your local grocery store, but the flavors won't compare to the ones you dehydrate at home.

Next, place all the powdered ingredients on a plate and add water. My basic recipe calls for:

⅓ cup (around 80 ml volume) nettle powder
2 teaspoons (6 g) onion powder
2 teaspoons (6 g) potato powder
1 teaspoon (3 g) garlic powder
1 teaspoon (3 g) French or Italian herb mix
⅓ teaspoon (2 g) each of both salt and pepper

Make sure you don't pour on too much water; you want to achieve the same consistency as bread dough. Too much water and you won't be able to shape your vegetable dough into cubes. I use a fork to mix the ingredients and obtain the perfect consistency.

Clean your hands, then shape the vegetable dough into a big ball and let it rest a bit—I usually allow it to rest for 30 minutes. I believe doing this leaves time for the various flavors to interact and blend with each other, but you can skip the resting step if you want.

If you let the dough rest for 30 minutes, clean your hands again and, using your fingers, create little cubes with the dough.

The final step is dehydrating the cubes. This takes a while in a conventional dehydrator, so it's not an energy-saving procedure by any means. We're talking around 10 hours of drying time at 125°F (52°C), but if you're using your dehydrator to warm up your house during the winter, it's a good option. Make sure the cubes are really dry before storing them in a closed container or jar.

To make soup, place the cube(s) in water, bring the water to a boil, and let it simmer for 10 to 15 minutes.

Let's be honest, though. While soup cubes are fun to make, you can also skip making the cubes and use the powdered soup mix to make your soup. It's easier to store in bags or jars, and you'll save some money from not using the dehydrator or oven.

1. Gather or forage your fresh ingredients. 2. Dehydrate your ingredients. 3. Using a stone or electric grinder, reduce them to a powder. 4. Gather all your powders as per the basic recipe. 5. Place the powders on a plate or in a bowl and add water. 6. Use a fork to mix your ingredients and make a dough. 7. With clean fingers, shape the dough into small cubes. 8. Dehydrate the cubes.

Making Cold Infusions

I started making cold infusions a couple of years ago after talking to chef Ludo Lefebvre (Trois Mec restaurant). He was interested in offering non-alcoholic pairings for his customers and asked if I could come up with some interesting beverages to complement their own creative drinks. Up to that point I was mostly brewing wild beers and making primitive wines, but I found it extremely rewarding to explore the possibilities nature was offering. I have since created countless wild infusions and offered workshops on the subject.

To begin I experimented with making warm infusions: basically boiling water, turning off the heat, and then placing my ingredients in the hot water. However, this method rather dramatically changed the flavor profile of many foraged plants. I discovered very quickly that you have to let the plants dictate what method to use.

I looked at the option of infusing my wild concoctions in the sun—otherwise known as brewing "sun tea"—whereby you place the container containing your ingredients in the sun and let the warm temperature speed up the infusion process. I scrapped the idea, though, because of the potential bacterial growth that can occur at somewhat high temperatures and make you sick. This issue was even more of a concern because I was dealing with fresh wild plants instead of dehydrated tea leaves.

Local mountain infusion: white fir and pine needles; manzanita, toyon and California juniper berries; elderflowers; and local mountain honey.

Chaparral infusion: manzanita berries, limes, wild peppermint, elderflowers, black sage, cactus pears, hibiscus flowers, honey, and organic cane sugar.

Forest infusion: wood mint, water mint, mugwort, manzanita berries, and organic cane sugar.

Foraging trip infusion: white fir, yarrow, elderflowers, wood mint, manzanita and California juniper berries, lemons, and raw local honey.

SIMPLE COLD INFUSIONS

I experimented with placing my wild infusions overnight in the refrigerator, where the temperature is very low and bacteria growth is not really a concern, and frankly I was amazed with the results. It worked beautifully with many of the aromatic plants, such as white fir, pine, yerba santa, mints, and my various wild berries, and to this date it's my favorite method.

Procedure

1. Forage your ingredients. These can range from aromatic flowers to plants and berries. Here are some of the ingredients I use in Southern California: elderflowers, various wild mints, fragrant or pearly everlasting, yarrow, white fir and pine needles, California juniper berries, mugwort, white sage, black sage, fennel, yerba santa, manzanita berries, toyon berries, Mormon tea, blackberry leaves, lemonade berries, wild currants, sweet white clover, cactus pears, passion fruits, pineapple weed, gooseberries, and dehydrated elderberries.

2. Work out your mix. There are no real rules; you just need to experiment until you are happy with the flavors. Your infusions will also change with the season and whatever is available. When I make my mountain infusion, I usually use 40% wild mint, 40% white fir needles and branches, 10% pine needles, and the rest a mix of various ingredients, such as around 20 cracked California juniper berries, around 40 cracked manzanita berries, and a couple of sliced lemons (or lemonade berries). If I use yarrow or mugwort, I do so very sparingly—maybe a leaf or two. Mints are an excellent base on which to build flavor, and we have over nine found locally, each one with different flavors.

   If you use white fir and pine, cut the needles first so it's easier to extract the flavors. You can also experiment with various woods; I've used California juniper wood chips with interesting results.

   Add sugar or honey to taste.

3. Clean your container thoroughly—this is critical if you plan to serve your infusions to others. After cleaning with soap and hot water, I often do a final rinse with very hot water.

4. Thoroughly clean your foraged ingredients, then place the ingredients and sugar (if any) inside the container and add cold springwater or distilled water. (Do not use tap water, which often contains chlorine and other chemicals.) Add as much water as possible and close the container. I often recycle old glass containers to make my infusions, and cover the top with plastic wrap.

5. Place the container in the refrigerator for at least 12 hours and up to 24 hours, then strain the contents. Place the liquid into a new (clean) container. Keep it in the fridge and enjoy whenever you want. For added food safety, I like to drink the infusion within 3 to 4 days.

Cold infusions don't have to be complex at all; you can easily take a single ingredient as a base and make a delicious infusion. I do this often during my foraging hikes by simply picking up and crushing a specific plant between my fingers then placing it into my water bottle. Infusions with herbs such as mints or sages can be enjoyed within a few minutes.

From a culinary perspective, some plants are much better tasting when they are cold-infused. A good example is yerba santa. I like to pick the young yerba santa leaves in late winter or early spring, as they are highly aromatic at this stage. I place them in my bottle with a couple of lemon slices to make a refreshing drink. Yerba santa is mostly used as a warm infusion for medicinal purposes (to relieve cold and flu symptoms), but the flavor can be extremely bitter if you infuse it too long. Taken fresh and infused cold for a few hours, you can experience the aromatics and little of the bitterness.

Here are some examples of the simple combinations I've used with success. These are just guidelines, and you can add more ingredients if you want added flavors. As a forager, there are countless aromatic plants you can use to make this type of simple cold infusion.

WILD FENNEL

3 to 4 medium-sized fennel leaves, finely chopped; 2 green apples, sliced; and honey to taste. Use a quart of water (around 1 l). Infuse for at least 24 hours in the refrigerator. I like to use Granny Smith apples.

BLACK SAGE

Take a couple of small black sage branches, and bruise them slightly and lovingly between your fingers to release their essences. Add 2 sweet oranges, sliced, and honey to taste. Use a quart of water (around 1 l). Infuse for at least 24 hours in the fridge.

WHITE SAGE

Use 3 to 4 fresh white sage leaves, and bruise them slightly and lovingly between your fingers to release their essences. Add 2 lemons, sliced, and honey or sugar to taste. Use a quart of water (around 1 l). Infuse for at least 24 hours in the fridge. Limes go very well with white sage too.

WHITE FIR

Use enough small white fir branches to fill one-third of a 1-quart (1 l) container. Cut the needles slightly so they release their essences, and place everything into the container. Add 1 lemon, sliced, and honey or sugar to taste. Infuse for at least 24 to 48 hours in the fridge.

LOCAL WILD MINTS (*STACHYS BULLATA*, *MENTHA ARVENSIS*, *LEPECHINIA FRAGRANS*, ET CETERA)

Use enough leaves to fill one-third of a 1-quart (1 l) bottle. Bruise them slightly and lovingly between your fingers to release their essences. Add 1 lemon, sliced, and honey or sugar to taste. Infuse for at least 24 hours in the fridge.

As you can see, I often use lemons, apples, or oranges to harmonize the flavors but, depending on your location, you can also substitute completely wild ingredients. For example, you can use pine needles, sumac, or lemonade berries instead of lemons, or use manzanita berries instead of apples. White fir is great to infuse some tangerine/lemon flavors.

Simple cold infusions: sumac, mint, and lemons; water mint, oranges, and honey; white sage, lemons, and honey.

Hot and Chilled Infusions

I feel a bit silly to be writing about hot infusions because making them is often a simple process, but at the same time it can be an art form. If you are obsessed with trying to capture the essence of an environment, it can become a more complex project, albeit quite fun. It's not unusual for me to spend a couple of days, or sometimes much longer, fiddling with a new recipe to get the flavors I want. Very often it's a slow evolution. I try something one day, change it a bit the next day, do it again a few days later when I think of a possible new ingredient or a better way to infuse one, and so on. Sometimes I'm basically happy with an infusion but will continue working on it for a month and test it for flavors on people attending my wild food classes.

Because I deal mostly with chefs, mixologists, restaurants, and our private dinners, my infusions are not meant to be medicinal; they are based more on flavors and aroma. They often represent a local environment, such as the local mountains, chaparral, or desert, and are meant to be paired with specific dishes.

If you want to chill your hot infusions you'll need to experiment a bit, as the flavors can change quite drastically over a short period of time. These have other culinary uses besides just as a beverage, such as making interesting granitas (semi-frozen desserts) or being included in salad dressings.

At this moment I don't have any truly set recipes. I play with what nature is offering me, so it's a somewhat intuitive process. One day, though, I'll probably write down the specific ingredients or possibly even package them.

Within the context of this book, it would be difficult for you to try to reproduce what I do if you live in a different environment, but maybe you'll find some ideas related to possible blends you can create and methods of making them.

When you're dealing with wild plants you have a very wide spectrum of ingredients to play with—each with specific characteristics. I often tell people that there are no rules, just flavors. It should taste awesome and you should be proud to serve it. Well, maybe there is *one* rule: Your infusion shouldn't be unhealthy or poisonous.

As a somewhat vague general approach, I use the cold infusion method with fresh ingredients and the hot/chilled infusion method with dehydrated ones.

Ingredients can include wood, barks, leaves, needles (pine, fir, et cetera), twigs, stems, berries, fruits, flowers, and so on—pretty much any part of a plant if it is appropriate. Sources of sugar can include regular sugar, molasses, brown sugar, tree saps, and even insect excretion, such as lerp sugar or honey.

I found out years ago that you can't simply steep your ingredients all at once in hot water for a determined amount of time and call it a day. I mean, you *can* do this, but I think if you do you'll miss out on some interesting flavors. This method may work with the usual commercial blends, but not in more elaborate wild concoctions. Here are a few tips:

EXPERIMENT WITH EACH PLANT, ANALYZING ITS FLAVORS, TO DETERMINE YOUR STEEPING TIME.

This is very important if you want to go deep into subtle flavors, which some woods or barks can provide. For example, a wood such as California juniper may take anywhere from 20 to 30 minutes to infuse flavors properly, if you are using a small dried branch. It's always better to use shavings when using wood.

Oak bark can provide interesting and complex accents (which is why it is used for wine barrels), but can become overwhelmingly bitter very fast depending on the oak species used. White oak is much less bitter than other oaks. Other woods have also been used in making barrels, such as chestnut, acacia, and various fruitwoods, but I have not yet experimented with them.

Conversely, some aromatic plants such as white sage, black sage, and yerba santa may require a very short steeping time, so you should either use a small amount or place it in the infusion for a short time and remove it.

Each ingredient is different, and if you are really interested in creating unique infusions, you need to take the time to experiment with each one. For example, steep some crushed manzanita berries (or manzanita powder) and taste the infusion every couple of minutes. Either take notes or trust your memory; by doing so you'll gain the knowledge and experience necessary to use each ingredient and extract its maximum savor.

LAYER YOUR TIMING.

Some infusions can take a considerable amount of time. For my local mountain blend, I will simmer my California juniper wood for 15 to 20 minutes, then remove it. Some other ingredients, such as manzanita berries, Mormon tea, or pine needles, benefit from somewhat longer steeping time in simmering water—you will want to place them in the water at the appropriate time.

Once I'm done with the simmering part and I turn off the heat, I then place the ingredients that I don't want too long in the infusion. These are usually highly aromatic ingredients such as white sage, black sage, sagebrush, and white fir. With these ingredients, it's all about quantity and steeping time. A little goes a long way. Strain and serve the infusion when ready.

Another option is to place the right amount of your highly aromatic herbs in a bowl and pour the hot infusion you have already made with the other ingredients in front of the guest.

Sometimes I use a different but fun and useful trick. Once my basic infusion is done, I serve it; to make sure it stays really hot, I'll place a small heated rock in it and then add a bit of some very aromatic plants such as white sage, dried fermented lemon, or yarrow. The small heated rock is always quite popular and works nicely.

CHOOSE THE APPROPRIATE SOURCE OF SWEETNESS.

There is a considerable number of choices for adding sweetness. Of course you can use regular white sugar, but I like the infusions themselves to dictate the source. For a mountain blend, I may use honey from beehives in the actual mountains; for a forest blend, birch or maple syrup may be more appropriate.

You can also make your own molasses with foraged fruits and berries. For my chaparral infusion I use my cactus pear molasses or I'll also use some of my lerp (insect) sugar.

STUDY THOROUGHLY AND KNOW THE PLANTS YOU ARE USING.

It's important not just from a culinary perspective, but also from a medicinal one, to recognize the potential allergies and reactions that your ingredients may cause. Some infusions may not be appropriate for specific people, including pregnant women or young children. Remember, safety is your responsibility.

HAVE FUN! THE CREATIONS ARE ENDLESS.

As a note, you can also let some of your finished hot infusion cool in the fridge and serve it as a cold beverage so long as the flavor profile doesn't change in the process. I've made ice cubes with some of my infusions and served them in a glass with carbonated water, with excellent results.

Preserving Herbs Through Freezing

Some herbs are actually better frozen rather than dehydrated. The dehydration process often eliminates the volatile essential oils in more refined herbs, such as mints and chervil, or affects the flavors too greatly with other plants. For example, black mustard or nasturtium lose their wonderful flavors if dehydrated but will retain them somewhat if frozen.

There are a couple of ways to freeze herbs. You can simply wash them, shake to remove excess water, and then place them in freezer bags. Removing air helps prevent freezer burn. I usually use my vacuum food sealer, but you can also use regular freezer bags. Simply slip a straw in at one side of the opening, seal the bag up as close as possible to the straw, and suck the air out. While still sucking, remove the straw quickly and close the bag.

Another option is to mix your herbs with a bit of water, and then make a paste using a blender. Place the paste in an ice cube tray. Once frozen, place the ice cubes in a freezer bag and try to remove as much air as possible. This is the method we use for black mustard leaves.

Herbs can also be frozen in oil instead of water. This method works well with sages, fennel, nasturtiums, and herb mixes. I usually chop the herbs, mix 2 parts herbs with 1 part olive oil (or melted high-quality butter), place the solution in ice cube trays, and remove the cubes once they are frozen. The cubes are then stored in freezer bags that has have as much air removed as possible. This is a good method if you intend to use these herbs for cooking later on.

Chickweed, chervil, and garlic preserved in olive oil.

Black mustard (*Brassica nigra*)
Wasabi flavors—used for making hot mustard and sauces. Flowers, leaves, and seeds are used.

Black sage (*Salvia mellifera*)
Strong aroma, works very nicely with fruity ingredients such as wild sodas and preserves. Awesome with chocolate; we often do black sage chocolate truffles or hot chocolate.

California bay (*Umbellularia californica*)
Same uses as regular bay but stronger flavors. Better if dehydrated for a couple of months.

California sagebrush (*Artemisia californica*)
We use it dehydrated and sparingly with other herbs and seeds in our spice blends. Strongly aromatic but bitter.

Wild celery (*Apium graveolens*)
Same uses as regular celery. We use the whole plant instead of just the stems. Seeds are also used as flavoring.

Burr-chervil (*Anthriscus caucalis*)
Carrot family. Highly aromatic and flavorful. Used fresh or dehydrated.

Sweet white clover (*Melilotus alba*)
Use sparingly; fantastic for adding flavors to various dishes. Needs to be foraged fresh—can become toxic if spoiled or fermented.

Wright's cudweed (*Pseudognaphalium canescens*)
Can lend interesting whiskey flavors to dishes. Best used for roasting or smoking.

Epazote (*Dysphania ambrosioides*)
Pungent and strong flavor. Used sparingly in spice blends and in many traditional Mexican dishes.

Wild fennel (*Foeniculum vulgare*)
Highly aromatic anise-flavored spice. Leaves, flowers, pollen, and seeds are used.

California juniper (*Juniperus californica*)
Berries used for flavoring; they have pine and lemon notes. Wood used to smoke meat or fish.

Lerp sugar (*Spondyliaspis eucalypti*)
A psyllid bug excretion composed of starch and sugar. Crunchy and sugary once dehydrated.

California peppertree (*Schinus molle*)
Used very sparingly, usually steeped lightly to extract flavors. Some people may have adverse reactions.

Currants (*Ribes* spp.)
Some native currants have incredible aromatic qualities. We use the leaves for infusions.

California mugwort (*Artemisia douglasiana*)
Very aromatic but bitter. Used sparingly as a spice; mostly used in making primitive beers and infusions.

Tasmanian blue gum (*Eucalyptus globulus*)
Leaves used as spice or infusion. Minty and mellow flavor.

Lemonade berries (*Rhus integrifolia*)
We use them instead of lemons by steeping the berries in infusions or sauces.

Mints
We have over nine different aromatic mints in the wilderness around Los Angeles.

Magnolia (*Magnolia grandiflora*)
Young flower buds and leaves used as a mild spice.

Sweet alyssum (*Lobularia maritima*)
Interesting flavors, spicy and slightly reminiscent of radish. The flowers are sweeter.

Woods and barks
California bay, juniper, oak, and mesquite. Used for smoking and as an ingredient for spice blends.

White sage (*Salvia apiana*)
Very strong flavors; used sparingly in spice blends and infusions.

White fir (*Abies concolor*)
Used as a spice (fir sugar), but mostly in infusions. Interesting lemony/tangerine flavors.

Yarrow (*Achillea millefolium*)
Used mostly in infusions and primitive brews. Bitter but highly aromatic. Can be used sparingly in spice blends.

Ashes and charcoals
Juniper, mesquite, California bay, oak, pine, and cedar.

Dehydrated fruits
Toyon berries, strawberries, elderberries, manzanita berries, cactus pear skins, wild currants.

Wild seeds
Fennel, black mustard, celery, various sages.

Insects
Ants, crickets, stink bugs, and others can also be used as an ingredient in a wild spice blend.

Chaparral wild spice blend: white sage,
black sage, California sagebrush,
California bay, salt, peppercorn,
and garlic powder.

Creating Wild Spice Blends

Spices are usually defined as aromatic or pungent vegetable substances used to flavor food. This would include dried herbs, seeds, barks, roots, and fruits. Although not a vegetable substance, I like to add insects to the mix too and call them a spice. A good example would be some of our local red harvester ants, which add a nice lemony accent to foods.

I'm currently experimenting with local aromatic woods such as California bay, juniper, and mesquite infused with other spices and grated over food. This work is still very much in the trial stage, but there are some interesting possibilities.

Although I've not seen it often in culinary uses recently, native peoples used a variety of ashes such as cedar, juniper, and so on, as food flavorings. I've been playing with a few of these—they indeed have some interesting but very mild flavors. Lye can be made from ashes combined with water, and thus mixing ashes in food can also chemically alter the ingredients and taste. Some native stew recipes call for the addition of ashes.

There are around 50 wild ingredients we use to create various spice blends, and every year I seem to find more. By adding these to other, more conventional spices such as peppercorns, garlic, onions, cloves, and so on, we can create an infinite number of interesting wild flavors.

As a word of caution, although I've never seen anyone having adverse reactions in my 16 years of foraging, I use wild spices sparingly. They often have intense flavors, so a little goes a long way. Like some commercial spices, herbs, or plants such as nutmeg, turmeric, parsley seeds, and licorice, some wild spices may be toxic in large amounts.

Most of my ingredients are dehydrated before use. This often helps with the flavors and, as is the case with store-bought spices, dehydration can also reduce or eliminate potentially harmful chemical compounds.

Using the berries of the California peppertree (*Shinus molle*) is still somewhat controversial. Some people use the berries as peppercorns, and I've purchased homemade products at the local market that used these berries in jams and sauces. However, whenever I eat them I experience mild stomach upset. Steeping them lightly for their flavors instead of ingesting the seeds seems to resolve that issue. If you research the plant you'll see a wide range of opinions about it, and although they were apparently once sold commercially as pink peppercorns and in pepper blends, it's not a spice I provide to local restaurants or chefs at this time. Using the dehydrated unripe fruits before the seeds are formed may be the solution, but I still have to research that possibility.

On the Use of Primitive Tools

Primitive stone grinders are my favorite tools for making spice blends. Because of their toughness, some ingredients (stems, for example) can damage or ruin an electric grinder, and some, such as California bay leaves, won't reduce into powder.

While foraging, I'm always on the lookout for nice flat stones, usually 1 inch high and with a rough texture. I find most of the smaller stones I use for grinding in local riverbeds. If you start looking for stone grinders you will realize very soon that there is an art to picking out the right stones. I often say that each flat stone needs a specific stone grinder to complement it, from both an aesthetic and a practical point of view. My job is to find the perfect set, and sometimes this can take weeks or months.

To effectively reduce the ingredients into powder or small bits, use rough ingredients such as whole peppercorns or coarse salt.

CHAPARRAL WILD SPICE BLEND

This is my favorite spice blend, and it's extremely versatile. We've used it on popcorn, french fries, fish, and even as a steak rub. I have expressed quantities in grams here to make measuring easier. The basic recipe is as follows:

Ingredients

6 grams whole peppercorns
5 grams white sage
4 grams California sagebrush
5 grams black sage
1 gram epazote (optional)
32 grams garlic powder
30 grams coarse salt
1 gram California bay

Procedure

1. Using an electric or stone grinder, reduce all the ingredients to a crude powder.
2. Place in an airtight jar right away so you don't lose any aromas and flavors.

This blend is extremely aromatic from the various sages; it's spicy and salty too. Feel free to play around with the ingredients; some may like less garlic powder or salt. I've made it so often that I've stopped weighing the ingredients and now just mix them instinctively. You can substitute chili powder for the peppercorns if you wish.

Use sparingly—a little goes a long way. When using with fish, I usually add a bit of fennel seeds in the recipe.

WHITE FIR SUGAR

This sugar is extremely simple to make and is quite delicious sprinkled on desserts or as an ingredient in ice cream, pastry, or drinks. It has some wonderful pine and lemon flavors.

I collect the white fir branches in the nearby mountains, usually at elevations between 6,000 and 8,000 feet. It's an ingredient I can forage all year long: The newer needles in spring have more of a lemony flavor, but they're good at any time of the year. Most of them I use fresh in cold infusions; I dehydrate the rest to use in our spice blends or to make fir sugar. For optimal flavor, I don't dehydrate the branches in the sun or dehydrator but simply hang them in the garage inside a large paper bag. In Southern California it usually takes 3 to 4 weeks for them to be fully dehydrated.

Making the sugar requires two or three stages. If you were simply to grind the granulated sugar with the fir needles in one step you would end up with bits and pieces of organic material left in the sugar and a mealy texture. By doing it in a couple of steps, the sugar grains will reduce the needles into powder properly.

Ingredients

12 grams cane sugar
5 grams white fir needles

Procedure

1. Place 6 grams of cane sugar and the white fir needles in an electric coffee grinder on espresso setting. Grind for 10 seconds. I like to shake the grinder as it's in motion to ensure even grinding.
2. Open the grinder and add another 6 grams of sugar. Grind for another 10 seconds.
3. Taste the sugar. If it is still a bit mealy, add another 2 grams of granulated cane sugar and grind one more time. As a last step I use a fine strainer to remove any unwanted particles—there are always a few.

WILD FENNEL SUGAR

This process is very similar to making the white fir sugar. Wild fennel sugar is really delicious sprinkled on ice cream and desserts.

Ingredients

10 grams cane sugar
5 grams wild fennel seeds

Procedure

1. Grind 5 grams of cane sugar and the wild fennel seeds in an electric coffee grinder on espresso setting. Grind for 10 seconds. I like to shake the grinder as it's in motion to ensure even grinding.
2. Open the grinder and add another 5 grams of sugar. Grind for another 10 seconds.
3. Taste the sugar. If the texture is still a bit mealy, add another 2 grams of granulated cane sugar and grind one more time. Use a fine strainer to remove any unwanted particles as the last step.

SUPER SIMPLE SPICE BLENDS

Spice blends don't have to be complex to start with: It's better if you venture into this world of wild flavors with very simple blends that are also easy to forage. As you gather and preserve more of your foraged aromatic herbs and spices, you can begin experimenting by adding more to the blend. It all comes naturally as you gain experience.

Here are some examples of tasty and yet simple blends. Just grind the ingredients together or place into a coffee grinder on espresso setting for a few seconds. It looks better ground by hand, though. I like my spice blends to be a bit rough instead of a fine powder. (See the On the Use of Primitive Tools sidebar on page 157.)

California Sagebrush Blend

Use as a steak rub, or with lamb, goat, game meats, or potatoes.

2 grams dehydrated California sagebrush powder
3 grams whole peppercorns
10 grams garlic powder
6 grams salt
2 grams sugar

Wild Fennel Seeds Blend

Use with fish, shellfish, roasted carrots, and various steamed or roasted vegetables.

4 grams wild fennel seeds
2 grams ground coriander seeds
1 gram whole peppercorns
3 grams salt
2 grams onion powder

White Fir Blend

For desserts, ice cream, roasted carrots, to name a few.

3 grams white fir needle powder
1 gram dehydrated orange zest
2 grams chili powder (mild or hot)
2 teaspoons sugar

Some restaurants I've worked with have used some very simple blends of garlic and white sage extremely sparingly (the flavors are very strong) on potatoes or steamed vegetables.

In my kitchen, I've sprinkled dehydrated California sagebrush leaves over grilled steaks, with excellent results. California sagebrush (*Artemisia californica*) was used as a spice by native peoples too, but it's important to understand that not all sagebrushes are edible and some can be somewhat toxic. You need to research each of your local aromatic plants thoroughly and carefully before use.

DUCK PROSCIUTTO FLAVORED WITH WILD SAGES

The straightforward recipe is packed with flavors. Anyone with a refrigerator can make it successfully. My herb mix features ingredients native to or naturalized in Southern California; you can use the same procedure with your local (wild) aromatics.

Ingredients

1 duck breast

Sea salt or kosher salt (quantity will vary depending on pan size)

2–3 medium-sized white sage leaves, crushed

1 teaspoon (3–4 g) cracked peppercorns

1 small California bay leaf (or 1 commercial bay leaf), crushed

Around 1 tablespoon (8 g) garlic powder

2–3 tablespoons (2–3 g) California sagebrush leaves

Procedure

1. Pour ½ inch of salt in a non-reactive pan. Place the duck breast on top and cover it well with another layer of salt. (If you use more than one duck breast, make sure they don't touch each other.) Use sea salt or kosher salt, not regular table salt (which contains iodine and other chemical agents).

2. Cover the pan with plastic wrap and place in the refrigerator for 24 hours (18 hours is fine if it's a small breast).

3. Remove the duck breast from the salt, rinse it with water, and pat dry with a paper towel. Place the breast on cheesecloth; add the wild aromatic herbs on both sides. Wrap it with the cheesecloth (you should end up with the cheesecloth being two or three layers thick), and tie with a string.

4. Weigh the duck breast at this point, as it will be ready to eat when 30 percent of its weight has been lost through dehydration. After weighing it, hang it in a section of the fridge (don't let it touch anything).

5. When the weight of the duck breast is reduced by 30 percent—usually in 10 to 12 days—your prosciutto is ready. Remove from the fridge, unwrap the cheesecloth, and enjoy. The wild sages infused into the meat during the dehydration process provide nice feral flavors.

6. You can wrap the prosciutto in plastic wrap and store it in the fridge for several weeks.

Local Mountain Blends

Wherever you live, the spice blends you can create with your local ingredients are pretty much endless. As you preserve more and more of your foraged goodies, you'll be able to experiment with much more complex blends. While I try to mostly use wild plants and my own preserves, such as dehydrated whole limes or lemons (limes or lemons boiled in salted water, 1 part salt and 6 parts water, for 5 minutes then placed in the sun until completely dry), some people may decide to just use one wild ingredient with regular spices. It's all good. From my perspective, the fun is in the creation of new, unusual, and delicious flavors.

MOUNTAIN "FISH" BLEND

This blend is sour, salty, and spicy with hints of pine. It's very nice used lightly on fish.

Chef Mia Wasilevich created an innovative and delicious use for this blend, sprinkling it on raw cashews that have been dipped in honey.

Ingredients

5 grams white fir
6 grams coarse sea salt
1 dehydrated lime or lemon (I prefer lime)
4 grams chili powder (mild or hot)
0.5 gram dehydrated yarrow flowers
1 gram wild fennel seeds
1 small white sage leaf
8 grams lerp sugar (or 4 grams white sugar)

Procedure

1. Using an electric grinder, reduce all the ingredients to a crude powder. I usually add the fennel seeds and coarse salt last, which helps grind the ingredients to a fine powder.
2. Place the spice blend in an airtight jar right away so you don't lose any aromas and flavors. It's always better after a few days.

HILLSIDE BLEND

This is another interesting blend that also tastes like the local hills and uses ingredients I usually forage there. It's sweeter and quite exotic.

Ingredients

7 grams white fir
15 grams dry-roasted elderberries (dehydrated at 220°F [105°C], which tends to give them a roasted flavor)
1 gram wild fennel seeds
1 dehydrated lime
1 gram chili powder (mild or hot)
7 grams manzanita berries
1 gram salt

Procedure

1. Using an electric grinder, reduce all the ingredients to a crude powder. I usually add the fennel seeds and coarse salt last, which helps grind the ingredients to a fine powder.
2. Place the spice blend in an airtight jar right away so you don't lose any aromas and flavors. It's always better after a few days.

Rediscovering a Spice: Wright's Cudweed

A couple of years ago during a morning foraging walk I had a new smell experience. It was a beautiful morning, the sun was just appearing on the horizon, and I was enjoying the unique chaparral perfume and sights. Early morning is a fantastic time to wander in the wilderness: The dew emanating from the local plants slowly evaporates and you are blessed with a thousand scents. The various essences are always changing as you walk among them. You may get hints of sages in one location, then walk another 50 yards and experience new accents such as mugwort or California sagebrush.

Overall it's always the same chaparral perfume, but the notes can vary immensely. Smell is a powerful foraging tool.

At one point during my walk, I got hints of a new scent that fascinated me. It was quite pungent but not overwhelming, with some definite curry-like qualities. I took note of where the wind was coming from, followed the scent trail, and came upon a very dry-looking plant that I had seen before but always discarded because of its underwhelming appearance. I knew every other plant in the area so the scent could only be coming from that one. I held a bunch of the dry branches to my nose, inhaled slowly—and it was as if I had been transported into an exotic Middle Eastern market. It had hints of curry, lemon, and even peppers: a very unusual smell, yet so amazing. It was an instant obsession to see if the plant could be used in culinary applications.

I took a bunch of photos and, within hours, thanks to the online feedback of local experts, I knew the name: Wright's cudweed (*Pseudognaphalium canescens*)—also called rabbit tobacco, although this common name can be confusing since many plants of the same genus are called that too.

Once I had the Latin name, I was able to do some research on it. Interestingly, this type of plant was often traditionally used as a cold and flu remedy (taken as a tea) or as a tobacco substitute (with no nicotine). I could find very little other information about this plant, but I did find an obscure reference in an ethnobotany book that the Cherokee had used it as a spice, which prompted me to investigate its potential culinary uses.

Playing with "wild spices" is not easy—usually they're much stronger than the varieties you can purchase or grow in your garden. For example, the difference between white sage and garden sage in terms of flavors and aroma is quite significant. So using wild spices is a game of moderation and of truly understanding how the flavors relate to one another. In the end, you want to create something that people would actually enjoy tasting in their food.

I tried all kinds of experiments with this new (to me) plant, such as making sauces, sautéing it in oil or butter with other spices, and adding it to stews. The difficulty I encountered was the plant's obvious bitterness when I cooked with it. So I set the project aside for a while.

A month later, while on a quest to forage more cudweed to play with, I came across some quails and thought that quail could be the perfect main dish for my culinary experiment with the "wild curry" flavor. Inspired by the fact that this plant was also used as a tobacco substitute, I tried something different. I wrapped the plant around a couple of quails and roasted them in the oven. Eureka! The whole house smelled fantastic and the flavors imbued in the birds were out of this world, with only the slightest hint of bitterness.

I introduced that technique to some local chefs I was working with and soon this very unique "new" spice and flavor was introduced in the Los Angeles culinary scene with the approval of foodies and critics. Chef Chris Jacobson from Girasol restaurant used it with salmon, and Los Angeles critic Jonathan Gold choose it as one of the best dishes of 2013. He described the flavor as follows: "The salmon has been smoked over a foraged herb called rabbit tobacco, which gives it an odd, almost whiskey-like edge."

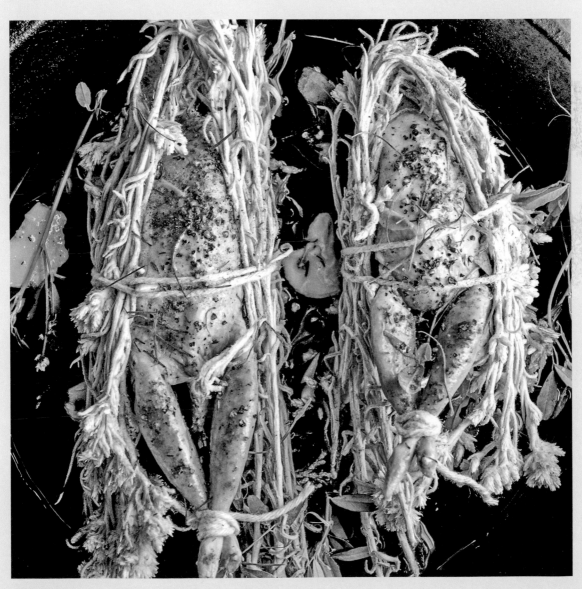

Quails wrapped in Wright's cudweed.

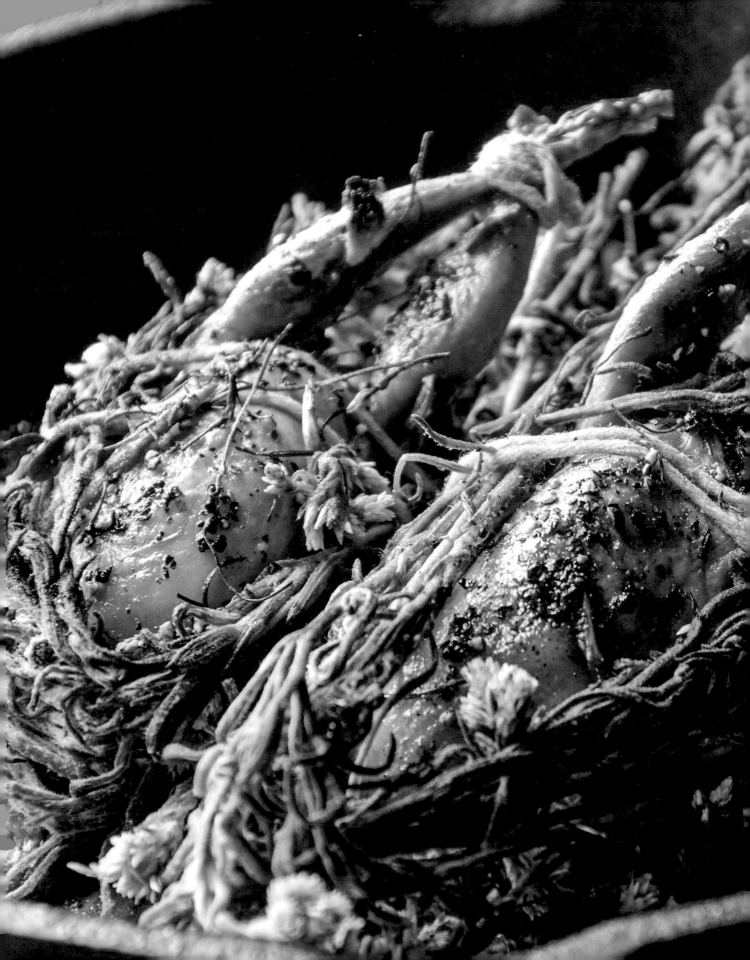

CHAPARRAL ROASTED QUAIL

Here is the original quail dish created in our wild food lab. I currently don't have a hunting license, so to keep it legal I purchased some quails at our local butcher.

Ingredients

2 quails
Around 20 California juniper berries, cracked
6 sprigs sweet white clover
8 sprigs Wright's cudweed
Olive oil
Black peppercorns, crushed
Chaparral Wild Spice Blend (see page 158), or use a regular spice blend, such as Italian or French
4 garlic cloves, crushed
1 medium-sized California bay leaf or 1 regular bay leaf.
2 ounces (11.3 g) butter
California sagebrush leaves (optional)

Procedure

1. Place the quails in a brine solution (1 cup of salt to 1 gallon of water). Quails are so small that you don't want to leave them in the brine for too long; usually 1½ hours is enough. Since I make my own forest beer and vinegar with wild plants, I also add ½ cup of mugwort vinegar to the brine. You could use a good-quality apple cider vinegar.

   You want the quails to stay under the surface of the brine, so place a small dish on top of the quails. Place in the refrigerator.

2. Preheat the oven to 425°F (218°C). When the brining time is finished, stuff the quails with the crushed California juniper berries (around 10 each) and sweet white clover (2 sprigs each).

3. Now, using the Wright's cudweed, create a wrap around the quail. Tie the wrap with string or with a wild fiber. To keep it true "chaparral" style, I could use local yucca (*Hesperoyucca whipplei*) fibers as a string.

4. Brush the quails with olive oil and sprinkle them with crushed black peppercorns and the Chaparral Wild Spice blend (or your own spice blend). Place the quails in a shallow roasting pan. Add the garlic, bay leaf, 2 sprigs sweet white clover, and butter to the pan. I also added a few dehydrated California sagebrush leaves. You need to use this herb in moderation; a little can go a very long way.

5. Roast the quail for 18 minutes at 425°F (218°C), then change the oven setting to broil. Broil the quail for another 4 minutes. Remove from the oven and let them rest for 10 minutes.

   Then plate the quail and enjoy.

I must say that the rabbit tobacco really shone brightly in this dish, and the sweet curry aroma permeated our whole house. I really liked the end result. Almost none of the bitterness of the Wright's cudweed had permeated the quails, but the curry-like flavors did. The quails were perfectly cooked, and nicely salted from the brine.

In my humble opinion, that dish reeked of chaparral (in a good way), but not overwhelmingly so. It was delicious.

Compound Butters with Wild Aromatic Herbs

Compound butters are super easy to make, and by using the strong flavors of wild aromatics they can really take your food up a notch. Some of our local herbs such as fennel, nasturtium, chervil, sages, sweet white clover, and countless others are really perfect for this application. We spread the butter on bread, place it on grilled vegetables, fish, steaks, quail, and so much more.

BURR-CHERVIL BUTTER

We could fill pages with a lot of recipes but, really, you'll have much more fun experimenting with your own local aromatic plants to create delicious compound butters. Here is one recipe to start (this butter is great with grilled steaks):

Ingredients

3.5 ounces (100 g) unsalted butter, room temperature
4 tablespoons (approximately 10 g) chopped burr-chervil
0.5 ounce (15 g) shallot
1 large garlic clove
Salt to taste

Procedure

1. Take the butter out of the refrigerator and let it come to room temperature. Finely chop the burr-chervil, shallot, and garlic clove.
2. When the butter is soft, mix all the ingredients thoroughly. I like to go old school and use a fork, but you can also use a blender or food processor if you want.
3. Wrap the butter in parchment paper. It helps if you spray the paper lightly with oil first. I usually roll it into a cylinder and twist both ends. If you want to go wild, you can also use a large dock leaf instead of parchment paper. Place in the fridge and use it within 4 to 5 days, or freeze it for up to a month.

You can use this same recipe with other aromatic ingredients, such as sweet white clover or fresh wild fennel leaves. A quick online research session on compound butters will introduce you to countless interesting recipes that use regular spices as well.

SALTS WITH WILD HERBS

I began making infused salts a few years ago. They not only provide a very pretty garnish but done properly are packed with flavors.

In order to make infused salts, you need to use highly aromatic and flavorful herbs or spices. Although I use mostly wild ingredients, there are many interesting salts you can create with regular spices too. One of my favorites is made with habanero peppers; it's super hot and bright red. A few grains are enough to bring some decent heat to a dish. The California bay salt is also very good, with mild but excellent flavors.

The principle is simple: You basically create a paste with plant powder, water, and salt. If the paste is saturated enough with salt, the crystals won't dissolve; through the process of osmosis they will become impregnated with the flavors of the herb.

Procedure

Dehydrate your herbs, such as California bay, sweet white clover, epazote. Using a coffee grinder on espresso setting, grind the dehydrated plant into powder. With some tough ingredients such as California bay leaves you may need to add a bit of coarse salt to the grinder, which will help to reduce them to a powder.

Using a spoon, mix the powder with salt and water to make a thick paste. I use the following amounts to start with:

1 tablespoon (10 g) dry aromatic or spicy powder
  (California bay, epazote, chili, sweet clover)
4 tablespoons (60 g) coarse salt
1–1½ tablespoons (15–25 ml) water

You want a rough paste; if it is still too liquid, add some more powder. If you're using a very hot chili powder, add it sparingly.

Place the paste into a plastic bag and let it rest for 30 minutes so that the salt really gets impregnated with the flavors. Then remove the salt from the bag and spread it out on a plate. Place in the dehydrator at a setting around 140°F (60°C), or in your oven at the lowest temperature. For air circulation and to allow the moisture to escape, prop the oven door open a little by placing a folded towel in the door.

After approximately an hour, using a fork or spoon, stir and crush the salt to pull apart the crystals before they are fully dehydrated. Repeat every 20 minutes or so. If you forget this step, you'll end up with a very hard salt block and you won't be able to separate the crystals. The whole dehydration process should take around 3 to 5 hours.

Once done, store the salt in tight sealed jars. Over time, depending on the plants you used, the colors may fade a bit from green to tan. I like to use the salts within 3 or 4 months for optimal flavor.

Roasted and infused California juniper wood.

ROASTED AND INFUSED AROMATIC WOODS

This is still somewhat experimental as I write this book, but so far, after a few trials, I've been very happy with the results. It all started when I used some California juniper wood for smoking meat—I fell completely in love with the smell emanating from it when the wood was beginning to roast. It had such a unique, pleasant, mellow cedar-type smell, which reminded me of the wide-open spaces of the local desert. I immediately thought that I had to find a way to use it as a spice.

Easier said than done. I tried roasting some California juniper wood and then scraping the outside to use it as a spice, but it did not work very well by itself. It was gritty, bitter, and tasted like burnt wood more than anything else. After experimenting for a while, I found out that it is best used as an additive flavor by roasting it in combination with other spices. Used that way, the wood essences provide a nice undertone. I plan to experiment much more with the technique and use a wide variety of aromatic woods, such as California bay, fig, and olive, but so far this is what has worked for me using juniper. At this time, the technique is somewhat lengthy—maybe, over time, I will develop a better one.

Procedure

1. Forage the juniper wood. This usually means making a trip to the local desert. Very often I have to remove the bark and outer layer, which is often damaged by the sun and harsh environment, to get to the nicer wood beneath. I then place the wood in the oven at around 200°F (93°C) for an hour to pasteurize it somewhat.

2. I create my custom spice blend. You want it somewhat liquid so the flavors will be infused into the wood. In this case I used lime juice, pequin chili, and garlic powder. A lemon- or vinegar-based spice blend would probably work well too. The spice blend and wood are placed in a Ziploc bag and left in the refrigerator for a couple of weeks.

3. After a week, I remove the wood from the fridge. I don't clean it, as the outside is quite saturated with spices. I place it in the oven on a tray and leave a pan at the bottom of the oven so excess spices can drip. I roast it at 350°F (177°C) for around 20 minutes. You want a nice dark, crusty, and roasted surface. It's not a necessity, but I even add some California bay leaves and Wright's cudweed during the roasting process to provide some additional flavors.

4. When the roasting is done, I remove the wood from the oven and let it cool a bit. Place it back into the Ziploc bag with the spices and leave it in the fridge for another week.

5. After a week, roast the wood again as per step 3, remove from the oven, and let it cool. It's not a must, but I like to leave it aside in a cool, dry place for a couple of days before making the next step. I believe some of the flavors still inside the wood will infuse the spices even more.

6. Using a spoon, knife, or other similar instrument, scrape the outside of the wood. You end up with a somewhat rough and dark powder made of roasted wood and spices. Using a grinder (electrical or manual), reduce it to a fine powder and set aside for use later. You're done!

Is all this worth it? I think so. It's still experimental, as I say, but when I followed these steps I had a definite juniper wood flavor, which created a nice, unique undertone when sprinkled over food. It is definitely different from smoking spices over juniper wood—using this method I actually taste the aromatic wood.

I can't wait to experiment with other woods and spices, possibly refining the technique as well. If someone comes up with a better method, please be in touch. I'm all ears!

Sea bass with roasted juniper wood and spices.

Wild Mustards:
Making Good with an Invasive

In spring, when the mustard flowers are in full bloom, the hills around Los Angeles have a beautiful yellow hue. The old story is that the Spanish explorers planted mustard seeds to create a golden pathway so they could find their way back home later on. Ever since then, we have been plagued—or blessed—with this non-native and invasive plant. Foraging it does a lot of good for the environment.

Mustard is easy to identify and I don't know of any poisonous look-alike where we live. The small abundant flowers, usually a half-inch across, grow outward along the stalk on long stems. With a magnifying glass you can see that each flower has four petals, four sepals, six stamens, and one pistil.

Locally we probably have eight or nine different kinds of mustards, with flavors ranging from broccoli-like to a strong wasabi taste. My favorite is the black mustard (*Brassica nigra*), which has that very interesting wasabi flavor. It looks similar to other wild mustards aside from its size, which makes it easy to find and forage. I often tell my students that if a mustard plant is taller than they are, then they're probably dealing with black mustard. Some specimens can be over 10 feet tall.

Grab one flower and chew on it. If it is the black mustard, it is sure to open your sinuses and make your eyes water—it's that strong!

Locally, the flowers and leaves can be foraged from February to April. The seeds ripen around June or July. If you want to store the seeds, you will need to dehydrate them first or they could mold. I store them in paper bags until thoroughly dehydrated, then place them in tightly closed jars.

The leaves can be cooked, but I mostly use them for making raw spicy sauces or salad dressings. From my perspective, the flavors are more pronounced in the flowers and leaves; the seeds are milder once dehydrated. The flowers make a wonderful wasabi-Dijon-style mustard. It is extremely easy to prepare with a *molcajete* (stone grinder) or a modern blender.

You need to go easy on eating the plant raw; some people experience stomach problems if they consume too much. Think of it as gourmet food: It's something you would serve sparingly as a nice condiment.

You can dehydrate the flowers and leaves, but you'll lose most of the flavors. If I want to use the plant to make spicy sauces in the future, I usually blend the fresh leaves with a bit of water to create a paste, place the paste in an ice cube tray, freeze, remove the mustard cubes, and store in plastic freezer bags for later use.

BLACK-MUSTARD-SEEDS MUSTARD

You can't buy mustard with this much flavor at the store. When I make my own mustard, I sometimes use homemade vinegar with local strains of bacteria. I use raw honey instead of sugar, and sea salt foraged from pristine seawater.

The basic recipe is fairly simple. You can use foraged or even store-bought ingredients. Either way, it is sure to be much better than any brand-name mustard. I've always used my *molcajete* (stone grinder) to make the mustard, so I don't know if it would work using an electric blender. You might try it and see for yourself.

Ingredients

⅓ cup (45 g) black mustard seeds
¼ cup (60 ml) red wine vinegar
¼ cup (60 ml) apple cider vinegar
⅓ cup (80 ml) white wine
2 teaspoons (12 g) honey or sugar
1½ teaspoons (9 g) salt

Procedure

1. I place the seeds in my mortar, add a bit of vinegars and wine, and grind for 2 to 3 minutes, then let the mixture rest for 5 minutes.
2. I add more wine and vinegar, grind, and let it rest again for another 5 minutes. I'll probably do this three or four times, then add the honey or sugar and salt. Taste and adjust the ingredients if you want it more acidic or more salty.
3. The fresh mustard is quite bitter. You'll need to age it for 2 or 3 days before using. I usually pour the contents into a clean jar and let it age in the refrigerator. The seeds can still expand, and you may want to add more wine, vinegar, or simply water to obtain the consistency that you desire. This mustard should last for many weeks in the fridge.

Photo courtesy of Mia Wasilevich.

MUSTARD FLOWERS MUSTARD

I make this recipe outdoors while I'm teaching, so I've never bothered to takes notes on the exact amount of ingredients. It is very much done to taste, so don't hesitate to subtract or add more to the ingredients. What's important is that it tastes good to you. Start with the following:

Ingredients

1 cup (235 ml volume) fresh mustard flowers

¼ cup (60 ml) white wine

¼ cup (60 ml) vinegar (I often use apple cider vinegar)

1 garlic clove

1 teaspoon (approximately 4 g) Italian spice mix or Herbes de Provence (optional)

1 teaspoon (6 g) salt

Procedure

1. Grind all the ingredients until you get a beautiful lime-green paste.
2. Taste, and adjust the ingredients to your liking.

This mustard is very similar in strength to the wasabi served in sushi restaurants, so you can serve it with raw fish as a wasabi substitute. The same basic recipe can be made with fresh mustard leaves (substitute chopped leaves for the flowers).

Photo courtesy of Mia Wasilevich.

Quail eggs sprinkled with sweet clover, cattail pollen, and pequin chili powder.

Appreciating Sweet White Clover

Although I'm talking about sweet white clover in this section, both sweet white clover (*Melilotus alba*) and sweet yellow clover (*M. officinalis*) can be used identically. These are two of my favorite aromatic herbs for roasting and sautéing. They're both packed with flavors and have very interesting vanilla and cinnamon qualities.

Sweet white clover is one of the most versatile wild herbs I forage. Mia makes a killer compound butter with it, and I love to infuse salt or make an herbal powder with it.

It's one of those herbs you want to use sparingly, as the plant contains a decent amount of coumarin, an organic chemical compound found in many spices and plants such as fenugreek, cinnamon, apricots, black currants, cherries, broccoli, strawberries, and some herbal teas. Medicinally, coumarin has blood-thinning and antifungicidal properties. Like nutmeg, sweet clover should not be taken at high doses over a long period.

Think of this herb as providing a gourmet touch. This plant has been used in many parts of the world as seasoning or flavoring in various dishes or teas. Sweet clover has also been used in many high-end culinary establishments such as L'Enclume, Red Medicine, the Nordic Food Lab, and others.

The leaves are edible raw, although the added bitterness makes it an acquired taste; from my perspective they're much better for cooking. I

Infused white clover salt.

often tell my students to start with a very basic recipe to uncover the flavors and potential of the herb, and suggest something as simple as a roasted potato cooked in foil with garlic, olive oil, salt, pepper, and one small branch of fresh sweet white clover so they can experience its qualities and go from there.

There is a word of caution, though: If you forage the plant, the real danger is if the plant is moldy. The mold is usually very visible, as the leaves are coated with some kind of white powder. The mold (fungus) transforms the coumarin into another chemical compound called dicoumarol, which is toxic and strongly anticoagulant.

So always make sure the plant is nice and fresh, avoid harvesting it if you see any sign of mold or even decay, and never use the plant in any sort of fermentation process. If you dry it, make sure it stays dry and does not mold. Otherwise, have some culinary fun and enjoy it sparingly!

Roasted mashed potatoes mixed with chickweed, clover, and chervil.

Oven-baked potato
with sweet white clover.

SUMMER

The Berries and Fruits Time

Summer Recipes

Summer is tough for a Southern California forager. The temperature can rise up to 110°F (43°C) by midday, which makes it pretty much unbearable to do any extended hiking. The strategy is to start foraging at sunrise and stick as much as possible to shaded areas and streams. Often, I have to call it quits by noon.

However, it's not always possible to avoid the sun and excessive heat. Such is the case when I have to forage for cactus pears or wild berries. I just try to keep my sun exposure to a minimum.

Even with just foraging during the morning hours, the days are long. I wake up around 4:30 a.m. and finish the day at around 7 p.m. While I call spring the "Greens Time," summer is really the "Berries and Fruits Time." Once the forage is done, my afternoons are often busy cleaning fruits and making wines, jams, and various other preserves. Last year I made around 10 gallons of elderberry wine, which I use mostly for cooking and making gourmet vinegars.

With so many berries available, it's also easy to collect wild yeasts for my brews.

The summer is also a good time to take a break from the heat and head to the mountains—the cooler temperatures at high altitude provide a welcome relief. From my experience, the flavors of many plants and trees such as pines, white fir, and yarrow are at their prime in the summer, and are perfect for making infused vinegars and other delicious concoctions.

I still give foraging classes and workshops during the weekend and thus make a lot of refreshing wild infusions to keep my students cool. Each year I seem to be able to find new plant uses to make cold infusions and other interesting drinks, such as vinegar-based shrubs. The fun and learning never stop.

Despite the fact that the wilderness around Los Angeles is turning into a desert, if you know what you are doing you can still find a substantial amount of wild greens, such as watercress, curly dock, and California speedwell, near shaded streams. Nature in our area can also be surprising; I once found chickweed—normally a winter green—in the middle of summer.

Working with restaurants during this season is challenging. I'm more limited with the quantity of fresh wild greens or edible flowers I can provide, although I am able to rely on preserves made during springtime. This is one of the reasons preserving is so important as a professional forager—it's one way to be able to make a living despite harsher conditions and to continue providing exciting ingredients to chefs.

Although in recent years California has experienced a terrible drought, you can learn a lot by being proactive. The drought and the necessity to keep finding wild ingredients has helped boost my creativity tremendously. I learned a lot about edible insects, foraged tons of wild seeds, and did a lot of research on those subjects. I also went deeper into what was available and developed interesting culinary uses for these plants and materials, such as smoked oak bark, spice blends, and so on.

Concocting Summer Drinks

Summer is a great time for making lots of different drinks, including cold infusions, wild sodas, and primitive beers and wines. One of my favorite drinks to make in the summer is Cactus Pear and Chia Seed Juice. Making this simple drink can take 10 minutes or, if you are a bit crazy like me, it may take a couple of days.

This is one of the non-alcoholic drinks I've made for chef Ludo Lefebvre at Trois Mec restaurant. It is extremely easy to concoct and embodies perfectly the local and native flavors of summer. You can do it the easy way by purchasing chia seeds and nopales cactus fruits (usually imported from Mexico and found at Hispanic markets), or you can do it the hard way by foraging the chia seeds and the fruits from the prickly pear cactus. Just so you know, there are many other cactuses with edible pears, but the prickly pear cactus (*Opuntia littoralis*) is the most abundant where I live.

As a forager, this is a perfect example of tasting the true flavors of the terroir. The difference in flavors between the purchased and foraged cactus fruit is as extreme as eating a store-bought orange or a perfectly ripe one just picked from the tree. Harvested at just the right time, it's very tasty and sweet.

Cactus pear and chia seed drink.

The chia seed sold in the local store is *Salvia hispanica.* It is different from the golden chia I find in the desert (*Salvia columbariae*). The wild seeds are pretty much the same size but more brownish in appearance, as if they have been parched in the harsh desert sun. The seedpods of the commercial chia are also bigger and contain many more seeds, which makes it easier to harvest and sell. The cactus fruits purchased at the store usually come from the nopales cactus. They are quite large, contain smaller seeds, and have the advantage of having very few needles, since they have been conveniently removed for you. There is no guarantee, however, that commercial chia or nopales are pesticide-free if that is important to you.

Making this drink the foraged way takes a couple of days: One day in late August for gathering the chia seeds and another one in September for foraging the cactus pears and making the drink.

For the seeds, I will spend my time driving a couple of hours to the high desert to find native chia and harvest the seeds. It's a somewhat slow process and quite meditative. While native peoples used to plant fields of chia, which made it easier to collect in large baskets, presently it's a process of finding areas where chia is still somewhat abundant and walking from one plant to another, picking the seedpods, and shaking them into a paper bag.

This is easier said than done, especially when the desert wind can be as high as 30 mph and the temperature over 100°F (38°C). On a good day it will take me a couple of hours to collect ½ cup. I'm happy if at the end of the day I come back home with one cup of chia seeds.

The second day is dedicated to foraging the fruits from local prickly pear cactus. They are usually half the size of nopales fruits and loaded with needles, the most dangerous ones being the tiny needles called glochids, which lodge in the skin easily, causing irritation.

I've been foraging these fruits for a very long time, and each year I learn new tricks from local natives on how to pick them properly and avoid getting stuck in the process. Maybe one day I'll be able to do it glochid-free.

CACTUS PEAR AND CHIA SEED JUICE

To make this drink you will need to forage around 30 large cactus pears or purchase 14 nopales fruits. I use around 2 tablespoons (approximately 25 g) of chia seeds.

Starting in late July and August, I'll drive to the town of Valyermo. There is quite an abundance of chia in the desert surrounding the town. Once located, the seeds are not too difficult to collect; it is just a time-consuming process. On the plus side, you get to enjoy the beautiful scenery. It is best to leave before sunrise and start your foraging day early in the morning, before the heat become unbearable.

Harvesting the prickly pear cactus fruit requires a little bit more know-how and some precautions. I don't like glochids and I'm sure you don't either, so here is a neat little trick that's often neglected by foragers. I learned it from an old native woman who was chuckling when I was picking up my cactus pears and getting stuck all over by the needles. It's a small detail but, gosh, did it make a difference!

Here it is: *Remove most of the needles before picking up the fruit.* It's easy to do; usually you can find whatever materials you need nearby. Simply pick up some dry twigs or tiny branches and make a small bundle. Remove the glochids by slapping and brushing the fruits with the bundle. Don't be gentle! Whack the spiny things forcefully (but with respect)—up, down, left, and center—around 10 seconds, and you'll be amazed that you can remove more than 99 percent of the potentially painful little buggers. Don't do this if you're standing downwind. I'm convinced that glochids have an intelligent guidance system that will find ways to prickle your skin through any clothing. So make sure you are standing upwind before slapping the fruit with your bundle. Trust me!

Next, twist and remove the fruit using kitchen tongs. Once removed, place it into your paper bag or bucket. If you did a good job at removing the needles, you don't even need kitchen tongs and can remove the fruit using your fingers.

Once you have the quantity you need, you're ready to make the juice!

Procedure

1. Once you've collected all your fruits and you're back home, place your cactus fruits in cold water for an hour. If by any chance there are some glochids remaining on the fruits, this soaking will make them tender enough that they won't penetrate your skin when you handle the fruits.

2. After an hour of soaking, remove the fruits from the water, cut them in two with a sharp knife, and remove the inside flesh with a spoon. You'll see that it's quite mucilaginous. Place the flesh into a bowl. You'll notice there are quite a few large seeds—we'll deal with them in future steps.

3. With the 30 large cactus pears or the 14 nopales fruits, you should end up with around 3 cups of flesh-and-seed mix. Add water to the mix: I usually use a ratio of 1 part water for 2 parts of cactus pear juice, so let's add 1½ cups (350 ml) of water.

4. Place the fruit flesh and seeds and water in a blender, and process at the lowest speed for a few seconds. You can also choose to go primitive and crush everything using your hands. Either way works—just make sure your hands are clean when you do this. (As an added bonus in using this approach, cactus juice is good medicine for the skin.)

5. Pour the juice through a strainer so you can remove the seeds. I use a wooden spoon to stir vigorously and push the juice through the mesh. It

Step 1

Step 2

Step 3

Step 4

Step 5

Step 6

usually takes a couple of minutes. Set the seeds aside; don't throw them away.

6. Once the seeds are removed, you end up with a beautiful, thick carmine-colored juice. The final step is to add the chia seeds. Take your wooden spoon and stir, stir, and stir even more while adding the seeds. If you don't stir, you will end up with big lumps of gooey seeds.

7. Stir for a minute or so and voilà! You're done. Let the juice and seeds rest for 10 minutes, during which time the chia seeds will continue to expand. Bottle it and place it in the fridge. I like to drink it within a week.

Step 7

No Waste: Cactus Pears Skins and Seeds

Foraging requires some substantial time and effort, so as much as possible I try to avoid creating any waste. Some plants, such as black sage, have numerous uses: Not only can you use the seeds as food and the leaves for flavoring, but you can even use the stems as aromatic skewers. This no-waste rule has been extremely beneficial in terms of creativity and has forced me to go deeper into possible culinary uses for countless wild ingredients. And in the process this dedication has expanded my pantry greatly.

In the case of cactus fruits, every part of the fruits has edible and culinary uses. Some people even blend the thick, juicy skins of the fruits with the flesh and seeds when making their juice. I tried this, and from my perspective it doesn't really add to the juice in terms of flavors and sweetness. You also face the danger of getting a few glochids into the juice, if you didn't do a good job prepping the fruits.

I make good use of the discarded cactus fruit skins and seeds. I usually slice the skins in strips and dehydrate them at around 140°F (60°C) until thoroughly dried, which can take a day. Living in Southern California, I can also place them in the sun to dry; they're usually dried within a day or two. They make a wonderful crunchy and sugary little snack, and can be used in infusions to add sweetness and color. You can also make a substitute red sugar by grinding them using a coffee grinder on espresso setting or with a stone grinder.

The seeds can be thoroughly cleaned and dehydrated as well. I usually dry the skins and seeds at the same time. I have used the seeds to make a flour. They're terribly hard to grind once dried, and primitive tools such as a large stone grinder and heavy mortar are much better than modern equipment. Once crushed, I use a manual coffee grinder to reduce them into powder. It's not a fantastic flour, and the historical use of them for this purpose by native peoples is contended by some. They probably used the seeds of the saguaro fruits but not the ones from our local prickly pear cactus.

Powder from cactus pear skin.

Dehydrated cactus pear skins and cactus pear seeds (*right*).

Fermenting elderberry juice.

The New Wildcrafted Cuisine

On Primitive Alcoholic Drinks and Flavors

Having followed many traditional recipes and made all kinds of wild concoctions using natural and foraged ingredients—from wild yeasts, berries, foraged fruits, aromatic herbs, tree leaves, barks, insects, and natural sugar sources such as tree sap, lerp sugar, fruit molasses, and honey—I've come to the conclusion that many native, ancient, and simply made foraged drinks have flavors that are . . . well . . . primitive.

Don't get me wrong, though. When I say *primitive* I don't mean unrefined, rude, or unsophisticated. I mean it in the sense of primal, unaffected, simple, and natural. For me this isn't a bad thing—in fact, I find it to be an appealing and beautiful aspect about these drinks.

If I make beer or wine, it's not going to taste like something you can buy at the local liquor or wine store. I have zero interest in even approaching those types of "civilized" flavors. I want my raw concoctions, my wild yeasts and plants, to talk to me completely untamed. Then, and only then, can I decide what to do with them—which might range from consuming them as is to mixing them in cocktails or with other plants, cooking with them, making vinegar from them, and so on.

For me, it's like traveling back in time. To a large degree we have forgotten the sacred origins of fermentation and primitive brews, whereby their effects on the psyche or the body were much more than just a quest for flavors or a simple desire to get drunk. The ancients also knew something that is now largely missed: the fact that plants *can* communicate with you through these primitive brews from a spiritual or medicinal perspective and, yes, through taste as well.

Sometimes the flavors are not for everyone. Some of the chefs I work with don't know how to deal with them, and I can't fault them for that. My foraged grape wine brewed with wild yeasts does not compare to a fine Bordeaux or Merlot, but then again, I'm not even trying to compare it to them. It is what it is. After centuries (or more) of winemaking experimentation—altering the raw ingredients such as grape varieties, yeasts, and even sugar—we humans have managed to produce extremely sophisticated and delicate alcoholic beverages. We have also turned the Near Eastern wildcat into a cute purring creature and wolves into tame and friendly dogs. As a forager in Southern California, I still deal with rattlesnakes, bobcats, mountain lions, black bears, and coyotes. I like to think of my brews as a reflection of the raw, untamed terroir.

On the plus side, though, there is a definite trend toward experimentation and rediscovering those long-lost raw flavors. In the beer world, natural yeasts and wild ingredients are making a very strong comeback, and sour beers are becoming popular again.

In the hands of talented and creative chefs or mixologists, the primal qualities these brews offer can really shine. Here in Los Angeles, genius mixologist Matthew Biancaniello can pretty much turn any of my foraged and primitive fermented concoctions into drinkable works of art. Chef Josiah Citrin at Melisse restaurant can transform my white sage cider into a delicate sorbet.

From a modern culinary perspective, the potential of the raw and undomesticated character of natural fermented drinks is pretty much like the wilderness around us—plentiful and amazing to explore.

Step 1

Step 2

Step 2

Step 3

Step 4

Step 5

Step 6

TISWIN (AKA COLONCHE)

Tiswin is an alcoholic drink brewed from corn or saguaro cactus fruits. It is the sacred drink of Native Americans who resided in the Sonoran Desert of Arizona and Mexico. Traditionally the wine is made with fruits from the saguaro cactus, but you can also substitute nopales or cactus pears to make a similar drink.

Ingredients

30 large nopales cactus fruits (or 60 cactus pears),
   cleaned and needles removed (see instructions
   for removing needles on page 192)
3 cups (0.75 l) springwater or distilled water
   (don't use tap water, which may contain chlorine)
Yeast (either wild yeast or packaged dried champagne yeast)

Procedure

1. Cut the nopales or cactus pears in two and scoop out the pulp using a spoon. You can also hold the sides of the halved fruits with both hands and push in the center with your thumbs to remove the insides.

2. Place the pulp in a blender and add the water. Blend for at low speed for around 5 seconds or so, then pour the raw juice into a strainer. You can also use your clean hands or other instruments if you don't have a blender. Once in the strainer, use a wooden spoon to stir vigorously and push the juice through the mesh. It usually takes a few minutes to separate the seeds from the juice.

3. Pour the juice into a large pot and bring the liquid to a boil, then reduce the heat to a low simmer. Simmer, uncovered, for an hour. Watch carefully as the liquid is coming to a boil; there can be substantial foaming and it can easily spill over. Trust me, I know!

4. At the end of the simmering time, strain the liquid again. You may notice that the color has changed from a dark red to a beautiful orange. Transfer to a strainer. This time, be gentle and don't force the pulp through the mesh; you want a nice golden liquid without any impurities. Return the juice to the stove and simmer, uncovered, for another 20 to 30 minutes. This will concentrate the sugar even more through evaporation.

   (By the way, there is little consensus as how much time the initial and second boiling should take; it can range from 20 minutes to 2 hours. I've found 2 hours to be excessive, and I had very little liquid left in my pot at the end, which didn't make sense. The longer time was probably necessary when making a large quantity of tiswin. The timing in this recipe is based on my own trial and error using a somewhat small quantity of cactus pears.)

5. Remove the pot from the heat, cover, and place into a pan filled with cold water. Keep the pot in the cold-water bath until the juice is lukewarm. You may need to change the cold water several times. I usually add ice to the water to speed up the process.

6. Once the juice is lukewarm, add the yeast. Place the liquid into a bottle and fit it with an airlock. From my research, like many primitive drinks this beverage would best be enjoyed before it is fully fermented, usually in 4 to 5 days.

In terms of flavors, unlike the fresh juice, which tastes a bit like watermelon, the flavors of this traditional brew remind me a bit of a fermented corn drink with fruity undertones.

If you want, you can also do a complete fermentation: Just leave the juice in the original container until you don't have any fermentation gas escaping—usually a couple of weeks. Then you can bottle your beverage for future use. It's a terrific base for interesting cocktails.

Elderberry Wine

The American elder (*Sambucus canadensis*) can be found throughout most of the United States. Here in Southern California, I mostly deal with the Mexican elder (*Sambucus mexicana*). To some degree I'm rather lucky in this respect: The berries from American elder are usually purplish black, but our local elders provide us with either white (actually, kind of greenish) or black berries. So I'm able to make either a white or red wine with the berries, depending on their color.

Making elderberry wine can be confusing the first time you try it. Not because it's complicated, but if you do search for recipes online or in books, it seems that everyone has a different recipe, and some of them can be as complex as making a fine wine, with added spices, aging in oak barrels, and so on.

Honestly, I'm not interested in making a very elaborate modern wine with my elderberries; I like the raw and wild flavors from the berries and the process that I use. The elderberry wine I make is not just for drinking, but also for cooking, making vinegar, blending into ice cream, and so on. So I tend to stick with very traditional recipes and create a brew that is likely very similar to what our ancestors would have drunk.

Some of the old traditional recipes were super simple. In Belgium and France we used to juice the berries, add some sugar and honey, then place everything into a container with a towel on top and forget about it for a few months. If we were lucky we had some wine, and if not, then we had some delicious vinegar. Most of the time we ended up with wine.

I even have a local friend who ferments her wine in open bottles; it is quite delicious after a couple of months, and it gradually changes into vinegar. She swears by her method for medicinal purposes. Some of the flavors, mostly when the wine is starting to turn into vinegar, are actually extremely interesting and unique. You can't tell if it's a wine or a vinegar, but either way it's fantastic for making salad dressings.

So if anyone is interested in making elderberry wine, don't be afraid to try. My advice would be to start with a very traditional recipe the first time around. Then, once you've been successful, research and create more complex ones.

To make wine, you basically just need to combine the ingredients, boil and then cool the liquid, strain, and add your yeast. Let it ferment for a few months, then bottle and forget about it for a few more months. I use the 6-month rule: Let the wine ferment for 6 months, bottle it, and then wait 6 more months before drinking it.

If you follow this basic recipe, the type of yeast you use will determine to a large degree whether your wine is strong, sugary, or dry. At this time I use mostly wild yeast, and the fermentation stops at around 5 percent alcohol with some of the sugar unprocessed; thus my wine is still somewhat sweet. If I used purchased champagne yeast, which converts more of the sugars to alcohol, I will end up with a very strong dry wine.

Honestly, I like both. The strong one, which I call Elderberry Schnapps, is fantastic as a base for cocktails.

BASIC COUNTRY ELDERBERRY WINE

This is pretty much the most basic recipe you can find, the way it was done in the old days. It's not a very sophisticated wine by modern standards but it has some nice primal qualities. Aside from just drinking it, you can also use it in sauces, for cooking, for creating cocktails, and for other interesting culinary applications.

Ingredients

3 pounds (0.45 kg) elderberries (I use 4 pounds [1.8 kg] with Mexican elderberries)

3 pounds (0.45 kg) white sugar

1 gallon (3.75 l) springwater or distilled water

1 teaspoon (5 g) citric acid (roughly equal to the juice of 3 lemons)

Yeast (either wild yeast or packaged dried champagne yeast)

Procedure

1. After you forage the berries, your first step is to remove the stems. In my experience it is much easier to remove the berries if you do so right away. Fresh, you can use your fingers to remove the berries easily. If you wait another day or more, the berries will get softer, making it a messier task, and you may need to use a fork to remove them from the stems. Another option is to freeze them. After they're frozen, just shake or lightly crush the clusters with your hands and the berries will fall from the stems. You may need to remove some small bits of stems here and there.

2. Weigh the berries and adjust your ingredients accordingly.

3. Next, using your hands or a food mill, crush the fresh berries and strain the juice. If you crush the berries with your hands, you may need a cheesecloth to strain the juice. Place the juice into a large pot. Add the sugar, water, and citric acid or lemon juice.

    (If your berries were frozen, place them in the refrigerator until they've thawed properly, then use the same technique to juice the berries.)

4. Bring the berry solution to a boil, then simmer for 10 to 15 minutes in a covered pot.

5. Place the covered pot in a pan of cold water to cool it down. Once the solution is lukewarm, add the yeast and strain the solution into a large bottle, then top it with an airlock. You can also use a food-grade bucket with a clean towel on top. The airlock or clean towel is there to protect your brew from unwanted critters, such as fruit flies and various unwanted bacteria, and to let the fermentation gas (CO_2) escape. As when making any other brews or wines, make sure you clean all your equipment before using it.

6. One week later, filter the liquid through a sieve or cheesecloth and place it into a new bottle or container.

7. Fit with an airlock again. The fermentation process will continue for many weeks. I usually leave the wine alone for 4 to 6 months at this point, replacing the water in the airlock if needed. If you're using a food-grade bucket, I would advise placing the cover loosely so

fermentation gas can still escape and putting a clean towel on top. Change the towel from time to time. Using an airlock is *much* better. Some beer or wine supply stores sell food-grade buckets outfitted with an airlock on top.

8. When the fermentation process is completed, carefully siphon the finished wine into bottles. Place your bottles in a somewhat cold and dark place, such as the basement, and wait for another 6 months before drinking. Enjoy!

Step 2

Step 3

Step 5

Step 6

A Simple Alternative Method Using the Same Ingredients

This method is very similar to what we used to do in Belgium and does not require any boiling. Although the wine is probably more prone to spoiling or turning into vinegar because of unwanted bacteria—bacteria that were not removed during the boiling process—I've personally never experienced any problems. Hygiene is key: Make sure your hands and all your tools, containers, and bottles are cleaned thoroughly.

Procedure

1. With clean hands, remove berries from the stems, crush them, and strain the juice through a cheesecloth or sieve.
2. In a clean pot, combine your juice with the sugar, water, lemon juice or citric acid, and yeast.
3. Place into a large (clean) bottle with an airlock and let it ferment for 6 months, then bottle. Wait another 6 months before drinking.

Elderberry Slime, aka Elderberry Green Goo or Gunk

In the first part of the fermentation, you may end up with some sort of green slime or goo on top of your fermenting liquid. Don't worry much about it, as this is fairly normal with elderberry fermentation. It's easy to clean with hot water later on. Just clean your container as soon as you have transferred your wine to the second container. You may still get some "goo" in the second container, but probably less. Again, just clean it with hot water as soon as you have bottled your wine.

Mexican elderflowers.

ELDERFLOWER CORDIAL

This elderberry cordial is a refreshing non-alcoholic alternative. Early summer is a good time to make this delicious drink.

Ingredients

4 cups (1 l by volume) elderflower blossoms
3 large lemons
6 cups (1.5 l) springwater or distilled water
5 cups (1.25 l) sugar
1½ teaspoons (7.35 g) citric acid

Procedure

1. Clean the elderflower blossoms. You may have quite a few bugs in your elderflowers, which is perfectly normal. After foraging them, I usually lay them outside on a bunch of newspapers for half a day (not in full sun); most of the bugs will vacate. I then leave the flowers in a large bowl overnight in the garage. Usually the next day the flowers will fall easily from the stems with a little convincing rubbing. You will need 4 cups of the little florets.

2. Slice the lemons and place them in a covered pot with the water and sugar. Bring everything to a boil for 15 minutes, then remove from the heat. Add the citric acid, then add the flowers. Stir all the ingredients to make sure they're well blended.

3. You can either transfer the elderflower brew to a new, clean container or simply cover the pot and let it cool. Set aside for at least 24 hours and up to 48 hours. I like to stir it once or twice a day using a clean wooden spoon.

4. Strain your cordial through a sieve or cheesecloth. With clean hands, squeeze the lemons and flowers to extract as much delicious liquid as possible. Store in sealed jars or bottles in the refrigerator for up to 3 months. To enjoy the cordial all year round, I usually preserve it in pint jars and process them for 20 minutes in a boiling-water bath.

Sacred Lerp Sugar Fermented Drink

This is a sacred brew that probably has never been made before. Let me explain that. I think it's sacred due to the fact that you have to have something spiritually "different" about you to attempt an eccentric drink like this, and also because it takes so damn long to forage the sugar. Trust me, should you attempt a similar project, it will feel sacred to you.

Lerp sugar is the excretion of a small insect that feeds mostly on gum trees. Originally from Australia, the insect can now be found in Southern California. From my research, this excretion is around 60 percent sugar and 40 percent starch, but from my experience it varies with the location and the season. July is the best time to collect the little excreted "crunchies." Once I find trees loaded with them, I do some taste checks and forage the excretions that have the most sweetness.

Collecting the sugar is not easy; you have to go from leaf to leaf and, using your fingers, remove the excretions and let them drop into a plastic bag. It can take most of a day to collect 4 to 5 cups. If I'm lucky and a tree is loaded, I can do it in a few hours. The sugar is then dehydrated for future use.

The brew is quite aesthetic. After boiling the water, sugar, and herbs, it looks like beautiful thick milk with greenish hues. As with many primitive drinks, because of the low sugar content, it's meant to be drunk following 3 to 4 days of fermentation.

The flavor is interesting as well, and probably not for everyone, but that's what I like about it—it's very unique. Think of it as fermented boozy sour milk. You can take the lazy approach and say it doesn't taste very good, but then you'll miss the exciting possibilities it offers as an ingredient in cocktails, sauces, salad dressings, and so on.

The brewing method is pretty much identical to the one I described in the tutorial for making primitive beer (see page 60). Basically, you take all the ingredients, boil them for about 20 minutes, cool the resulting liquid, then strain it and add the yeast (wild or packaged). Bottle and let it ferment for 3 or 4 days. We're looking at around 2 percent alcohol content after 4 days.

Instead of using an airlock, I tie a fig leaf with a yucca (*Hesperoyucca whipplei*) fiber on top. The leaf has a pinhole to allow the fermentation gas to escape and prevent critters such as fruit flies from infecting the brew. Basically, I have created a primitive airlock.

The ingredients are as follows:

½ gallon (2 l) springwater or distilled water
2½ cups (200 g) lerp sugar
0.1 ounce (3 g) dehydrated mugwort leaves
2 fermented/dehydrated lemons (fresh lemons are fine too)
3 medium-sized yarrow flower heads
Wild yeast from local juniper berries (or packaged dried champagne yeast)

Making "Wild" Sodas

Wild sodas are excellent alternatives to the sodas you buy commercially. Nowadays the sodas that you purchase at the store are almost all made with some flavoring and corn syrup; then CO_2 is pumped into the liquid to create the carbonation. Not exactly a health product.

The old way of making soda was through a simple fermentation process. You make juice or an infusion, add yeast to it, let it ferment for a short time in a container (carboy, large bottle, or jar), then transfer it to a closed bottle (plastic soda or swing-top glass bottle). It's a probiotic process with live yeast. As fermentation continues within the closed bottle, pressure is building, and this is what creates the carbonation.

The Hot Method for Making Soda

Making a soda using the hot method is super simple; it's very similar to making beer. You basically boil all the ingredients, cool the solution, add yeast, let it ferment for 12 to 24 hours, then bottle it.

As you experiment with foraged or purchased ingredients, you'll discover that boiling your solution works in some cases, but can alter the taste too much with specific herbs. For example, you lose a lot of subtle flavors when cooking mints, chervil, fennel, basil, or white fir, while some herbs such as mugwort, yarrow, and dehydrated berries take this method very well . You don't always have to boil the ingredients, either; you can make some infusions by boiling the water, removing it from the heat, and then placing your herbs in the hot water and letting them steep for a specific amount of time. Once the solution has cooled down, you add the yeast, then strain and place into your fermenting vessel.

A SIMPLE "WILD" SODA FROM SCRATCH

I make all kinds of sodas and, although the basic principle is the same, you have slight variations in the preparation. The ingredients you use will dictate the best method to use: hot (boiling them first) or cold infusion to start with. Some plants, such as mint, white fir, or yerba santa (*Eriodictyon californicum*), are much better when using the cold method, while others—including dehydrated berries, white sage, and mugwort—are better boiled first to extract the flavors. Feel free to experiment with plants using both methods—it's all about flavors.

You don't need a lot of equipment to make soda. Here is the basic list for making a 1-gallon (3.75 l) batch using the hot method.

Ingredients and Equipment

¾–1 cup (170–225 g) white sugar, or ¾ cup (236 ml) honey
Yeast (wild yeast or packaged dried champagne yeast)
1 gallon (3.75 l) springwater or distilled water—
   don't use tap water, which may contain chlorine
Large pot with lid (if you boil the juice/infusion)
1-gallon (3.75 l) bottle or glass container
Sieve and funnel
Soda bottles (recycled plastic soda bottles or swing-top glass bottles)
Measuring cup
Airlock and stopper (available online or at local beermaking
   supply stores), or you can top the gallon bottle with a clean
   paper towel and a rubber band

Procedure

This is the basic procedure for making soda. Step-by-step instructions and recipes follow.

To make soda you basically make your tea/brew, infusion, or juice, then let it ferment for 12–24 hours in a bottle or container with an airlock. The airlock is there to let the gas from the fermentation escape and to prevent fruit flies, bacteria, or any other unwanted critters from getting into the brew.

After 12 to 24 hours of fermentation, transfer your soda to closed bottles and wait for another 8 to 24 hours. Pressure builds up inside the bottles and creates the carbonation. After that period of time, you can place your soda in the refrigerator. The low temperature will slow down the fermentation process.

There is a bit of an art involved to getting the right amount of carbonation in the bottles. If the original fermentation is very active (lots of bubbling), after bottling the liquid you don't need to leave it fermenting in the closed bottle for 24 hours, since it may be too much and will build up lots of pressure. It's not always a good thing when you open the bottle and experience a gusher.

During the initial fermentation, I use the airlock to see how active the fermentation is. If I see a bubble coming through every second I know it's super active; when I bottle it I will leave the soda in the closed bottle for maybe 8 hours then place it in the fridge. If I see a bubble going through every 2 seconds during the initial fermentation, I usually leave the soda in the closed bottle for 12 to 16 hours. You can always check the pressure by opening a bottle carefully and very slowly. See Feel the Pressure on page 220, for more tips on pressure and carbonation.

BLUEBERRY-FENNEL-MUGWORT SODA

Here is a recipe example for a ½-gallon (1.8 l) batch of wild soda.

Ingredients

½ gallon (1.8 l) springwater or distilled water

2 lemons

2 tablespoons (14 g) lerp sugar (optional)

½–¾ cup (65–90 g) dehydrated blueberries (feel free to try other berries)

½ teaspoon (1 g) wild fennel seeds (or commercial fennel seeds)

A small handful (1 g) dry mugwort leaves

⅓ cup (75 g) organic white sugar

¼ cup (60 ml) honey

Champagne yeast (or wild yeast starter)

Procedure

1. Pour the water into a pot and add all other ingredients except the yeast.
2. Covered the pot, bring the solution to a boil, then simmer for 20 to 30 minutes.
3. Remove the covered pot from the heat and place it a pan filled with cold water. You want to bring the temperature of the solution down to lukewarm. You may need to change the cold water a few times as the liquid cools. The main reason for cooling is because, if the liquid is too hot when you add the yeast, it will kill the yeast and defeat its purpose.
4. Clean your fermentation bottle thoroughly. You can find ½-gallon (1.8 l) or 1-gallon (3.75 l) bottles at most regular grocery stores; look in the aisle for cheap wine. Place a funnel in the bottle's neck, then pour the solution through a sieve and into the funnel. With very clean hands, you can also squeeze the ingredients left in the sieve to extract more flavors.
5. Open your champagne yeast packet (a 5-gram packet is usually good for 5 gallons) and pour some of the yeast inside the bottle—I use around one-fifth of the yeast packet contents.
6. Place the clean stopper and airlock on top of the bottle. Wait 12 to 24 hours. Usually after 10 to 12 hours, sometimes sooner, you will see fermentation activity and gas escaping in the form of bubbles. That's what you want. When your fermentation is quite active you can bottle it.
7. Pour your fermenting soda into plastic soda bottles or swing-top glass bottles. Close the bottle tops. If your fermentation was very active, check the pressure after 8 hours by opening the top slowly and carefully. If there is not enough pressure, keep fermenting the soda and check again after 8 more hours. When satisfied, place in the refrigerator, which slows the fermentation process.

Step 1

Step 2

Step 3

Step 5

Step 6

COLD-INFUSED WILD SODAS

When making beer and some sodas, I usually boil all my ingredients first, then let the solution cool down before adding the yeast. Boiling kills any bacteria that may be present on the ingredients you use. These bacteria could eventually alter the flavors or possibly spoil the brew over a long period of time. Once they've been eliminated through pasteurization (boiling), you add your yeast, giving the yeast a higher chance of success and a better guarantee that your end product will taste the way you want.

You don't always need to boil your ingredients when making wild sodas. Soda fermentation is rather quick, and during the fermentation, the yeast that you put in the brew is taking over and—at least for the time being—it is the obvious winner in the war against unwanted bacteria. Over time this might change, but because we're drinking the sodas soon after the initial fermentation, the potential spoilage doesn't have time to occur. We enjoy the taste of victory!

As I explained earlier in describing the hot method for making soda, my main reason for boiling or not boiling the ingredients when making sodas is simply related to flavors. Some herbs will unleash their flavors through boiling, but other herbs or plants are much better enjoyed fresh. If you boil mint, the flavor changes considerably. I really like the taste of some fresh pine and white fir needles, but I don't enjoy the taste as much when boiled.

It's clearly a question of preferences. As you experiment with wild brews and sodas, you will need to determine the appropriate methods. That's the fun part.

Aside from brewing for flavor, some sodas can also be made for medicinal purposes—a pine needle and lemon soda, for example, is packed with vitamin C. Often some vitamins and nutrients are altered through the boiling process, so if you're brewing for medicinal purposes, a cold infusion can be more appropriate.

Procedure

1. Decide on the appropriate herbs, fruits, aromatics, juice, and whatever else you want to blend to create your soda. Forage or purchase the ingredients.
2. Thoroughly clean the ingredients and any containers and utensils you will be using. You can go to the extreme of placing your container in boiling water to pasteurize it, but I have never had any problem with just a thorough cleaning with hot water and regular dish soap.
3. With clean hands, mix your herbs, fruits, and other ingredients. Add springwater or distilled water (not tap water, which contains chlorine) and a sugar source (white sugar, honey, brown sugar, molasses, birch or maple syrup, et cetera). For 1 gallon (3.75 l), I'll use around ¾ cup (170 g) of sugar or honey (180 ml). You can experiment with less, or more if you want a very sweet soda.
4. Mix everything so your sugar base is well diluted, then add the yeast. You can use either a yeast starter that you have made yourself from wild berries or a commercial yeast strain. I often use champagne yeast purchased online or at the local brewing supply store.
5. Place a paper towel on top of the container and tie it up. If you used a jar, screw the metal top over the paper towel. Stir three or four times daily with a clean wooden spoon.
6. Wait 24 hours (or up to a couple of days if you used a wild yeast starter); the fermentation bubbling should be quite obvious. Strain the fermenting solution into recycled plastic soda bottles or swing-top glass bottles. Check for pressure after 8 hours or so, then place in the refrigerator when appropriate. I like to drink my fermented sodas within a week or two.

STINGING NETTLE, WILD MINT, FOREST GRASS, AND LEMON SODA

This medicinal soda has interesting herby flavors. It was inspired by the herbs that grow in Los Angeles after our first rain of the season, usually in November or December. It's a very nice green refreshment, after having experienced a few months of desert-like conditions.

I didn't weigh the ingredients when I made this soda, so I've instead given a breakdown of the ingredients by percentage. You can play with the amount of ingredients relative to one another as you like.

Ingredients

30% forest grass

40% stinging nettle

20% wild mint (you can also purchase your mint at the store)

10% fallen leaves (I used willow and cottonwood, which are a tad bitter)

3 lemons, sliced

1 gallon (3.75 l) water (not tap water)

1 cup (236 ml) honey

Wild yeast starter (or champagne yeast)

Procedure

1. Clean your foraged ingredients. Roughly chop the stinging nettle, grass, and the mint.
2. Loosely fill the container with the grass, nettles, leaves, and lemons. Add water, honey, and yeast starter. (I made my yeast starter from California juniper berries.) I usually use around ¼ pint (118 ml) of liquid from my wild yeast starter.
3. Stir three or four times a day. The wild yeast provides a slower fermentation—I waited 36 hours before bottling this brew.
4. It takes another 24 hours in the swing-top bottle to get the carbonation I want. Once the soda has reached your desired level of carbonation, place it in the refrigerator. I usually drink within a week. The resulting flavor is quite spectacular—it's lemony, but you can taste the green too.

PINE NEEDLES, WHITE FIR, AND LEMON SODA

This mix is composed of mostly pine needles (60 percent) and some white fir needles (40 percent) along with two lemons. I make sure to cut the pine and fir needles with scissors so they can release their flavors quickly.

The flavor of this soda is like drinking the local mountains. It has some nice pine and tangerine flavors, which are extremely refreshing. As an added benefit, this soda is packed with vitamin C.

Ingredients

Pine and white fir needles, packed very loosely in the container—around 60% pine needles and 40% white fir
2 lemons, sliced
1 gallon (3.75 l) water (not tap water)
1 cup (225 g) organic cane sugar
Champagne yeast (or wild yeast starter)

Procedure

1. Fill half of the container loosely with the pine and fir needles and lemons. Add water and sugar.
2. Add the yeast, stir, and place a paper towel on top. I usually use champagne yeast for this soda. Stir three to four times a day; usually it takes a couple of days to get a good fermentation (you'll see the liquid bubbling). When the fermentation is active, using a sieve and funnel, strain the solution into soda or swing-top bottles.
3. It usually takes the soda another 12 to 16 hours in the swing-top bottles to get the carbonation I want. Once the brew has reached your desired level of carbonation, place it in the refrigerator. Drink within 2 weeks.

Here is the scoop: When you deal with wild ingredients, including wild yeasts, you may also have to deal with some interesting variations in terms of fermentation activity. Some herbs, such as nettles or grass, can create a beautiful and very active fermentation, while some sages will create a more finicky and slow one. Other ingredients, such as pine or white fir, induce a more regular—albeit a bit slow—fermentation. In the beginning, it's a good idea to take note of the content of your creative concoctions, the fermentation time, and the delicious (or not) result.

The yeast you use is also very important. For example, commercial champagne yeast is very reliable, but once you start dealing with wild yeast starters, you're entering the fermentation wilderness. Some strains seem to be super active while others are slower.

Then you still have other variations to deal with, such as temperature, how active your yeast starter is, and little details such as the position of the moon (just kidding on that one).

So what do you do? The answer is simple: observe!

Is the rule of fermenting a soda for only 12 to 24 hours sacred? Nope. Sometimes you'll have a very active fermentation overnight, and you may choose to bottle the soda at that stage; other times you may need to go a bit longer than 24 hours. There are no set rules. The key is to observe. You want to see a nice active fermentation, healthy bubbling, and the brew should smell good. Then you can bottle it.

Let's assume you've had a nice bubby concoction and you've bottled it in a recycled soda bottle or a swing-top bottle. Now what?

A very active fermentation inside a closed bottle can create a lot of pressure; I've had my share of liquid spurting out aggressively from the bottle. In the beginning, you may want to start with recycled plastic soda bottles because you can gauge the carbonation by pressing the side of the bottle with your fingers. The first times I made soda I used recycled plastic bottles and compared the pressure with a regular store-bought Coke bottle by pressing the side. When I was satisfied that the pressure with my soda was similar to the Coke, I would place my soda in the fridge. The cool temperature would slow down considerably or stop the fermentation process.

Additionally, if you look at the bottom of plastic soda bottle, it is designed to pop out in the event of too much pressure. If one day you see that the bottom of your plastic soda bottle has expanded and the bottle is starting to look like a balloon, you better find a safe space (outside) to carefully open the bottle, because the liquid inside will expel with a lot of force. Swing-top bottles are technically designed to release pressure inside in case of too much pressure, but I've had one case of a bottle exploding, probably because of a manufacturing defect.

You really should not have any problems if you observe and take care of your sodas. With time you gain experience and confidence; it's really an easy process. Just don't do as one of my students did once: go on a weekend trip and forget that you had a very active fermentation going inside a soda bottle.

Now I use swing-top bottles and, if the initial fermentation is very active, I check one of my bottles after 8 hours or so by holding and pushing on top with my left hand and slowly releasing the side handles with my right hand. If I'm satisfied with the carbonation, I just place the bottles in the fridge. I do the same before serving a batch to guests. Once in a while I would miscalculate the pressure and found out the hard way that it was too much. Simply hold and release slowly a few times and, bit by bit, you'll get rid of the excess pressure without losing some of your precious liquid. If I don't have enough pressure when the bottles come out of the fridge, I let them come back to room temperature for a few hours. The fermentation process will restart and you eventually get the right amount of carbonation.

MAKING SODAS WITH FRUIT JUICES

If you don't have time to go foraging or pick up ingredients at the local farmer's market, you can make excellent sodas using fruit juice purchased at the local store. Sometimes I make sodas using organic fruit juice and add some wild ingredients such as black sage, wild mints, yarrow, white sage, or mugwort.

Be aware that some (usually cheap) "juices" are not actually made from juice but arc instead a mix of high-fructose corn syrup, colorants, preservatives, chemicals to preserve flavors, juice from concentrate, et cetera, and they may not ferment for obvious reasons. Even yeast would not like them and help them to ferment!

I usually don't boil the juice (most of them are already pasteurized) unless I add other ingredients. For example, if I make a blend of blueberry juice and add a bit of mugwort to it for added flavors, I would take a portion of the juice, maybe 20 percent, boil a few dry mugwort leaves in it, then let it cool before straining and pouring it back into the original juice.

I've also made sodas with freshly made juice using the cold infusion method. Fermentation is a very safe process. If a fermentation goes bad, the resulting liquid will not smell good—definitely not something you would want to use. In my 10 years of fermenting, I've never had one batch go bad. Just use good hygiene, wash your hands often, clean the containers and bottles you're using, and you should be fine.

Some purchased fruit juices already have sugar in them, so you may not need to add any more. I make this decision by taste. If a fruit juice is very sweet, I won't add sugar. If it is not too sweet, I may add ¼ cup (57 g) or ½ cup (115 g) of white sugar or honey per gallon.

Procedure

Clean your fermentation bottle and pour the juice inside. (Very often I add water to the juice, too, if it is very sugary, around one-fourth the volume.) Open your champagne yeast packet (good for fermenting 5 gallons) and pour some of the yeast inside the bottle. You can also use a wild yeast starter.

Place the clean stopper (cork) and airlock. Wait around 12 to 24 hours. Usually after 10 to 12 hours, sometimes sooner, you will see fermentation activity and gas escaping. That's what you want. By the way, if your fermentation is really active before 12 hours, it's completely okay to proceed to the next step; it's not unusual for me to bottle some of my fermenting juice after 10 hours or so.

Pour the fermenting juice into plastic soda bottles or swing-top glass bottles. Close the bottle tops. Check the pressure from time to time. When you're satisfied with the level of carbonation, place in the fridge and enjoy later on.

Even if you purchase fruit juices from your local market or buy fresh fruits such as pomegranates, apples, watermelons, or oranges and make the juice yourself, you can still add some wild flavors to your drink by adding foraged ingredients.

I often use wild berries to add interesting flavors. For example, recently I made a fruit juice soda (cherry) and

Making soda with
blueberry juice,
lemons, mugwort,
and yarrow flowers.

Wild yeast starter with California juniper berries.

added dehydrated manzanita and toyon berry powder, a few black sage leaves, and a couple of lemons.

One of my favorite sodas is made using a locally purchased pomegranate and blueberry juice. It is already pasteurized, and I simply pour most of the juice into a clean 1-gallon (3.75 l) bottle and set aside around 2 cups (0.5 l). I don't need to add sugar to the juice as there is already enough.

I pour the 2 cups (0.5 l) of juice in a pot and add a bit of yarrow or mugwort leaves. I juice 3 lemons and throw them in the pot as well. I bring the liquid to a boil, then simmer for around 10 minutes. The pot is then placed in cold water with the lid on. The cold water is changed two or three times until the juice is lukewarm.

My next step is to strain the juice into the bottle and, with clean hands, squeeze the ingredients so I can extract all the flavors. The final step is to add the yeast (commercial yeast or wild yeast starter) and place the airlock on top of the bottle.

After a short fermentation, between 12 and 24 hours depending on how active it is, I bottle it and check the pressure after 8 hours or so. When I'm satisfied with the pressure, I place it the bottle in the fridge.

The interesting flavors you can create by mixing regular juices and wild ingredients are infinite.

Wild yeast starter made with California juniper berries and sugar water (3 parts water and 1 part sugar), stirred 3 times daily. Photo taken on Day 5.

SODAS WITH WILD YEAST FROM RAW HONEY

You can make sodas without using champagne or other commercial yeasts by using a wild yeast starter or raw honey. If you want to make a yeast starter, see The Quest for Wild Yeasts on page 79. Once you've made your wild yeast starter, follow the usual procedure for making a soda, and simply pour some of your starter in the solution instead of using commercial yeast. I usually use around ⅓ to ½ cup of starter (80 to 120 ml) for a 1-gallon (3.75 l) batch.

The procedure that I detail below, which I call a raw honey soda, is basically a sort of herbal mead made with a smaller amount of raw unpasteurized honey. Use around 1 cup (236 ml) of honey per gallon (3.75 l) of liquid.

Raw unpasteurized honey contains enough yeast from pollen and countless flowers to start a fermentation. It has never failed in my case. It usually takes anywhere from 2 to 4 days to get a fermentation going. This is a cold method (no boiling).

Here is a recipe for my wild mint soda using raw honey. You can substitute other flavorful herbs and berries for the mint, or buy some organic mint at your local store. For making this drink, purchase raw unpasteurized honey (often available at farmer's markets, or contact a local beekeeper).

Procedure

Clean thoroughly the container you will use for the fermentation process. This could be a vase, a food-grade plastic bucket, or a very large jar. Use ¾ (178 ml) to 1 cup (236 ml) raw honey for a 1-gallon (3.75 l) batch.

Mix the honey and the water in the container; make sure it is nicely dissolved. Use 3 to 4 bunches of mint (I've never weighed it, but it's basically 2 handfuls). Chop the leaves and stems roughly so the mint releases its essence in the water. Add the mint to the solution of raw honey/water and cover the container with cheesecloth or a loosely fitting lid so that flies and other critters don't get in.

To get the fermentation going you will need to stir the solution three or four times a day. Take a clean spoon (or whatever else you decide to use) and stir, stir, stir for a couple of minutes. There's no need to do this during the night, but do it before you go to bed and first thing in the morning. Always make sure you replace the lid or cheesecloth when you're done stirring.

In 2 to 4 days depending on the temperature, you will start to see some bubbling happening. Congratulations, your fermentation is active. If it smells good, or at least okay, you're good to go. If it smells like you really would not want to drink it, discard the liquid. I never had a failure with raw unpasteurized honey; the only failure I had was when a purveyor lied to me when I thought I was purchasing unpasteurized honey. The honey had been pasteurized, which kills the yeast and makes it inactive.

Using a sieve and funnel, transfer the solution to your plastic soda or glass swing-top bottles. Discard the herbs. Check the pressure from time to time. When you're satisfied, place in the fridge and enjoy later on.

As a note, most raw honey purchased at a store won't ferment. These honeys are actually processed at low heat, which kills the wild yeast. Find a beekeeper and get some true raw honey.

Active fermentation using
wild yeast from raw honey—Day 3.

Making SoBeer

I call this beverage SoBeer because it's a cross between a non-alcoholic soda and beer. The idea came to me out of necessity when we booked a private event on short notice and the client wanted to have some wild brew on the menu. Usually my beers need a minimum of 3 to 4 weeks of aging in the bottles before they are drinkable, but in this case I only had a bit more than 2 weeks from making it to actual consumption.

Having experimented a lot with sodas and native brews, which don't require a long fermentation time, I decided to try a new method to make the deadline. It's probably the same way low-alcohol beers are made, but not being a traditional brewer, I wouldn't know.

My logic was as follows: The recipe for my most popular beer (mugwort and lemons) asks for 1¼ pounds (0.55 kg) of brown sugar for 1 gallon (3.75 l) of liquid. The initial fermentation in the carboy (large

bottle used for fermentation) is 10 days. Based on the fact that 1 pound (0.45 kg) of sugar renders a rough estimate of 5 percent alcohol, I concluded that I could make a lower-alcohol beer by cutting down the brown sugar to 10 ounces (284 g) and still get a beer with around 3 percent alcohol and the regular flavors. The fermentation would theoretically take less time because there is less sugar.

Faced with no other choice, I made a gallon of beer with half the sugar, fermented it for 6 days in the carboy, and bottled it for 2 weeks. It worked! People loved it.

Since then I've gone further and made all kinds of low-alcohol wild brews with even less sugar and fermentation time. When a reporter from *LA Weekly* wanted to interview me for an article about the wild brews I created, I managed to make a tasty forest beer composed of seven wild ingredients within a week by using 7 ounces (198 g) of sugar, fermenting it for 4 days,

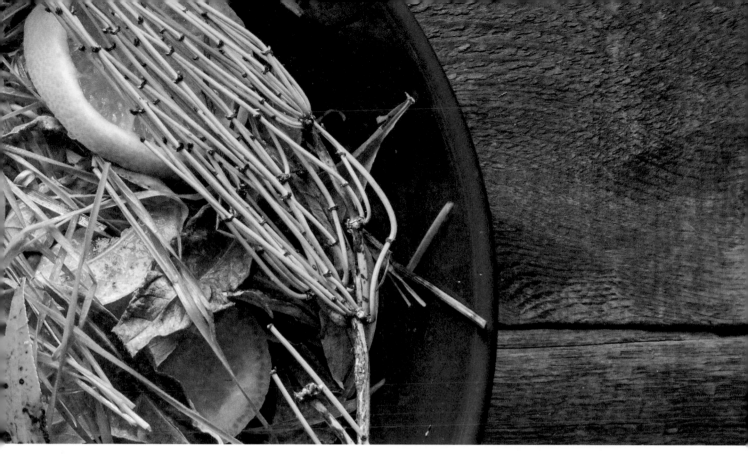

Forest SoBeer—mugwort, forest grass, willow leaves, turkey tail mushroom, lemons, Mormon tea (*Ephedra viridis*), California sagebrush, dried elderberry, brown sugar, and lerp sugar.

then bottling it for only 3 more days. The end result was very similar to a sour, fruity Belgian beer with some hints of grapefruit.

She asked me what kind of beer it was and, not knowing how to properly name the thing, out of the blue I told her it was a SoBeer, a low-alcohol primitive brew that is a kind of cross between a soda and a beer. I actually like the name as it doesn't sound too serious, so I've been using it ever since.

The more I get into primitive fermented brews, the more I realize that, aside from the basic preparation methods, there are no real rules—it's all about flavors. If you can make a wild brew in 10 days and make it taste like a low-alcohol beer, why not? A lot of native brews were simply fermented for a few days with wild yeasts, then enjoyed.

I think nowadays there are too many rules about making beers or wines, like how beers can only be made of hops and grains. We've forgotten the fun of

throwing all the rules aside and going wild. The amount of interesting alcoholic concoctions and flavors is really infinite. Never be afraid to create and learn from the failures.

SoBeer has the following ingredients for 1 gallon (3.75 l): a small handful of dry mugwort leaves, a bunch of forest grass, 3 lemons, 7 to 8 bitter willow leaves, a few turkey tail mushrooms, a branch of Mormon tea, a teaspoon (1 g) California sagebrush, 3 tablespoons (30 g) dried elderberry, 8 ounces (226 g) brown sugar, and 2 tablespoons (14 g) lerp sugar. I boiled everything for 20 minutes, cooled down the solution like any other beer, strained it, and added some wild yeast from a yeast starter made with local juniper berries. I fermented it for 5 days in the carboy, then bottled it, adding ½ teaspoon (2 g) sugar to each bottle. I drank it 2 or 3 days later. This was the brew that tasted a bit like a sour gueuze with hints of grapefruit.

Primitive carbonation system for wild brews.
Photo courtesy of Mia Wasilevich.

Primitive Carbonation

I've always wondered if primitive beers or wines were carbonated. Despite a decent amount of research on the subject, I've not come to a definite conclusion.

Presently, all the beers we buy at the store are carbonated. We've come to take it for granted, and carbonation is now seen as a quality and aroma enhancer.

There are two types of carbonation: forced and natural. In the forced process, CO_2 is introduced into the beer under high pressure; in the natural process, carbonation is a normal by-product of fermentation within an enclosed container capable of sustaining a decent amount of internal pressure. Fermentation

releases CO_2 and, under pressure, it is absorbed back into the brew.

It's probable that some ancient beers or wines could have achieved some level of carbonation when stored in closed oak barrels or amphorae, but the consensus seems to be that carbonated drinks came with the invention of stronger glass bottles that were capable of sustaining the internal pressure from the trapped CO_2.

Nevertheless, and just for curiosity, I decided to experiment creating carbonated brews with primitive containers such as gourds and clay. Until historic evidence turns up, it's probably the next best thing to show that it was a possibility, and if it is something that our ancestors even desired.

Most primitive brews are consumed after a short fermentation process, usually a few days. Such is the case with sorghum beer in Africa. Going further than the main fermentation period is risking that the brew goes bad. Some herbs, such as hops or mugwort, will help preserve the beer for a considerable amount of time and add flavors, but a native primitive brew made only with the juice of cactus pears, for example, will not last very long after the initial fermentation.

My first attempt at creating some carbonation using a primitive vessel (a gourd) was through the use of a similar system to a swing-top bottle. I crudely pasteurized the cleaned gourd by placing boiling water inside, then let it sit for 10 minutes. I then poured some light mugwort beer (using about ¾ cup [136 g] of brown sugar for ½ gallon of water) into the gourd with some wild yeast starter, and let the fermentation proceed for 4 days. This was an open fermentation; a clean towel was placed on top of the gourd so fruit flies would not get in.

The fermentation was very active for the first 3 days and, on the 4th day, I created pressure by using a primitive bow system on top. First I made a couple of grooves on the side of the gourd's neck and tied up two sticks. Then I made a groove on the top and placed another stick. I connected the top stick with the others with yucca (*Hesperoyucca whipplei*) cordage and created a bow under tension, basically forcing the top to connect tightly with the gourd. In between I placed some dry mugwort leaves, which sealed the system somewhat, and the leaves also acted as an insect repellent. Overnight, I managed to get a slightly fuzzy beer. So it is possible to create a light carbonation with very primitive tools and containers. With this system, had there been an excess of pressure inside the gourd, the bow would not have been strong enough to hold and the pressure would have been released. Too much pressure inside the gourd could have resulted in a cracked gourd.

After trying this with a gourd, I decided to work with my friend Melissa Brown, who is an extremely talented pottery artist. She created a couple of designs of possible primitive clay containers for making wild brews that would allow some carbonation inside. The system was pretty much a duplicate of the gourd system, but a bit simpler by only using a stick placed on a grooved top (which can be used as a cup, too) and yucca string guided by grooves at the bottom. Dry grass is placed between the cup on top and the container to create a seal and not allow little critters to infect the brew. Deerskin would probably work extremely well too.

The stick is not a necessity; you can also use a small rock placed on top during the initial fermentation (or do an open fermentation with a clean towel on top), and then place a heavy rock overnight to achieve the carbonation.

Both systems worked quite well and a light carbonation was achieved.

NON-CARBONATED PRIMITIVE FERMENTATION (AKA BOOZY SODAS)

After doing all these experiments trying to get some carbonation using basic tools and vessels, I became interested in making primitive fermentations in clay pots. There is something quite magical about clay. This type of fermentation is probably the closest to actual native brews. It's like using everything the earth is offering as raw ingredients, from clay to plants, to make very tasty and somewhat alcoholic concoctions.

My inspiration came from studying native pottery, but also understanding the principle of fermentation and how to make it easy and somewhat foolproof for anyone to use. The problem with simply covering a clay pot with a lid, leaf, or clean towel is the fact that some bacteria can still potentially infect your brew after a while.

A known and tested system for fermenting food is a traditional fermenting crock, into which vegetables mixed with salt are placed with a weight to keep them under the brine. On top of the crock is a gutter that, once filled with water and covered with the lid, creates a liquid seal. The carbon dioxide created during the fermentation process can escape, but bacteria can't get in.

My idea was to mix traditional crock technology with primitive pottery, pretty much taking an archaic clay fermenting vessel and adding a gutter and lid on top. As with the regular fermenting crock, water is added in the gutter, then the lid is placed and creates the seal. While it was fine in my head and on paper, I'm not a potter, so I worked with my talented friend Melissa Brown, and together we started producing some prototypes and tested them. After making a few corrections and revisions, we ended up with beautiful fermenting clay vessels (thanks to Melissa's talent) that worked perfectly and required minimal supervision.

This type of vessel is perfect for making primitive brews, which are usually fermented for a few days and then drunk. It's a bit like making the soda-beer (SoBeer), but with less sugar and less fermentation time, and we don't bottle it. The beverage is slightly alcoholic—kind of a boozy soda with maybe 2 percent alcohol and a tad, if anything, of natural carbonation occurring from the active yeast. From my research, quite a few ancient sacred or medicinal beverages were enjoyed this way.

You don't need a lot of sugar for this. An adaptation of my original mugwort beer recipe for this kind of brew would be something like this:

Ingredients

⅓ gallon (around 1.25 l) springwater or distilled water

2 lemons

0.1 ounce (3 g) dry mugwort

A bit less than ½ cup (90 g) of some sugar source—feel free to experiment with white sugar, honey, brown sugar, maple or birch syrup, homemade molasses with wild plants such as prickly pears, and lerp sugar, or mix them

Yeast

Procedure

Cut and squeeze the lemons into the water, then add the mugwort and sugar. Boil all the ingredients for 20 minutes. Place the covered pot in cold water and cool the liquid to 70°F (21°C), then add the yeast. One small packet of yeast is usually enough to make 5 gallons, so you don't need to use the whole packet.

Clean your funnel/sieve, then strain into the clay vessel. Place the lid and fill the gutter with water. Let it ferment for 4 to 5 days before serving.

There are a lot of boozy creations you can make. For example, you can take some juice (purchased or homemade) and add a tad of sugar (if necessary) and some champagne yeast. Ferment this for 5 days and voilà! With experience, you can make some truly delicious drinks.

If you are interested in purchasing these clay fermentation vessels, we offer them for sale through my website (www.urbanoutdoorskills.com) and through Melissa's website (www.melissabrownceramics.com).

Primitive clay fermenting bottles with gutters for water.

Elevating Vinegar

The advantage of making a lot of interesting primitive and native brews is the fact that you can take the process to the next level and create some truly unique vinegars. As I write this, I probably have 5 gallons of various vinegars aging in wooden barrels in the garage—vinegars that we use both for our own cooking and to provide to some of the chefs I work with.

The main reason I create my own vinegars is simple: flavor. The subtle qualities obtained through the slow, natural approach to making home-made vinegar don't even resemble the industrially produced vinegars you purchase at the store. While most commercial vinegars are made within 2 or 3 days using a process called oxygenation to speed up the fermentation, some of my homemade vinegars are aged for months, sometimes with aromatic woods such as roasted oak bark, juniper twigs, or fig wood infusing in them.

Add to that the interesting ingredients used to make the original brews or wines and you'll realize there is an infinite number of possibilities in terms of flavors. You can nearly taste the connection to the land, traditions, and people when you take a native brew like *tiswin* (native prickly pear cactus wine) and turn it into an acidic delicacy.

I mostly use two methods to create vinegars. The first is fairly typical: I just use a culture (mother of vinegar) that was given to me a few years ago by a friend. The acetic acid bacteria in the mother converts the ethanol contained in the brews into acetic acid (vinegar).

The second method is a bit unusual. In my quest for local and wild flavors, I also did some experiments and came up with another way of making vinegars using local bacteria from fruit flies. This method is my favorite because it enables me to create a wide variation of unique flavors with sourced bacteria from my terroir.

I've also tried to make vinegar with my beers and wines by pouring the liquid in a container, placing a clean towel or cheesecloth on top, and letting nature run its course over time. In theory, bacteria in the air would infect the brew and turn it into vinegar, but, perhaps due to my location, I've never been successful with that method.

My vinegars are usually started in a jar protected with a fine mesh or cheesecloth. Every 3 to 4 weeks or so, I feed them with more of the original alcoholic beverage. Once I have a decent quantity (usually ½ gallon or 1.9 l), I store them in toasted oak vinegar barrels (which you can purchase online) and continue to feed them in the barrels.

TO GIVE YOU SOME EXAMPLES, THE "WILD" VINEGARS I'VE MADE SO FAR INCLUDE:

Mugwort beer vinegar—bitter and highly aromatic

Water mint mead vinegar—fresh, light, sweet, and lemony

Forest beer vinegar—bitter and musky, with hints of mushrooms

Elderberry wine vinegar—fruity and quite acidic

Black currant wine vinegar—fruity and acidic

White sage and lime cider vinegar—hints of sage and lime, quite light

Tiswin vinegar—light and fruity

MAKING VINEGAR

My first method to make vinegars with wild brews and mother of vinegar is super simple. So far it has worked every time. Here is the procedure I use:

Procedure

Get a starter culture, also called mother of vinegar, from a friend; you can also purchase it online. Usually you get one in a jar with some actual vinegar too. The mother is mostly composed of bacteria and cellulose. I usually compare the texture and look to a jellyfish. The color will depend on the type of vinegar; you make. A red wine vinegar will have a red mother, a beer vinegar will have an amber mother.

You can also try to start vinegar by purchasing raw vinegar such as Bragg's organic raw and unfiltered apple cider vinegar. Some people have used that method, but I've never tried it.

You will need to mix your brew/wine with your starter. The acetic acid bacteria present in the mother will turn the alcohol into vinegar. Depending on the temperature, this can take anywhere from 3 weeks to a couple of months. When adding beer or wine, I use a ratio of 2 parts beer/wine to 1 part vinegar (including the mother). If my wine is too strong (above 10 percent alcohol), I usually add 20 percent water to it. It's just based on experience; some of my elderberry wine

that had a high level of alcohol by volume never turned into vinegar until I added water to reduce it.

Make sure that the container you use to make the vinegar is not made of material that reacts to acids, such as aluminum, plastic, or iron. Wood, ceramic, glass, and stainless steel are fine. Although vinegar is antiseptic, good hygiene is still important. Clean your containers thoroughly before using them. Dish soap, or very hot water for wooden containers, works fine.

Mix your alcoholic liquid with the starter in the appropriate container. If you don't have a lot of starter, use a small glass jar. Oxygen is necessary for the acetic acid bacteria to grow, so choose a container that will allow for a large liquid surface area. I often use wide-mouth jars or even recycled vases.

Cover the top with a clean towel, paper towel, thin mesh, or cheesecloth. Tighten it with a metal band, string, or rubber band. The idea is to not let any insects contaminate your vinegar while still allowing it to have access to oxygen.

Mothers from red wine vinegar.

Place your container in a somewhat warm and dark place. Many people store their jars in a closet. Living in Southern California, I use my garage. The ideal temperature is between 60° and 80°F (16° to 27°C). As you can imagine, I routinely experience temperatures much higher than that during the summer and have seen no ill effects.

From my experience, the average time it takes to change your alcoholic beverage into vinegar is usually around 3 weeks, but it can take much longer, sometimes a couple of months, if you start with higher-alcohol wines and you live in a colder climate.

Some people like to oxygenate their vinegar by stirring it every couple of days, but I prefer to leave it undisturbed and let nature and time do their work. If you want, you can smell the liquid after 3 or 4 weeks through the cheesecloth or mesh. When it is ready it should have a strong vinegar odor.

Also check to see if a new mother of vinegar has formed on top of the liquid. That's what you want.

Try not to move the container too much, as the mother may be displaced and fall to the bottom. If that happens, usually a new mother will form on the top, but you don't want that to happen too often. It's best to leave it alone.

I've had vinegars that smelled like acetone or nail polish after a week or two. This has occurred from time to time with wild brews that had a high volume of alcohol. I used to worry about it; now I simply see it as a temporary stage that goes away after a week or so. It has never affected the final flavors.

You can enjoy your vinegar and bottle your vinegar when it is ready based on the smell test, or you can use it as a starter to make a larger quantity of vinegar. By using 2 parts of alcoholic beverage to 1 part starter, you end up pretty quickly with a large amount of vinegar.

If you decide to bottle it, it's a good idea to filter the contents to remove various particles. Don't forget to set aside the newest mother and some of the vinegar to use as a new starter to make more vinegar.

To produce better flavors, I like to make and age my vinegars in toasted oak vinegar barrels. Once I have around ½ gallon (1.9 l) of starter (vinegar and mother), I pour the liquid into the barrel, add more wine/brews, and simply wait. Every 3 to 4 weeks or so, I add fresh alcoholic beverage with the usual ratio (2 parts of alcohol to 1 part vinegar). When the barrel is nearly full, I let the vinegar age for a couple of months before bottling.

The whole process is really easy. The only time I was not able to make vinegar was when I purchased a strong red wine (14 percent alcohol). It simply never turned into vinegar. Probably because at the time I didn't use my little trick of adding 20 percent water and the wine wasn't organic (it contained sulfites, which suppress microbiological activity).

In more than five years of experimentation with my homemade natural brews and wines, I've never experienced a failure in making vinegars.

Starting your vinegar. I mixed 2 parts beer, 1 part old vinegar, and some vinegar mother my friend gave me. Within 3 weeks a new mother had formed on the surface and my vinegar was ready.

Making more vinegar. The contents of the jar have been transferred to a larger vessel and I added twice the amount of fresh beer. The new vessel is covered with a thin mesh. A new mother will form on the surface. Note that I discarded some old mothers that were in the jar but transferred the newest one in the vase.

Filtering the vinegar before bottling to make a nice and clean vinegar.

VINEGAR FROM SCRATCH—FRUIT FLY VINEGAR

In my quest for the true flavors of the local terroir I became interested in the possibility of making vinegar using actual bacteria from the environment. I made a lot of experiments that didn't work out well. In fact, every single attempt ended up as a failure until I had my "Eureka!" moment with an ingredient I had completely neglected: fruit flies!

The concept may sound rather disgusting to some, but it's probably how vinegar was made in the first place. If you research making homemade vinegars there seems to be some sort of obsession about fruit flies and how to protect your vinegar from them. Here in Southern California we are loaded with them—when I open a bottle of vinegar or one of my wild beers, within minutes I have a crowd of fruit flies trying to feast on it.

Interestingly, as I found out, fruit flies are really helpful in creating your own wild strains of vinegar. This discovery came from a simple observation. One of my friends makes elderberry wine each year, and some of her bottles would always turn to vinegar. As I'm constantly on the lookout for a new mother of vinegar, I gladly accepted some of this starter culture from her. The interesting part was that I would always find a substantial number of dead fruit flies at the bottom of her elderberry vinegar.

I found this rather unappetizing and would filter the vinegar to get rid of them. But the observation of the dead flies became the key to realizing success in my attempts at making "wild vinegar" from scratch with my mugwort beer.

From my research I found it was possible to make your beer turn to vinegar by exposing it to the air. It's supposed to be simple: Pour the beer in a jar, place some cheesecloth on it so critters don't get in (houseflies, bees, fruit flies, ants, and so forth), and the bacteria existing in the air will inoculate your beer and turn it into vinegar.

The process sounds simple; the only problem is that it never worked with my homemade "wild beers." Maybe it's because we live in California and it's usually hot outside, but after a week or so I would get some weird white mold and the smell was quite bad—not something you want to drink, for sure.

So I decided to do an experiment. Instead of fermenting my mugwort beer for just 10 days, then bottling it, I let the beer ferment until it was done (around 5 to 6 weeks), and then poured it into two jars. On the first jar I placed cheesecloth on top and screwed on the lid. I left the other jar wide open with no cheesecloth protection. Within minutes I had a lot of fruit flies getting in and enjoying themselves. Some of them would fall into the beer, and within an hour I had around 20 floating fruit flies. I then placed the cheesecloth on top of this jar and screwed the lid down.

My "Eureka!" moment occurred a week later. After a quick sniff I realized that the beer with the fruit flies was turning into vinegar while the other one hadn't done anything.

It took 6 weeks to get a thin mother of vinegar on top of the fruit-fly-infused brew—much slower than the regular mother of vinegar I was using (usually it's around 3 weeks).

My next step was to strain the vinegar through a coffee filter. I removed the dead flies and kept the mother of vinegar, which I used on a new batch of mugwort beer.

I'm very happy with this vinegar; I call it the Shadow Hills mugwort beer vinegar, after the neighborhood where I live. This method is great for creating your very own vinegar with local wild strains of bacteria. It has a unique flavor profile compared with my regular vinegar: It starts slowly—kind of lemony—and it takes a second or two before you get the acetic bite.

If you use this method, because you're dealing with wild strains you may end up with vinegar that you don't like. So expect some failures—but the successes are worth it. You're basically creating your own unique vinegar, unlike anything you could buy at the store and, heck, even anywhere else in the whole world.

Interestingly enough, this method has not worked very well so far with purchased white wine or red wine, probably because of the sulfites used in winemaking, which inhibit the "natural" vinegar bacteria. When using purchased wines, I won't do the fruit fly method but will instead use my regular mother of vinegar.

If you want to experiment with this method, make sure you only let fruit flies "contaminate" your brew, not regular houseflies or other critters. Have fun, expect a few failures, and, if you're into brewing, there is an almost infinite number of unique vinegars you could make. I'm already thinking about sagebrush beer vinegar, wild grape vinegar, and many others.

Here is a step-by-step summary of the method used to make this vinegar.

Procedure

1. Use your own brew or purchased beer/wine. If you use a purchased beverage, make sure it is of high quality. Most alcoholic beverages sold at the store contain chemicals, which may interfere with the process, so try to find organic beer or an organic wine that is free of added sulfites.

2. Pour the beer or wine into a jar and leave it outside. For a quart jar, I usually allow around 20 fruit flies to infect the brew. You want them swimming around. Attracting this many flies can take anywhere from 10 minutes to an hour where I live (in Southern California).

3. Once the fruit flies are there and enjoying their swimming time, cover the top (use cheesecloth or a clean paper towel), secure it by screwing on a metal canning jar ring band, then wait. Place the jar in a dark place—a temperature between 70° and 80° F (21° to 27° C) is best.

4. After a couple of weeks it should smell like vinegar. In around 4 to 6 weeks it should be ready. Taste the vinegar. If it is not to your liking (some wild strains may create some flavors you don't like), start again. The best strategy is to make several batches at the same time.

5. If you love the vinegar, save the mother and use it to start your next batch—there's no need for more fruit flies. Once you've removed the mother, filter the vinegar and then either use it raw or bottle it and pasteurize it.

Turkey-tail-mushroom-infused vinegar
(turkey tail mushrooms, honey, and apple cider vinegar).

Elderflower-infused vinegar
(elderflowers and apple cider vinegar).

Elderberry-infused vinegar
(dehydrated elderberries and rice vinegar).

Sweet-white-clover-infused vinegar
(sweet white clover and rice vinegar).

Infused Vinegars

I think infused vinegars are one of the best approaches to capturing the essence of various plants and environments. The uses are also countless: We use them in soups, salads, and sauces, or sometimes just brush a small amount on a dish to add some extra sparkle. The type of vinegar you use is very important: You want at least 5 percent acidity, and from experience you will also learn which type of vinegar works well with some herbs. For example, apple cider vinegar has fruity qualities, while rice vinegar is more mild and neutral.

They're also very easy to make. I have two methods that I use, choosing the method based on the ingredients I want to infuse. The hot method works well with dehydrated ingredients such as wild spices or dehydrated fruits and berries. I use the cold method when doing complex blends to re-create the complex flavors of whole environments, such as when I'm making mountain, desert, or forest vinegars.

HOT METHOD

Take a bottle, jar, vase (make sure it's lead-free), or other container and clean it thoroughly or sterilize it (place in boiling water for 10 minutes). Make sure that the container you use to make the vinegar is not made of a material that reacts to acids, such as aluminum, plastic, or iron. Wood, ceramic, glass, or stainless steel is fine.

If you need lids or caps, make sure you clean them as well. To do so, I wash them in hot soapy water, rinse, and scald in boiling water. Some people place them in a bleach solution of 1 teaspoon per gallon for 5 minutes, and rinse them

thoroughly with hot water before use. If using corks (for bottles), use new ones and dip them in boiling water three or four times. I cover some containers, such as vases, with plastic wrap once the infused vinegar has cooled off.

Place your ingredients in the jar or bottle. You can use dried aromatic plants, fruits, and spices. If you use fresh plants/herbs, make sure to wash them and gently pat dry afterward.

In a non-reactive pot, heat the vinegar until it nearly reaches the boiling point (190°F/88°C), then pour it into the container containing the aromatics. Close the jar or bottle and let it steep for at least 3 weeks in a cool dark place. It's good to shake the container once every couple of days, or more frequently if you wish.

Certain ingredients may cloud your vinegar. You will need to strain it again through a clean cheesecloth or coffee filter several times until the vinegar is no longer cloudy, then pour it into a new sterilized or clean container.

COLD METHOD

The cold method for making vinegar is the easiest.

Sterilize or thoroughly clean your container. Wash your ingredients and pat them dry. Place your ingredients in the container and pour in vinegar with at least 5 percent acidity. Close the container and place it in a cool, dark place or your refrigerator for at least 3 weeks.

Strain/filter the vinegar and bottle it. When dealing with chefs or restaurants, it's a good idea to pasteurize your vinegar. For personal use, I usually don't pasteurize it and use it rather quickly.

MOUNTAIN-INFUSED VINEGAR

This is my favorite infused vinegar that I've made so far. Some of the ingredients may change a bit based on the seasons and what's available. Like any good forager, I taste the plants as I forage them to ensure they're packed with the essences I'm looking for. Depending on their location, age, soil composition, exposure to the sun, and other factors, the savor and aroma may vary quite profoundly. It's extremely obvious with trees, which can live for hundreds of years. A young white fir will have a flavor

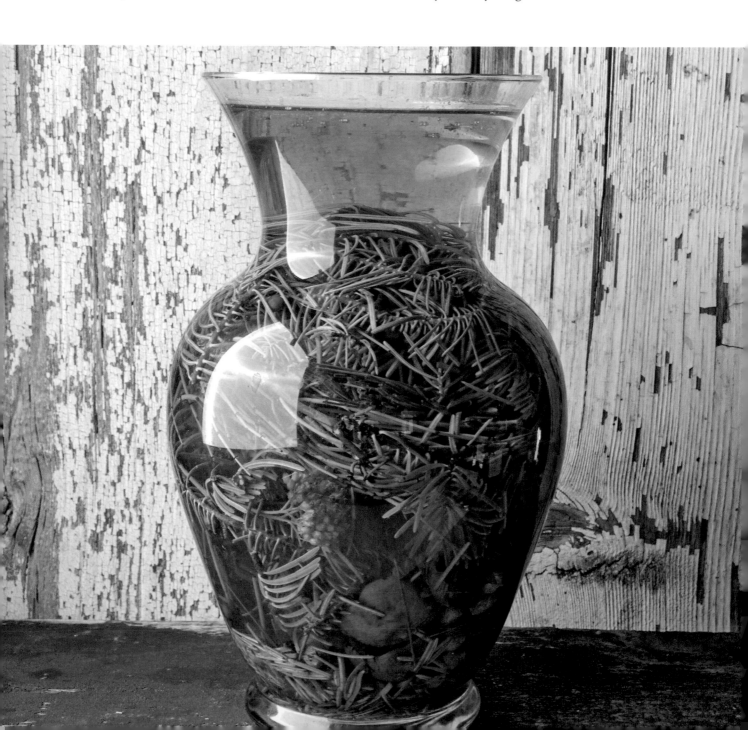

profile comparable to the spirit of a child—light, happy, playful, and full of life—while a much older tree will have more soul, with a tremendous amount of character and complex undertones.

This vinegar is a very nice representation of the environment: It feels and smells like the local mountains. For me, it also evokes wonderful memories of the foraging trip itself and the location of each ingredient. I can even tell which trees they came from. In my culinary world, context is a powerful taste enhancer.

Although it is quite a complex blend, it's very easy to make. The main flavor profile comes from the white fir, which has not only piney qualities but also tangerine-like accents. The juniper berries and pine needles add subtle layers of lemons and pine. During the summer I will add berries such as manzanita or currants, while in winter I may also add some dehydrated toyon berries, which have some cherry-like notes.

I never use a precise recipe for blends—the amount and composition are based on how they taste. I usually age the vinegar in a recycled vase, filled to the top to reduce oxygen exposure and with the mouth wrapped tightly with plastic wrap. The ingredients are packed very loosely, making up maybe 60 percent of the total volume.

A typical mountain vinegar blend for 1 gallon would be as follows. The manzanita and other berries are really added for their light notes; the main flavors come from the white fir, pine, and juniper berries.

Ingredients

70% white fir needles

15–20% pine needles

5–10% percent Mormon tea branches (*Ephedra viridis*—not the same one used for weight loss), if I have them

Around 20 crushed California juniper berries

30–40 crushed manzanita berries

30–40 other berries as appropriate, depending on the season

Around 1 gallon (3.75 l) good-quality apple cider vinegar with 5% acidity

Procedure

1. Thoroughly clean all your ingredients and pat them dry. Cut the white fir and pine needles. Place ingredients loosely in the container to around 60 percent of the volume.
2. Pour in the apple cider vinegar and fill the container to the top. Cover tightly with plastic wrap or a clean towel.
3. Place in a cool, dark place and let the vinegar age for 3 weeks or more. It's a good idea to shake it from time to time to remove any bubbles that may come out from the organic ingredients during the infusion process. Age it based on flavor: If you're happy with the flavor you can stop infusing after 3 weeks. Inspect your vinegar. If you see any sign of mold, any bubbling, or anything unusual, you must discard it. (This has never happened to me, by the way. Pine has excellent antibacterial and antifungal qualities. Interestingly, sometimes a new mother of vinegar will form on top, although the original vinegar was store-bought and pasteurized.)
4. Once you're satisfied in terms of the flavor, strain the contents and bottle the vinegar. For added food safety, you can pasteurize the bottles using the low-temperature pasteurization process (see the Pasteurizing Your Vinegar sidebar on page 252).

PICKLED TROUT IN MOUNTAIN VINEGAR

I'm not the best fisherman, but somehow I managed to get a couple of large trout from a local lake in the mountains. Inspired by the beautiful environment and having a fondness for rollmops, I thought it would be a good idea to pickle one in its own surrounding by using my homemade mountain vinegar. It's a very simple preparation.

Ingredients

1 large trout, filleted with skin on
½ cup (136 g) salt
1 quart (1 l) springwater or distilled water
1 small sweet onion
Mountain vinegar (enough to fill the jar)—
    see recipe above

Procedure

1. The first step is to brine the fish. I made a brine composed of ½ cup (136 g) sea salt in 1 quart (1 l) of water and poured it into a 1-quart (1 l) container.
2. Place the fillets in the brine container with a pasteurized stone on top as a weight to keep them under the brine. Leave the fish in the refrigerator for 10 hours.
3. Remove the fillets from the brine, rinse them under cold water, then place them in cold water and back in the fridge.
4. After a couple of hours, take the fillets out of the water and pat them dry with a paper towel. Put them in a clean quart jar. Slice the onion and place the slices in the jar, then fill the jar with mountain vinegar. The jar then goes into the fridge. The contents are best enjoyed after a couple of days and should keep for at least a week. For plating, I roll up the fillets with onion slices and some wild greens (chickweed, watercress, or whatever is in season) then secure them with a small oak twig.

FOREST-INFUSED VINEGAR

Recently I was hiking in a nearby forest. It had just rained and everything was green. The scent was musky from the humidity, old leaves from last fall, and mushrooms, but at the same time it had some floral qualities from all the flowers popping up here and there.

As I usually do when I create wild sodas and brews, I decided to grab various aromatic herbs, mushrooms, and berries, but this time my goal was to create a vinegar packed with all the scents, flavors, and aromas I was experiencing.

Procedure

1. Forage the ingredients. To do sophisticated blending, I'm aware that it requires some experience with foraging, but you can also infuse vinegar with one ingredient, such as elderflowers, wild mint, or white fir needles.
2. Clean your foraged ingredients properly.
3. As a base I like to use apple cider vinegar or rice vinegar (which is milder). You can use the vinegar of your choice. Make sure, though, that it has at least 5 percent acidity. Also check the labels. Many apple cider vinegars are flavored instead of being the real thing. It makes a big difference in the final result.
4. Sterilize the jars (I place them in boiling water for 12 to 15 minutes), let them cool, then place your ingredients inside.
5. In a non-reactive pot, heat the vinegar until it nearly reaches the boiling point (190°F/88°C), then pour it into the container or jar. I like to use the hot vinegar method if I have some very fresh herbs or plants that don't have the same kind of antibacterial and antimicrobial qualities as pine, fir, or juniper berries.
6. Close the lid tightly and let the jar cool down.
7. Place in the refrigerator or in a cool, dark place and let the flavors infuse for around 3 weeks.
8. Taste it and see if you need to add anything to it, such as a bit of salt, sugar, or honey.
9. Filter and bottle your vinegar. As an added food-safety precaution, I usually pasteurize the vinegar (see Pasteurizing Your Vinegar on page 252) by placing the bottles in water and bringing the temperature of the vinegar to 145°F (63°C) for 30 minutes. Clean the caps, close the bottles, and place them upside down until cool (the high temperature will further sanitize the caps).

How far can you go?

If you are an expert forager, you can create the most complex blends featuring the true flavors of the forest. For example in a recent "forest" vinegar I used the following ingredients in various ratios:

Burr chervil
Cottonwood and willow leaves
Grass
Turkey tail mushrooms
Manzanita berries
Toyon berries
Sweet white clover
Roasted oak bark
Old dried-up mugwort leaves
California bay (just a tad)
Foraged sea salt
California sagebrush leaves (just a few)

Elderberry-Infused Vinegar

If you make elderberry wine you can make elderberry wine vinegar, but I think you get more flavor if you infuse the dehydrated berries. You preserve more of the fruity accents by doing so. I like to use rice vinegar instead of apple cider vinegar, simply because I don't want the stronger flavors of cider vinegar to compete with the berries.

The method I use is very basic. Take any size jar and place enough dehydrated elderberries in it to fill up around one-third of the volume. Pour rice vinegar in the jar and leave a ¼-inch (0.6 cm) headspace as the berries may expand a bit, then close the lid tightly. Check your jar a couple of days later. If you see any signs of pressure due to the expansion of the dehydrated berries, open the lid to release pressure and remove any vinegar if necessary, then close the lid again.

Place the jar in a cool, dark place for at least 3 weeks, then enjoy. I never remove the berries—I think they're really pretty in dishes or salads—but you can strain the vinegar, bottle it, and also pasteurize it if you wish.

Feel free to experiment with other vinegars, such as white wine or red wine vinegars. You can also add a bit of sugar or honey.

Elderflower-Infused Vinegar

This vinegar is extremely easy to make and has very delightful floral qualities. I usually use a good-quality apple cider vinegar as a base, but rice vinegar works very well too. The elderflowers I forage come from our local Mexican elder; they are usually half the size of the elderflowers from the black elder (*Sambucus nigra*), so you need to take this into account for this recipe.

The process is quite simple. Basically you forage a bunch of elderflowers, take them home, and remove as much of the stems as you can. Sometimes I use fresh elderflower and remove the flowers from the stems with my fingers; other times I just leave the flowers in a bowl for a day or two and the flowers fall from the stem easily with some convincing shaking.

The idea is to pack as many of them in a jar as possible. With Mexican elder I can easily pack the florets from 60 flower heads in a quart jar, so I imagine that with the black elder you might need 20 or 30 of the flower heads. When done, simply pour as much apple cider as you can into the jar, close the lid tightly, and place the jar in a cool, dark place. I usually let it age for a month or so before straining the infused vinegar and bottling.

In the past I used to filter this vinegar before bottling using coffee filters to remove the yellow pollen, which makes the vinegar cloudy; but over time I've learned to appreciate that particular beauty as well.

For added food safety, you can pasteurize the bottled vinegar.

Turkey-Tail-Mushroom-Infused Vinegar

Because of their earthy aroma, turkey tail mushrooms are one of my favorite ingredients to add to vinegar. They're also extremely medicinal—they enhance immune system functioning and have anticancer properties. There is a definite bitterness to them as well, so I like to add some sugar or honey to my vinegar solution to balance the flavor, though it's not a must. Bitter is a flavor that some people like and, from my experience, the flavor tends to mellow over time.

To make the infused vinegar, I simply pack my jar with the mushrooms. If they are too big, you can cut them so they fit the opening. I fill around 80 percent of the jar with mushrooms, then pour in apple cider vinegar and add a bit of honey or sugar.

I place the jar in the refrigerator for at least 3 months, then taste it. If necessary, I'll add a bit more sugar or honey to taste. When you're satisfied with the flavors, strain the vinegar and bottle it. For added food safety, you can pasteurize the bottled vinegar.

Herbal Vinegars

As I've said before, the more I delve into wild edibles, the more I realize there are no rules, just flavors. If you practice food safety and good hygiene and know the ingredients that you are working with, there are countless combinations of new and unusual flavors you can create. Not all of them will work (and I have made a lot of mistakes), but it's all part of experimenting.

Every time one of my concoctions doesn't produce the desired effect, I learn something new. As you gain experience, you will get better at it and will be able to make truly delicious ingredients.

Don't be afraid to experiment with different vinegars, plants, and combinations of plants and berries. For example, a tiny bit of black sage in an elderberry-infused vinegar can really add an extra zing to the flavor profile, but by itself I found that black-sage-infused vinegar was pretty much unpalatable. Often it's about the quantity of herb you use, as many wild aromatic plants have extremely strong flavors. You can also get a lot of surprises: A plant that smells wonderful can end up tasting horribly bitter, or, conversely, a plant that didn't smell too good ends up tasting amazing, as was the case with our local native wood mint (*Stachys albens*).

You probably have hundreds of possible combinations that you can make from your local terroir. Even after 12 years of foraging, I find new ones each month.

Water mint vinegar.

Wood mint and juniper vinegar.

White fir vinegar.

Pasteurizing Your Vinegar

Not everyone will agree with pasteurizing vinegars. Some people think it's an unnecessary step because vinegar itself is antiseptic and would kill most harmful bacteria and mold. For purists, the health benefits would also be eliminated in the process. I don't disagree with them, and frankly, for personal uses, I don't pasteurize them, but if I create a vinegar blend for a chef I usually will do so because I don't always know how he will store the vinegar and when he will use it. Some of my blends also have numerous and very unusual ingredients, so I prefer to err on the side of safety if I know other people will consume it.

To preserve the flavors, my favorite method to pasteurize vinegar is using the same method used for milk, sometimes called low-temperature pasteurization, or thermization.

First I filter the vinegar to remove any impurities. If it was vinegar I made myself using a mother, it is usually somewhat cloudy, and filtering will help clear it. If I made an infused vinegar using purchased commercial vinegar, I usually use a simple strainer to remove organic bits and pieces.

Once the vinegar has been strained into the bottles, I place them in water and bring the temperature of the vinegar to between 145°F (63°C) and 150°F (65°C) for 30 minutes. The caps are cleaned thoroughly and screwed on the bottles, which are stored upside down until cool (the high temperature will further sanitize the caps).

Once cooled, store the bottles in a cool dark place.

INFUSED VINEGAR SAUCE WITH WILD BERRIES

I often use this type of infused vinegar as a sauce for game meats such as rabbit, venison, or quail. It works well with a wide variety of wild berries, such as elderberries, blackberries, blueberries, or currants.

Ingredients

For fresh berries I use around 50% fresh berries and 50% apple cider vinegar

For dehydrated berries I use around 30% dehydrated wild berries and 70% apple cider vinegar

Sugar or honey to taste

Procedure

1. Mix the vinegar with fresh or dehydrated berries. With fresh berries, I use a ratio of around 50 percent vinegar and 50 percent berries. Because the flavors are usually more concentrated with dehydrated berries, I often use a ratio of 70 percent vinegar and 30 percent dried berries. Don't get too hung up on these ratios—use them as a guideline to start, but feel free to experiment.

2. Bring the solution to a boil, then simmer for 10 minutes. Check the flavor, adding sugar or honey to taste. For my dehydrated-elderberry-infused vinegar, I used approximately 1½ tablespoons of honey for a half-pint jar.

3. Remove from the heat and let the sauce cool a bit. Pour the contents into somewhat hot jars (I clean them with hot water before pouring the vinegar) and close the lid. In the fridge, this will keep for several weeks. I like to let it infuse a couple of days before using it, as some berries (including elderberries) have hard seeds inside, and the infusion period makes them more tender.

4. When you plan to serve, reheat the sauce and let it simmer until you achieve a consistency to your liking. You may want to strain the sauce, which I do with some berries, such as currants, because they contain so many seeds. Feel free to mix ingredients and even spices. In my latest batch of elderberry vinegar sauce, I added some lemon peel and a tiny amount of cinnamon.

Feel free to experiment with other types of vinegar as well such as white wine, red wine, or rice vinegars.

Deer sausage snack with wild spice blend wrapped in a curly dock leaf, with homemade elderberry wine vinegar/eucalyptus honey reduction and mugwort, black mustard flowers, and crunchy lerp sugar.

MAKING SHRUBS

For a long time I was wondering what I could do with some of my "wild" vinegars, aside from using them in sauces, condiments, or preserving. A couple of years ago, I was making a new batch of elderberry wine vinegar and, as usual, tasting it. Probably because I was doing research on all the possible uses for vinegars, the taste reminded me of a drink a gentleman once made during a desert survival class a long time ago. He called it "jungle juice," and it was supposed to help rehydrate and help the body cope with the scorching desert heat. Instead of using alcohol, he used water, vinegar, and chunks of fruits. I remember the drink was really delicious, a perfect blend of sweet, sour, and fruity flavors.

A quick search online for vinegar drinks and voilà! I came across an old recipe for a vinegar drink from the 17th century called "shrub." Traditionally a shrub was a way to preserve berries and fruits by infusing them in vinegar. Once the berries or fruits were eaten, the remaining juice could be drunk with the addition of water and, if necessary, sugar or honey.

Making shrubs is once again popular with mixologists, and there is a good reason for that. Done properly the drink is fantastic, and some well-made shrubs can be compared to flavored champagne.

The basic procedure for making a simple shrub is extremely easy:

Procedure

1. Infuse some vinegar with fruits, berries, or even plants. My favorite shrub is made with my infused mountain vinegar, but you could also use ingredients such as cherries, fennel, blackberries, figs, blueberries, and so on. (Recently I infused a vinegar with elderberries in the refrigerator for a couple of weeks; I filled 30 percent of the jar with dehydrated elderberries and filled the rest with apple cider vinegar.)
2. Strain your infused vinegar, place it in a pot, and add the same volume of sugar or honey. You're basically making infused vinegar syrup. To make it simple, for every 1 cup of vinegar, you add 1 cup of sugar or honey.

    Don't limit yourself with just sugar or honey in your shrub experiments; you can also use other sources of sweetness such as tree sap (maple or birch syrup), for example. For one of my shrubs, I used apple cider vinegar and local prickly pear cactus molasses.
3. Bring the liquid to a boil and let it simmer for a minute. If you used sugar, make sure it is fully dissolved—stir if necessary.
4. Strain, let it cool a bit, then pour into a clean jar or bottle. Screw the lid on tightly or cork the bottle and place into the refrigerator or in a cool, dark place. It's a very acidic syrup, and should preserve well for months.
5. When ready to use, place ice cubes in a glass and pour enough vinegar syrup to fill around 20 to 25 percent of the volume. Fill the rest of the glass with carbonated water and voilà! You've made a delicious simple shrub.

There are huge numbers of creative drinks you can make with shrubs, so don't limit yourself with this very basic procedure. Do your own research on the subject. Some people use fresh fruits or even fruit juices, while others like to leave the infused berries in the vinegar. You also have the option of making lighter syrup by using less sugar or honey. My friend even uses another procedure, which is to make syrup first by mixing water or juice, sugar, and fruits, berries, or plants; bringing it to a boil; then adding the vinegar. This method works very well too.

Going Native

Summer is the time to forage for more native plants; in fact, it's mostly what's available at that time. During the rest of the year, I would say that over 60 percent of the plants I pick up are non-native. Curly dock, chervil, mustards, and many others were all imported from other parts of the world.

Because Southern California is pretty much a desert, some plants are able to thrive even if there is a terrible drought and just a couple of days of rain for the whole year. When people ask me about how the recent drought has affected me, my answer is simple: "It made me more creative." I learned a lot about wild edible seeds, went to the desert and the mountains to look for unusual foodstuffs, and did lots of research and various experiments. I also connected much more with the Native American community.

I did a lot of preserving and cooking with cactus (pears, pads, and flower buds) and the various kinds of yucca, experimented with a lot of infusions and native brews, collected bags of various unusual seeds, studied and took workshops on native cooking methods, and so on.

When dealing with native ingredients, respect and sustainability are key. Before foraging any plants you need to find out if they are protected or rare—and, if that is the case, simply don't touch them. I make a point of actually helping the ones I find by offering them whatever water I have available.

Respect the plants too—like us humans and like the animals, they are living entities. Don't kill them by uprooting them unnecessarily or taking too much. For example, if I find a field of watercress or chickweed, I don't take more than 20 percent of what I find so that the plants can continue to reproduce and prosper. Fail to do so and next year you'll realize it wasn't a smart move.

Ethical foraging is extremely important, mostly because these days foraging is quite trendy in the culinary world. We now have chefs or newly hired and often inexperienced foragers picking up plants for restaurants without the proper knowledge and understanding of sustainability. I have seen a field of chickweed decimated after a chef and his team came through—the lack of respect was heartbreaking. The quest for profit and foraging don't go well together.

It's also important to know where you can and can't forage. Don't break the law: Foraging native plants in some areas is strictly prohibited. It's your responsibility to find out; often the information on what you can and can't do in a specific location is available online.

In order to enjoy some plants, I've actually created my own wild garden. For example, since I started foraging many years ago I planted some yucca (*Hesperoyucca whipplei*) plants in various locations and private

lands owned by friends. In the last few years, some of these plants have been flowering and have gone to seed; thus I'm able to enjoy some special native food in a very sustainable way. For every yucca I pick up, I replant at least three (or many) more.

I think the biggest lesson I've learned during the drought years is that, no matter what, there is a true abundance of food around us. Local native people knew so much more than we do that they were able to survive in sometimes extremely harsh environments through ethical foraging, understanding sustainability, and properly preserving seasonal ingredients.

One of the most useful plants I know from my terroir is yucca. There are around 50 types of yuccas, mostly found in the Southwest of the United States and also in Mexico and Guatemala.

Where I live, although there are many more which are often planted for decoration, the most abundant yuccas I find in the wilderness are the chaparral yucca (*Hesperoyucca whipplei*), datil yucca (*Yucca baccata*), Joshua tree (*Yucca brevifolia*), and soap tree yucca (*Yucca elata*). Joshua trees are protected thus should not be foraged.

Most of them are easy to identify, as the long leaves grow in a rosette formation. Each leaf has very sharp, saw-like edges and ends with an extremely tough, thin needle. Some yuccas, such as our local chaparral yucca, have a life span of around seven years, and at the end of their life, usually around May, a flower stalk sometimes up to 15 feet tall will rise and be covered with clusters of white flowers. Around July and August, the fruits will develop. Other yuccas, such as the Joshua tree, will flower and produce fruits yearly.

In my local wilderness, the most abundant yucca is the chaparral yucca. Due to their saponin content, the root and leaves can be used to make soap. The tough, fibrous leaves were used by native peoples to make cordage, baskets, and even sandals. Once the plant dies and the stalk emerges, every part can be used as a food source.

The young asparagus-looking stalk can be cut, usually when it is around 3 to 5 feet tall (1 to 1.5 meters) and before it starts flowering. Some people just peel them and eat the tender flesh, which has a texture a bit similar to potato but tastes more like cucumber. My throat gets a bit itchy if I eat it raw, probably because I'm super sensitive to saponin, so I suspect there is a negligible amount in the young stalk. I use the same technique as the natives, which is to roast it or boil it with one water change, which eliminates the problem. As you'll see, there are some interesting culinary creations that can be done, and I know I've barely scratched the surface on the possibilities.

The flowers can be eaten raw or cooked. From my own experience and based on advice from a native elder, the raw flowers should be eaten in moderation; in large quantity they may have a laxative effect, so don't make a wild food salad with just the flowers. The flavor from the cooked flowers reminds me a bit of Belgian endive.

The green fruits are usually harvested in midsummer, around July and August. You need to pick them at the right time, before the seeds are formed inside. I usually do a test before harvesting the fruits from a stalk by cutting one with a knife. It should cut through easily, as if it were a potato or apple. If it's too hard or your knife gets stuck inside, it means the seeds have already formed and it's too late to harvest.

Traditionally the green fruits were roasted, but when I attended native cooking classes, we cut them in two lengthwise and boiled them first with a couple of water changes to remove the low amount of saponin, then sautéed them. I also preserve the boiled fruits in vinegar.

The taste of the green fruits is somewhat peculiar and hard to describe. Some people love it and some people, like me, are not too impressed. But every year, I'll still make a couple jars of pickled fruits to meet the demand.

The fruits of the other local yuccas are also edible; the flowers, which are thicker and tougher than those of the chaparral yucca, are usually cooked or, in my case, pickled.

Before foraging any yuccas, you need to research whether the plants are protected or if there are laws prohibiting taking any parts of the plants in your area. If so, you may be reduced to planting your own yucca garden or purchasing them from a local native plants nursery.

Pickled Yucca Recipes

Yucca is so versatile that you can pickle any edible parts of the plant, from the stalk to the flower buds, flowers, and fruits. The flowers of our chaparral yucca (*Hesperoyucca whipplei*) are too fragile to be pickled and usually turn into a mush during the process, but you can use the unopened flower buds instead, which are tougher. If I want to pickle flowers, I use the ones from the soap tree yucca (*Yucca elata*), as they are thicker and hold up well during the pickling process. Think sustainability: Don't harvest too many flowers—just pick a few from each plant.

The pickling solution is what determines the flavors to a large degree. Aside from the young fruits, which have a specific taste, the stalk and flowers are pretty neutral. You can follow my very basic recipes, which are the ones that people have liked the most in recent years, but there is a lot of room for creativity through using various spices and vinegars.

Pickled chaparral yucca stalk.

PICKLED YUCCA SHOOT

This recipe calls for a medium-sized yucca shoot. It will fill approximately four pint (500 ml) jars.

Ingredients for each jar

Yucca shoot

2 teaspoons (10 g) grated ginger, or 2 small pieces of fresh ginger (½ inch [1 cm] each)

¼ California bay leaf (or ½ regular bay leaf)

2 small chili pods—optional, but good if you like a little spicy kick (I usually use dried whole Japanese chili peppers)

1 teaspoon (5 g) sea salt

Pickling solution

3 cups (709 ml) apple cider vinegar (5% acidity)

2 cups (473 ml) sweet white wine

Procedure

1. Yucca skin is pretty tough, so you want to remove the green skin and get to the white flesh of the stalk. Use a knife to remove approximately ¼ inch (0.5 cm) of skin. Cut the stalk into ½-inch (1 cm) slices, or you can also cut it into chunks. If you have a large-diameter stalk, you may need to cut the slices in half so they can fit inside your jar.

2. Follow Basic Water Bath Canning on page 38. Clean the jars thoroughly, then place the slices and other ingredients in them. I keep the jars somewhat hot by standing them in a couple of inches of hot water.

3. Bring the pickling solution to a boil and pour it slowly into the hot jars, leaving ½ inch (1 to 1.25 cm) headspace. Remove any air bubbles with a clean spoon or knife. Wipe the jar rims and adjust the lids.

4. Place in the refrigerator and enjoy after a couple of weeks. If you want to can them using water canning, I usually process them for 25 minutes in a boiling-water bath (pint jars).

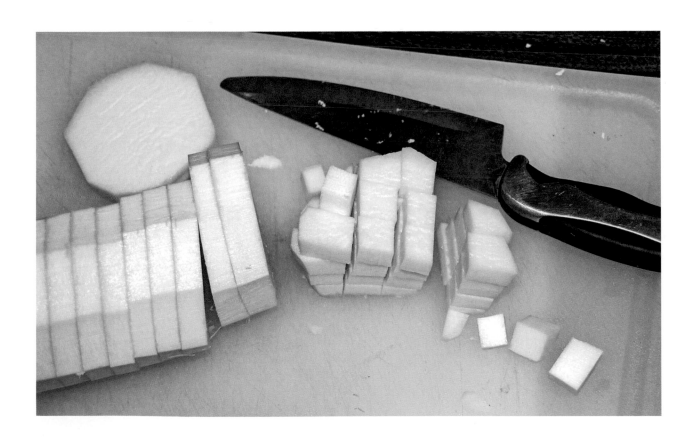

PICKLED YUCCA FLOWERS

You cannot use chapparal yucca to make this recipe, as the flowers are too tender. You need thick yucca flowers similar to the ones found on datil yucca (*Yucca baccata*). This recipe makes approximately four pint (500 ml) jars.

Ingredients for each jar

30 yucca flowers
2 teaspoons (10 g) grated ginger
2 teaspoons (12 g) sugar

Pickling solution

3 cups (709 ml) rice vinegar (5% acidity)—
    apple cider vinegar works well too
2 cups (473 ml) white wine

Procedure

1. Remove the flowers from the stems and clean briefly. Pat carefully with a clean towel and set them aside for 10 to 15 minutes to dry a bit, then place them into the (clean) jars with the ginger and sugar. I keep the jars somewhat hot by standing them in a couple of inches of warm water.
2. Follow Basic Water Bath Canning on page 38. Bring the pickling solution to a boil and pour it slowly inside the hot jars, leaving ½ inch (1 to 1.25 cm) headspace. Remove any air bubbles with a clean spoon or knife. Wipe the jar rims and adjust lids.
3. Place in the refrigerator and enjoy after 2 to 3 weeks. If you want to can them, process for 25 minutes in a boiling-water bath.

Pickled yucca gloriosa flowers.

PICKLED YUCCA FLOWER BUDS

I use this recipe with our local chaparral yucca (*Hesperoyucca whipplei*). The mature flowers are too tender to pickle, but the unopened flower buds are strong enough to withstand the high temperature of the pickling solution during canning.

The unopened flower buds also contain air and will float wildly when you pour the hot pickling solution into the jars if you don't cook them first for 2 to 3 minutes in boiling water.

This recipe makes approximately four half-pint (250 ml) jars. The pickling solution is very basic. By all means, feel free to experiment with creative variations.

Ingredients for each jar

50 unopened chaparral yucca flower buds (use more or fewer buds, depending on their size)
2 teaspoons (10 g) grated ginger
2 teaspoons (12 g) sugar

Pickling solution

2 cups (473 ml) rice vinegar (5% acidity)—apple cider vinegar works well too
1 cup (236 ml) white wine

Procedure

1. Remove the flower buds from the stem, clean briefly, and blanch them for 2 to 3 minutes in boiling water.
2. Place the buds into clean jars with the ginger and sugar. I keep the jars somewhat hot by standing them in a couple of inches of warm water.
3. Follow Basic Water Bath Canning on page 38. Bring the pickling solution to a boil and pour it slowly into the hot jars, leaving ½ inch (1 to 1.25 cm) headspace. Remove any air bubbles with a clean spoon or knife. Wipe the jar rims and adjust the lids.
4. Place in the refrigerator and enjoy after 2 to 3 weeks. If you want to can them, process for 15 minutes in a boiling-water bath (½-pint or 250 ml jars).

Pickled chaparral yucca flower buds.

PICKLED YUCCA FRUITS

Yucca fruits have an "interesting" flavor that, frankly, I'm not too fond of, but some of the students attending my wild food classes really like them, so I keep making this every year. Like the other recipes, it is very basic. I plan to work on more interesting pickling solutions, including brining and possibly fermenting the fruits first to see if I can improve the flavors. I've also used a pickling solution of just white vinegar and sugar (to taste) with good results.

This recipe makes approximately four pint (500 ml) jars. You will need 120 medium-sized, tender chaparral yucca fruits.

Ingredients for each jar

30 medium-sized, tender chaparral
    yucca fruit
2 garlic cloves (I usually cut them in two)
¼ California bay leaf (or ½ regular bay leaf)
2 small chili pods—they're optional but I
    like a little spicy kick. (Your choice of chili
    will determine how much kick you want.
    I usually use dried whole Japanese
    chili peppers.)
1 teaspoon Italian or French spice mix
1 teaspoon sea salt

Pickling solution

3 cups (709 ml) apple cider vinegar
    (5% acidity)
2 cups (473 ml) white wine

Procedure

1. Clean the fruits and cut the stems. Cook the fruits in boiling water for 10 minutes. Strain and set aside.
2. Place the fruits into clean jars with the other ingredients. I keep the jars somewhat hot by standing them in a couple of inches of warm water.
3. Follow Basic Water Bath Canning on page 38. Bring the pickling solution to a boil and pour it slowly into the hot jars, leaving ½ inch (1 to 1.25 cm) headspace. Remove any air bubbles with a clean spoon or knife. Wipe the jar rims and adjust the lids.
4. Place in the refrigerator and enjoy after 2 to 3 weeks. If you want to can them, process for 30 minutes in a boiling-water bath.

Pickled chaparral yucca fruits.

Traditionally, yucca fruits are roasted or baked. When I attended a native cooking class with some members of the Cahuilla tribe, the yucca flowers and fruits were boiled first (sometimes cut in half lenghtwise), then sautéed with garlic and onions. The flowers were also cooked and dehydrated to be used later on as a mush.

From my research, some native people also boiled the fruits and dehydrated them for future uses, usually pounded into a mush. I've barely scratched the surface myself in terms of the possibilities, but here are some interesting uses.

To make a chapparal yucca jerky, forage the young emerging stalk and remove the skin. Cut the stalk into long, thin strips. Boil the strips for 10 minutes, change the water, and boil for another 10 minutes. Strain and set aside.

Make a basic jerky marinade: For my recipe I use soy sauce, brown sugar, red wine, chilies, fresh garlic, and pepper. Unlike a marinade for meat, it should be quite light. I add around 40 percent water to it. For whatever reason, the flavors really concentrate during the dehydration process. Feel free to experiment with your favorite marinade.

I usually leave the stalk strips marinating for 5 to 6 hours, then dehydrate them at 160°F (71°C) until done. The look and texture are amazing. Some people who ate this jerky were convinced it was some sort of meat.

Yucca flowers can be cooked into a jam with regular white sugar and a bit of ginger or other flavorful plants, such as black sage or mugwort. Instead of water I use my white elderberry wine. The whitish color is not too appealing, so I usually add a bit of red beet juice. The end result is really beautiful and quite delicious.

Boiled yucca stalk chunks can be used like potatoes in stews and various dishes. The texture is quite interesting and the chunks are a bit transparent; they taste like a cross between a regular potato and a cucumber. I change the water twice when boiling the chunks. As when boiling acorns, make sure you use hot water when changing the water.

I also like to cut thin strips of yucca stalk, boil them twice for 10 minutes, then dehydrate them. I use them later in Asian-type soups or dishes like I would use bamboo shoots.

Boiled chaparral yucca fruits, quick pickled and served with vinegar, oil, and wild spices (*left*). Sautéed chaparral yucca fruits with garlic and wild spices (*right*).

Chaparral yucca stalk jerky (soy sauce, brown sugar, red wine, chilies, fresh garlic, and pepper).

Chaparral yucca flower jam (white sugar, ginger, elderberry wine, and red beet juice).

Boiled chaparral yucca stalk chunks in a beef bourguignon.

Cooked and dehydrated chaparral yucca stalk (used in Asian soups, similar to bamboo).

Collecting and Cooking with Cattails

Cattail (*Typha latifolia*) is one of the most versatile plants growing in the wild and can be found pretty much anywhere in the United States.

This plant loves water and can be found growing on the edge of lakes, in streams, marshes, swamps, or in very wet soil. It is usually 5 to 8 feet tall once mature. It is easily recognizable with its stiff, flat leaf blades. In the center you will find an erect, rounded stem reaching up to 6 or 7 feet (around 2 meters) in height. At the end of the stem, the flower head forms a cylinder densely packed with tiny male flowers in the top cluster and tiny female flowers in the bottom cluster. When the male cluster is loaded with pollen it looks bright yellow. The pollen is extremely easy to forage in large quantity.

Picked at the right time, the bottom of the stem can be eaten either raw or cooked. It is extremely important to make sure the water is not polluted; don't pick cattails where there is lot of human activity, horse riding, and so forth, as there may be harmful bacteria or even parasites in the water.

The bottom end of the stem looks very much like a leek. Using a knife, cut the lower stem (around 10 to 12 inches [20 to 25 cm]) and place it in your foraging bag. Once you're back home, clean the stems thoroughly; I usually use three changes of water to clean the stems. The inside of the stem is very tender—you may need to remove a layer or two to get to the tender stalk.

You will need to get your hands dirty if you want to collect the rhizomes, which are loaded with starch. In spring, I'm always interested in collecting the very young white shoots coming out of the root; those shoots are quite tender.

The season to forage cattail shoots is usually early spring, while the pollen is harvested in May or June. In Southern California we sometimes have both a fall and spring season.

Aside from food uses, native peoples used the long, flat leaves for making hats, roofing, sandals, and woven baskets. The dried leaves were even twisted to make dolls and various children's toys.

From a medical perspective, the crushed roots can be applied to burns, bruises, or cuts to promote healing and soothe pain.

Foraging and Culinary Tips for Cattails

ROOTS

The roots are usually found a few inches belowground. Harvesting them can be a dirty, messy job. You often have to get into the mud, dig with your hands, and pull them out. The first time I foraged them I was

Male flower head loaded with pollen. Can be cooked when still green and pollen collected when yellow.

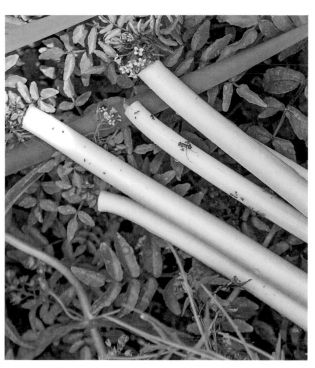

Tender cattail shoots. Can be cooked, pickled, or eaten raw.

Green and immature female flower head. Boil for 15 to 20 minutes and eat like corn on the cob.

White shoots from cattail roots. Can be cooked, pickled, or eaten raw.

a bit baffled by the fact that they're very fibrous and spongy. I was expecting them to be somewhat tender. Cattail root is not something you can eat or cook as is. They are loaded with starch, which must be extracted to make flour by chopping the roots into small pieces and grinding them in water. Another option is to scrape the starchy substance with a knife. The resulting starchy juice can be used in primitive bread recipes, or the starch can be collected for future use after settling at the bottom of a container and dehydrated.

The true delicacy is the young and tender white shoots coming out of the roots in spring. Forage them carefully, as they break easily. You can cook or pickle them. At Melisse restaurant they are cut in thick slices and cooked like scallops with the appropriate sauce.

SHOOTS

The bottom end of cattail stalks is my favorite forage. You can eat it raw or cooked. It looks very much like a leek, and you can cook them as such. It's quite awesome sautéed, but more often than not we cut it in thin slices and use them raw in salads.

The flavor is similar to a cucumber with a nutty accent. It's delicious. I usually pull back the two main outer leaves, then grab the other inner leaves and pull gently. It is best to do this when the plant is growing in water. Depending on the season, location, and age of the plant, the first 4 to 10 inches are tender and edible.

FLOWERS

Around May or June (and again in the fall here in Southern California), the cattail pollen can be collected from the top cluster (male flower part) by shaking it into a bag. This pollen can be used as a very colorful yellow flour in bread and pastries. In a good location, I've been able to collect 2 or 3 cups per hour.

Usually there is a decent amount of fluffy material mixed with the pollen. Remove it by straining the flour using a regular kitchen strainer.

Before placing the pollen in a jar or paper bag, you need to dehydrate it. I place it on a large flat plate in the dehydrator for a couple of hours; you can also use your oven at the lowest temperature setting, leaving the door open an inch or two. Failure to remove the moisture may result in your pollen molding and going bad.

The still-young and green bottom cluster (female flower part) can be eaten like corn on the cob after 15 to 20 minutes of boiling. Just add some butter, salt, and pepper and you have a delicious treat. The immature and still-green male flower can also be boiled for 10 to 15 minutes and is very nice sautéed.

Boiled cattail female flower head, yucca flowers, cattail pollen, and pickled unripe walnut sauce.

Foraging cattail pollen. *Photo courtesy of Mia Wasilevich.*

EXTRACTING CATTAIL STARCH

Cattail rhizomes are loaded with starch, but that doesn't mean it's easy to extract. There are two main methods for extraction that I know. One is to dehydrate the roots, then pound or scrape them to remove the powdered starch from the abundant fibrous material. Alternatively, you can pound the fresh root, pour the juice in a container, and add water. Over time the starch will settle and accumulate at the bottom of the container.

I once gave a workshop on making primitive breads and using native seeds. During the workshop, I used fresh rhizome juice instead of water to make primitive flatbreads, with the starch acting as a binder. Without any starch or gluten, the flatbreads would have crumbled too easily.

The basic method I use to extract starch with fresh rhizomes is as follows:

Procedure

The most difficult part of collecting cattails is actually finding the right location to forage them; you really want to make sure there is no pollution. Once you find the right location, it's time to get dirty—get into the mud and pull the cattails out slowly and nicely. You can clean them initially in the water, as they're usually quite muddy, then take them home and clean them even more thoroughly, which often requires several changes of water.

Using my primitive mortar, or *molcajete,* I pound the fresh rhizomes into a mush. They're quite fibrous and tough; it may take 5 to 10 minutes to do a good job. You can add some water to make your job easier.

I then place a sieve on top of a container and, using my hands, I squeeze the juice out. It is quite slimy.

Add water to the container and leave it alone for a while. Within an hour you'll see the starch beginning to accumulate at the bottom. Wait a few more hours, then carefully pour out the water and set aside the liquid starch.

Lay the wet starch on a plate and place it in a dehydrator or leave it in the sun. Once the water is evaporated, you end up with a dry powder. Congratulations, you've just made pure cattail starch. Save it in a jar and you can use it later on to thicken soups or sauces, make interesting primitive breads, and so on.

As with many other wild ingredients, extracting cattail starch is a lot of work, but it's also a very unique and beautiful product in its own right, even if it tastes like . . . plain starch.

PICKLED CATTAIL SHOOTS

This is a very basic recipe to make four pint (500 ml) jars. You'll need approximately 32 medium-sized cattail shoots. Feel free to experiment with your favorite spices.

Ingredients for each jar

8 medium-sized cattail shoots
¼ California bay leaf (or ½ regular bay leaf)
2 small chili pods—they're optional,
    but I like a little spicy kick (your choice
    of chili will determine how much kick
    you have—I usually use dried whole
    Japanese chili peppers)
1 teaspoon (6 g) sea salt

Pickling solution

3 cups (709 ml) apple cider vinegar
    (5% acidity)
2 cups (473 ml) sweet white wine or white
    elderberry wine (from Mexican elder)

Procedure

1. Clean your cattail shoots thoroughly and keep the tenderest parts, usually the first 5 inches or so. Remove the outer layers if necessary.
2. Clean the jars thoroughly, then place the shoots and other ingredients in them. I keep the jars somewhat hot by standing them in a couple of inches of hot water. That's because I've had a couple of (cold) jars crack when pouring the hot pickling solution in them.
3. Follow Basic Water Bath Canning on page 38. Bring the pickling solution to a boil and pour it slowly into the hot jars, leaving ½ inch headspace. Remove any air bubbles with a clean spoon or knife. Your cattail shoots will have a tendency to float; you will need to push them down when putting the lids on the jars.
4. Place in the refrigerator and enjoy after a couple of weeks. If you want to can them using the water bath method, process for 25 minutes in boiling water.

Moving to the Mountains

A special feature of Southern California is the large number of existing microclimates, which truly allows you to forage at any time of the year. Where I live, I'm an hour's drive from the mountains, the ocean, and the desert, and 10 minutes away from the forest. Even during the deadly heat of summer, I can find a decent amount of wild edibles in a forest where there is shade and a stream. It's just a bit more work and often requires some travel time.

The end of summer, when most of my surroundings have turned into a desert, is the perfect time to head to the surrounding mountains. They were formed millions of years ago, during major geologic movements, and even today new mountains are still slowly forming through tectonic activity along the San Andreas Fault, which provides us with the earthquakes that Southern California is also known for.

I live close to the Angeles forest and the San Bernardino Mountains. The highest mountain in the area is San Gorgonio, which tops out at 11,849 feet. Some years it's still possible to see snow in the middle of summer. Snow also means that there are numerous streams and springs, offering a tremendous biodiversity in plants and animals.

Over the years I've contacted and made friends with several people who own private properties and allow me to forage there, often in exchange for some of my wild brews. Being able to make wild beers has probably been one of the valuable skills I've learned. Bring some beers and, very often, doors will be opened and friendships created.

The higher elevation and lower temperatures in the mountains offer me a large amount of interesting ingredients, such as white fir, pine needles and sap, mugwort, sagebrush, yuccas, manzanita and currant berries, various types of aromatic barks, wild rosebuds, juniper berries, cattails, and many more.

During the terrible drought we had in 2014, the mountains allowed me to keep foraging and to provide wild greens, berries, spices, infused vinegars, and unusual drinks to the local chefs and restaurants I work with. Several of the non-alcoholic drinks I made for chef Ludo Lefebvre at Trois Mec restaurant were directly inspired by our high-altitude bounty.

Interestingly, as a forager I find myself doing pretty much what the natives did. The mountains were home to the Gabrielinos, Cahuilla, Serrano, and Chemehuevi peoples. At the end of summer, they also moved to higher ground to set up camp, forage what was available, and get ready for the fall bounty of pinyon pine nuts and acorns. In modern times, I have the luxury of owning a car and am able to just drive for a couple of hours, forage, and come back home. What is a fun day trip for me was a true survival activity for native people.

The altitude and shade from the pines and oak trees also offer a nice relief from the overwhelming heat. At around 8,000 feet the temperature can be in the low 80s instead of around 110°F, as it is in my usual foraging ground.

I still have much to learn in terms of foraging in the mountains, and that's the fun of it. Every time I go there, I take a lot of photos of plants I don't know so I can identify them later and learn about new potential ingredients. Spending time and taking cooking classes with native peoples has helped me a lot too.

PINE NEEDLE VINEGAR

I'm not a pine identification expert, but I know that all pines are edible. The only dangerous trees that look like pines and are truly considered poisonous are the yew and the Australian pine, but they're not from the pine family.

Some people claim that ponderosa and lodgepole pine should not be used, and yet pine needle tea has been made for eons with these pines with no known record of ill effects that I've ever found through my research. We're not animals; we're not eating pine needles by the pound. Vinegars are condiments and often used sparingly. Feel free to do your own research and make your own conclusions.

My method for foraging pine needles is simple. I usually like to find young pine trees, which have more flavors than older trees, and sample the needles. I'm looking for a nice lemony, piney taste. Once satisfied with the flavors, I prune that pine lightly and move on to the next tree.

Procedure

To make the pine-infused vinegar, I'll cut the needles and pack them in my jar. When done, I fill the jar with apple cider or rice vinegar and place it in the refrigerator or a cool, dark place, then wait about 3 weeks before using it. You don't have to wait that long, however—taste your vinegar after a few days. If you're happy just stop there, strain the vinegar, and bottle it. For added food safety, you can pasteurize the bottled vinegar.

Pinyon Pine Resin Vinegar

It took me the longest time to research and experiment with the culinary uses of pine resin. It's one tough ingredient—the flavor can easily be overwhelming, and it's often an acquired taste. Retsina, a Greek wine flavored with pine sap, is a good example of a food use for pine resin—and an example of an acquired taste!

If you do some research, you'll find some interesting traditional uses for the sap, often medicinal purposes. For example, in the old days Icelanders used to mix pine sap with honey for lung problems. Pine sap candies were quite popular, and I remember eating some as a kid while traveling in the Alps region of France. Natives and early pioneers also used pine sap to make chewing gum.

Presently, I've found very few examples of pine resin uses by chefs and restaurants. Pastry chef Dana Cree uses pine resin in some of her ice cream making, and some mixologists have used sap in various cocktail creations.

From my research, what you're looking for is not the young sticky sap, but the old crusty resin, usually collected from old wounds on the tree. In the older sap, some chemicals, such as turpentine and various other terpenes, have long since evaporated. This sap looks very much like amber.

The procedure for making the vinegar is very simple: Place a chunk of old pine resin in vinegar and let it infuse for a few weeks. It's strong stuff, and I use it very sparingly, often just brushing a bit of it on a pickled trout after it is plated.

Cooking with Pine and Fir Needles

Whenever I go to the local mountains, I probably encounter over 15 different types of pines. The most common ones are Jeffrey, ponderosa, sugar, and pinyon pines. I also see a lot of my favorite tree, the white fir.

At high altitude the forest floor is covered with a very thick and slippery layer of dead pine needles, which reeks of pine essence whenever there is a little bit of rain or humidity. If sages are the main fragrance of the chaparral, pines are truly the signature aroma of the mountains.

As usual, I always try to find as many culinary uses as possible for what nature is offering us, and although I've never seen or heard of local chefs using dried pine needles in their cooking, from my upbringing in Belgium I have some vague memory of them being used to create a special dish. I decided to forage some, and it only took me a couple of minutes to collect a very large bag of them.

While driving home, I was still obsessed with figuring out what the dish was when it hit me: mussels éclade!

Mussels éclade is a traditional dish in France (Charentes)—foraged mussels are spread on a large stone and covered with pine needles and bay leaves (optional), which are then set on fire. The technique is very simple: A small piece of bread or a potato is placed in the middle to support the first mussels, and the rest are placed hinge-side up (so ashes don't fall inside when they open) in concentric circles. The cooking time for mussels is around 10 minutes, so you need around 4 inches (10 cm) of dry pine needles on top.

A friend who grew up in France also told me that they often used a mix of whatever dry materials they could find nearby in making this dish—usually pine needles, dry leaves, and seaweed.

Since that trip in the mountains, I've made éclade several times, not only with mussels but also with clams and even with crawfish. The powerful mix of strong flavors from the shellfish and pine smoke is quite unique, in a good way.

I found that this method of cooking in burning pine needles and dry leaves also works well with specific ingredients such leeks, wild garlic, and onions. I usually cook the ingredients until they are nearly done, and then finish them with the burning needles. The first or outer layer, which has the most overwhelming flavor, is peeled off, and you still get a nice smoky touch to the inner layers that does not irritate the palate.

My favorite food to cook using this method is cattail shoots. The outer layer is not meant to be eaten anyway (the fibrous stalk is too tough and the smoked flavor overwhelming), so you're interested in the tender part inside. I usually serve it with a wild chimichurri sauce made with acorns, yarrow, mugwort beer vinegar, California juniper berries, watercress, garlic, pepper, salt, and chili flakes, and crumbled raw feta cheese (thanks to my friend Gloria for that idea).

I have also used white fir needles sparingly with grilled meat, potatoes, and other vegetables with good results. It's all about knowing the right proportions to use—a little goes a long way.

Mussels cooked in burning pine needles.

Cattail shoot cooked in
burning pine needles with wild
chimichurri sauce and crumbled feta.

Pine Rosin for Cooking

A couple of months ago, after a foraging day in the mountains, I became obsessed with pine resin. It's one of those ingredients that's truly plentiful in our local forests, and pretty much every time I go there I love to take a bit of the sticky sap between my fingers, bring it to my nose, and inspire slowly. A little drop of pine sap seems to concentrate all the aroma of the mountains. Each type of pine will have variations, but overall it's a complex blend of aromatics: fruity, lemony, woody, sweet. For some people, ponderosa pine sap even has hints of vanilla or cinnamon.

While I find the smell delightful, using the sap for culinary purposes is another matter. Fresh pine sap can contain harmful components, such turpentine and other organic compounds (terpenes), in various amounts. Although resin was sometimes used as medicine in the old days, it's really not something you want to ingest in large amounts. On the good side, turpentine and other terpenes are volatile over time and thus will be present in much smaller amount in old crusty pine resin. This was actually the key to being able to use the resin in cooking.

Searching for culinary uses, I came across something called rosin. At first I thought it was a typo and we were talking about resin, but rosin has a specific definition: "A translucent amber-colored to almost black brittle friable resin that is obtained from the oleoresin or deadwood of pine trees." So we're talking about old, crusty resin, not the fresh stuff—although there is mention made of a method for making it by heating fresh resin at a temperature between 212° and 320°F (100° and 160°C) to vaporize the volatile terpene components.

Now I was getting somewhere, and a quick search for culinary uses of rosin lead me to an obscure southern recipe for cooking potatoes in rosin. I found it fascinating, so of course I had to try it.

Rosin was a by-product of turpentine production, and apparently it was not uncommon in the old days for sawmill workers and country folks to harvest the pine sap, bring it to a boil, and drop potatoes in it. It was popular enough that a "rosin potato cooker" and even rosin itself were sold in local hardware stores.

Potatoes cooked in rosin are supposed to be the most delicious potatoes in the whole universe. Apparently the boiling rosin seals the skin and the quick cooking keeps the flavors and moisture at near perfection, if you believe the claims of rosin baked-potato connoisseurs.

Interestingly enough, if you do some research online you'll find that there are a couple of sites selling "Rosin Baked Potato Starter Kits" and rosin.

But I'm a forager, so buying my rosin is not an option, and besides, I'm still looking for the flavors of my local mountains. Enthusiasm is a good thing, and you'll need a lot of it if you plan to forage old crusty resin. You may get lucky and find the mother lode, but it took me several weeks and quite a few trips to the mountains to get enough for my culinary experiment. You also need to know your pines somewhat; Jeffrey pine resin is highly flammable due to the presence of a volatile hydrocarbon (N-heptane). I tend to err on the side of caution and don't use that resin.

Most the resin I collected was from pinyon, ponderosa, and Aleppo pines. Probably 80 percent was from pinyon (thank you, Gloria, for letting me forage on your property). I tried my best to collect old resin to avoid an excess of terpene components.

By the way, if you get confused a bit with the terminology of pine sap, resin, and rosin, think of it this way. Sap is somewhat fresh, an oozing liquid a bit similar to honey. Resin is more solid, although fresh resin can still be somewhat tender. If you forage it you're looking for hard, rock-like resin. There is a fine line between old resin and rosin, but think of rosin as resin that has been purified of terpenes through time, boiling, or other processes.

ROSIN BAKED POTATOES

You'll probably need at least 7 to 10 pounds of rosin to start experimenting with this recipe. If you forage your own old resin instead of purchasing it, don't assume it is pure. Before attempting to cook potatoes in it, I go through the process of bringing it to a boil a few times at temperatures of 300°F (148°C) to remove the volatile terpenes. Usually I do this three to four times for 20 minutes at a time over a couple of days. In the process you will also need to remove any unwanted materials, such as pine needles, bark, and so forth. It's pretty easy to do this with a metallic strainer, simply scooping up the odd bits as they float on the surface. Once done, let it cool: Your resin will become darker, hard, and brittle.

Cooking in rosin or purifying resin is an activity you should do outside, as the amount of smoke and the smell can be somewhat overwhelming. I also assume that the fumes are not very healthy for you. Resin is highly flammable; make sure you supervise the cooking at all times. I always have an old large bathroom towel ready to throw on top of the pot in case it starts to flame (this has never happened to me, by the way). Monitor the temperature carefully; it can go pretty high extremely fast when it begins to boil.

Once you've finished the purification process, your resin has technically become rosin. You can reuse your rosin pretty much indefinitely.

To cook potatoes in the rosin, I use the following recipe.

Ingredients

Purified rosin (see headnote)
2 potatoes (I use russet potatoes)
Condiments: butter, sour cream, garlic, salt, pepper

Procedure

1. Bring the rosin to a boil at a temperature of 275° (135°C) to 300°F (148°C). You will need to monitor the temperature during the whole cooking process.
2. Carefully place your potatoes in the rosin.
3. Boil until the potatoes start floating on the surface, usually around 30 minutes for medium-sized potatoes. If they don't start floating, just use 30 minutes as a guide for medium potatoes and around 40 minutes for large ones.
4. After that initial cooking period, continue simmering the potatoes for another 20 minutes or so. You'll probably need to experiment a bit with the type of potatoes you're cooking.
5. Using metallic kitchen tongs, remove the potatoes. Traditionally they were wrapped in brown paper with both ends twisted, but I like to plate them on actual pine needles.
6. The skin is not supposed to be eaten. Slice the potatoes open and serve with the condiments and herbs of your choice—butter, garlic, salt and pepper, sour cream, or anything else you might like. Enjoy!

This cooking method can also be used for sweet potatoes, but I plan to experiment with other interesting wild produce such as sunchokes, wild onions, and others.

The question remains, though: Are these the best potatoes in the whole universe?

Of course they are!

Fermenting Mountain Flavors

I make sauerkraut from time to time, and around 10 years ago I bought a couple of fermenting crocks. They have served me well all these years—they're one of the best investments I ever made, along with my *molcajete* (stone grinder). Fermentation is a great medium to experiment with wild flavors; it's probably the safest method for food preservation.

There are many interesting and tasty mixes you can create by adding wild edibles to your cabbage. The wild ingredients I've mixed for flavors or as an additional ingredients include: dandelion, wild mustard or radish greens, wild radish pods, watercress, chervil, dehydrated turkey tail mushrooms, epazote, white fir, pine needles, wild seeds, juniper berries, and various sages.

I've even used roasted oak bark or wood for smoky accents. The clean oak bark or wood is pasteurized in the oven at around 200°F (93°C) for 20 minutes, then roasted and placed with the cabbage in the crock. You can use a wide variety of woods, such as juniper or mesquite.

My favorite approach is to make sauerkrauts that reflect our local environments. For example, if we host or cater a private dinner featuring the local mountains, I may ferment my sauerkraut with white fir, pine needles, and roasted juniper wood and berries. You end up with some very interesting pine, tangerine, and lemon flavors and some "smoke" accents, if you also use the roasted wood.

I never use exact recipes, as the flavors vary quite a lot depending on the seasons, locations, and soil conditions. I like to taste the ingredients first and decide how much of each of them I need. However, I can give you some guidelines.

MOUNTAIN SAUERKRAUT

Making sauerkraut is *very* easy and, living in our digital age, you can find plenty of tutorials and videos online. Like beermaking, sometimes making sauerkraut becomes a bit overcomplicated, but basic sauerkraut is simply a mix of salt, water, and cabbage. Here is how I make my mountain sauerkraut.

Ingredients

3 large cabbage heads, grated or chopped

Sea salt (foraged or purchased—
    make sure there are no additives such
    as anticaking agents in your salt)

3–4 white fir branches

1 small pine branch (all pines are edible;
    I forage by tasting the needles and
    choose the ones I like the most)

30 green California juniper berries or any
    other edible juniper berries, crushed

1 piece toasted California juniper branch or
    oak bark (optional—see note.)

Springwater or distilled water

Procedure

1. Place the prepared cabbage in a clean bowl and weigh it. Based on the weight, sprinkle sea salt in the ratio of 2 teaspoons (11 g) salt per pound (0.45 kg) of cabbage, or 2½ to 3 tablespoons (42 to 50 g) of salt for every 5 pounds (2.25 kg) of cabbage.

2. Using clean hands, mix and massage the cabbage thoroughly and quite forcefully. I usually do this for 3 to 5 minutes; the salt will extract a lot of juices from the grated cabbage. That's what you want.

3. Now it's time to clean and add your wild ingredients. For the white fir and pine, I take the time to cut the top of the needles so the flavors can be extracted easily. I also crack the green California juniper berries for the same reason. If you are using juniper wood or oak bark, include it in the mix. Place them into the same container as the cabbage and mix thoroughly for 30 seconds or so.

4. Place the mixed ingredients into your fermenting crock and top them with the weights that were provided when you purchased it. The ingredients *must* be under the brine (the salted juice you created by massaging forcefully the shredded cabbage). Use your hand to pack it down forcefully to release more brine. If there is not enough brine, wait 15 minutes and try again. The brine should come, but if you end up with not enough brine to cover the ingredients and the weights, you will need to make more.

    To make the additional brine use clean water (not tap water), add salt, and stir to make sure the salt is dissolved properly. The ratio of salt to water is 1 tablespoon salt (17 g) for every 2 cups (473 ml) of water.

5. Once the ingredients are under the brine, close the lid. My fermenting crock has a groove that, when filled with water, acts as an airlock and lets the fermentation gases escape while protecting the contents from airborne bacteria and little critters such as flies.

    I usually leave my fermenting crock in the kitchen. Living in Southern California, usually 3 to 4 weeks is enough to ferment the kraut in the summer (4 to 5 weeks in the winter).

    If you don't have a fermenting crock and use another type of container, see page 119 on making wild food kimchi. It's a very similar procedure.

6. When the fermenting process is completed, remove the fir and pine branches as well as the juniper berries if you left the seeds in them. Place the sauerkraut in clean jars. Store it in the fridge. I like to eat it within a month.

Note: To prepare the oak, I dry it, then pasteurize it in the oven for 20 minutes at 200°F (93°C). I then roast the bark using a butane torch or over my gas stove burner. White oak is less bitter than others.

Manzanita

I call manzanita berries Southern California's wild apples. They taste like and kind of look like apples, but they're much smaller. It's fairly easy to recognize the small manzanita trees due to the characteristic orange or red bark and twisted branches. Manzanita is very abundant on the lower West Coast (California, Arizona, and New Mexico) but can also be found from Oregon up to Washington.

I forage manzanita berries during summer and fall. In early summer the berries are still green and tart, while in fall they turn red and a bit sweeter. The clusters of berries dehydrate over time; often they stay on the plants for a few months and eventually fall on the ground.

There are various kinds of manzanita berries. My favorite ones are the smaller and fleshier type, but in a bad year I'll take whatever I find, including the larger ones with a sticky coating and large seeds.

I've used the green unripe and dehydrated berries to make a primitive cider, basically crushing and boiling the berries with white sugar, cooling the solution, adding the yeast, and letting it ferment for a few weeks. The cider made with the green berries is much more sour and tart. Once you've made the cider, you can also turn it into vinegar and make your own wild "apple" cider vinegar. It tastes just like it.

My favorite use is to crush the dried ripe berries, remove the seeds, and save the powder. The powder can be used to flavor dishes; it's somewhat sweet and sour at the same time, with definite apple flavors. It's wonderful in cold or hot infusions and, if I have a large quantity, I use the powder to make carbonated sodas as well.

As with apples, you can also make some interesting sauces.

Creating Wild Hot Sauces

Some strong-flavored wild ingredients are a nice fit for making hot sauces—a few of my favorites are nasturtium, sweet white clover, burr-chervil, wild radish, black mustard, and watercress.

Of course, flavors are important, but you can also make hot sauces that are more medicinal and loaded with vitamins. A good example is stinging nettle or miner's lettuce hot sauce. Nettles being fairly neutral in terms of taste, most of the flavor will come from the choice of chili peppers you will use, but you get the health benefits from the plants.

Hot sauces can also become a reflection of the seasons or the environment. For example, in early spring I may use a small amount of chickweed to add some "green" accents to the sauces. In fall, some roasted mushrooms can make their appearance in some of the recipes, and in summer I may add some black mustard seeds for an added spicy kick.

If you made infused vinegar with aromatic plants, the vinegar itself can be the main flavorful ingredient in the recipe. By simply using my mountain vinegar and somewhat neutral chili peppers, such as jalapeños, I can end up with a hot sauce that is the reflection of the local mountains.

Nasturtium and watercress hot sauce.

Making Your Own Basic Hot Sauce

In case you've never made hot sauces before, I thought it would be a good idea to explain the basics of making them.

If you reduce most hot sauces to their basic ingredients, you usually have three main components: chili peppers, vinegar, and salt.

You can substitute lime or lemon juice for the vinegar and sugar for the salt. Some Asian hot sauces are made with peppers, lime juice, and sugar as their main ingredients.

The creative challenge lies in artfully mixing two elements—the pungency or heat you want to impart in the sauce by your choice of chili peppers, and the flavors you can create by adding savory ingredients (herbs, aromatic plants, and spices, for example). Cooking techniques such as roasting or smoking your peppers can add to the complexity of the sauce.

Because we're talking about making hot sauces, let's take a look a main ingredient, chili peppers, and what can make them taste so incredibly hot.

To keep it simple, chemical compounds (called alkaloids or capsaicinoids) create the heat of a pepper. Not all peppers are equal; some peppers have much more heat than others: Habaneros are a good example.

There is an actual scale of "hotness" calculated by extracting the chemical compounds from a known weight of pepper. In the old days, these compounds were mixed in various concentrations with sweetened water, and human tasters were asked to identify the point at which water neutralized the hotness. The volume of water required for each sample was assigned a rating in Scoville units. (The name of the units comes from the fact that a gentleman named Wilbur Scoville invented the test in the early 1900s.) Today the hotness is tested in modern laboratories, but the measurements are still expressed in Scoville units.

Peppers have a wide range of hotness, starting from zero with bell peppers to over 1,500,000 units with a pepper called the Carolina reaper.

So how hot is that? Well, most habaneros are in the range of 200,000—and if you've ever tried eating one, you would have a good idea where that sits on the scale. It's insanely hot!

The process of making hot sauces is really not complex; it usually requires choosing the ingredients (peppers, spices, and aromatic plants), adding some vinegar (or lemon/lime juice), and blending them together. For a light sauce, you can strain the liquid after blending the ingredients, but most manufacturers like the sauce to be somewhat thick, and they achieve that by adding a food a thickener, usually xanthan gum.

Next time you go to the supermarket, look at the labels and ingredients on some hot sauces. You'll see how simple most of the recipes are.

BASIC HOT SAUCE

For your first hot sauce, let's make a super-simple and very basic recipe.

Ingredients

1½ cups (473 ml by volume) jalapeño peppers, seeded and chopped

1½ cups (473 ml by volume) Anaheim chili or similar wild peppers such as banana or poblano, or plain green bell peppers

2½ cups (590 ml) apple cider vinegar (5% acidity)

2 teaspoons (10 g) salt (kosher or pickling)

1 tablespoon (10 g) garlic powder

Procedure

1. Combine all the ingredients and blend until smooth.
2. Strain for a thinner sauce (or keep it as it for a thicker sauce).
3. Transfer to pasteurized* jars or bottles and cover.
4. Refrigerate at least 1 week, then enjoy. Shake the bottles before serving.

* To pasteurize your jars or bottles, place them in a pot and fill the pot with water. Cover and bring the pot of water to boil. Continue boiling for at least 10 minutes. Remove the bottles/jars using tongs, hold upside down to remove the water, and set them aside.

NASTURTIUM AND WATERCRESS HOT SAUCE

There is a lot of room for experimentation and creativity with all the wild ingredients available—I've barely scratched the surface with the sauces I've made using my homemade or infused vinegars and the large number of wild ingredients available. Here is an example of a simple nasturtium and watercress hot sauce.

This recipe makes two half-pint (250 ml) jars.

Ingredients

2 cups (473 ml by volume) nasturtium stems and leaves

1 cup (236 ml by volume) watercress

5 jalapeño peppers, seeded

1½ cups (355 ml) homemade vinegar or commercial apple cider, wine vinegar, etc.

4 teaspoons (14 g) garlic powder

1½ teaspoons (7 g) foraged or commercial sea salt

3 tablespoons (45 ml) raw honey

Juice of 1 small lemon

3–4 tablespoons (30–40 g) native golden chia seeds (or commercial chia seeds)

Procedure

1. Place all the ingredients except the chia seeds in a blender. Blend until smooth.
2. Place into a bowl and add the chia seeds slowly as you stir, so they won't clump together. Place the bowl in the refrigerator for 15 minutes to let the chia seeds do their work by thickening the sauce, then bottle. I like to start using this sauce the following day and consume within a week.

Most commercial hot sauces use xanthan gum as a thickener. For my part I like to use what my terroir is offering. Chia or broadleaf plantain seeds are a healthy and nutritious alternative to the xanthan gum and, besides, they look great in the sauce and keep the ingredients in suspension.

Canning or Bottling Your Own Hot Sauce

While the basic recipe I provided above is safe for storing in the refrigerator and consuming within a few weeks, if you decide to make your own sauces and want to make them shelf-stable for long-term storage, you need to learn something about acidity level and food safety.

If you don't can or bottle your hot sauce properly, you could get seriously sick from bacteria. Botulism is a rare but serious illness caused by the *Clostridium botulinum* bacterium. This bacterium can thrive in an oxygen-free environment and thus may live in improperly canned or preserved food.

On the good side, the bacteria cannot reproduce in a highly acidic environment. In order to can or bottle your sauce properly, you need to make sure that the solution is acidic enough—we use the pH scale for this. The pH scale measures how acidic or basic a substance is. The pH scale ranges from 0 to 14—a pH of 7 is neutral; a pH less than 7 is acidic; a pH greater than 7 is basic.

To avoid botulism in preserved hot sauce, we need a pH that is less than 4.6. From a food-safety perspective, it is recommended to use a pH of 4.2 or below. The acidity of your sauce comes mostly from vinegar (or from lemon/lime juice).

To calculate the pH you can use special paper strips, which will change color when you dip them into your sauce, and you can then determine the pH by looking at the color. If your sauce is too thick and dark, you may not be able to read the pH using paper strips. In this case you need to determine the pH level through a digital pH meter. I use a digital pH meter myself, and the investment was well worth it.

CANNING YOUR SAUCE

Make your hot sauce based on an existing recipe (such as the basic hot sauce in this book) or your own recipe. Use a strainer if you want a light sauce. Use a pH paper test strip or a digital pH meter to calculate the pH (the sauce should be below 4.2). If the pH is too high, add more vinegar. Then you can preserve your sauce following these steps.

Equipment you will need

A jar lifter
Canning jars with lids
A water bath canning kettle
A pot for the sauce
A blender or food processor

Procedure

1. Bring your sauce to a boil, then reduce the heat and simmer for 15 to 20 minutes (some recipes may vary). I usually taste as I go along using a clean spoon.
2. Pour the sauce into jars, leaving ½ inch (1 cm) headspace. Screw the lids on finger-tight and place the jars into boiling water. Process half-pint (250 ml) jars for at least 20 minutes. I process pint jars (500 ml) for at least 25 minutes.
3. Remove the jars from the canning bath. The jars should seal themselves. For more complete and illustrated instructions about proper canning, go to: http://www.freshpreserving.com/guides/IntroToCanning.pdf

Step 1

Step 3

Step 3

Step 4

Step 7

BOTTLING YOUR SAUCE

Bottling your hot sauce follows a similar process as canning the sauce. First, make your hot sauce, using a strainer if you want a light sauce. Determine the pH using a pH paper test strip or a digital pH meter (the sauce should be below 4.2). If the pH is too high, add more vinegar. Then you can bottle your sauce.

Equipment you will need

Hot sauce bottles with caps
Funnel
A pot with boiling water
A pot for the sauce
A blender or food processor for making
   the sauce
A strainer
A thermometer
pH paper test strips or a digital pH meter

Procedure

1. Transfer the sauce to a covered pot and bring it to a boil; reduce the heat, then simmer for 10 to 15 minutes. Taste the sauce as you go along—add salt, more chili, pepper, etc. to taste.
2. Place the empty bottles in boiling water for at least 10 minutes to sterilize them. I also clean thoroughly the caps in very hot water and dish soap.
3. Using a clean funnel, transfer the hot sauce into the sterilized bottles. If your sauce is too thick, you can strain it first then transfer the sauce into the bottles.
4. Place the bottles in a pot containing lukewarm water; the top of the bottles should be ½ inch (1.25 cm) above the water. Bring the temperature of the sauce to at least 190°F (88°C) for 15 minutes.
5. When done, carefully remove the bottles with tongs or a jar lifter.
6. Immediately cap and turn the bottles upside down; this will further sterilize the caps.
7. Leave the bottles upside down until they are cooled off. The bottled sauce should last at least a year.

FERMENTED HOT SAUCE WITH WILD GREENS

Very often, after a private event or a foraging workshop, I have leftover wild greens in my refrigerator. During the summer, when all kinds of chilies are abundant, I like to create various fermented and spicy concoctions with them.

You should turn to the Wild Food Kimchi section beginning on page 119 to understand the process if you've not experimented with fermentation before. You can use all kinds of wild greens and not be limited by what I used in this recipe. Other wild edibles to include might be watercress, ramps, thistles, wild radish leaves and pods, among others.

The only difference with the wild kimchi is that I don't use cabbage for making the sauces, but you could use some cabbage if you wanted to. Feel free to experiment and make you own hot sauces.

Ingredients

Wild greens: curly dock, dandelion, arugula, wild celery, and black mustard leaves—enough to pack around 60% of a 1-gallon (3.75 l) container

40 small organic habanero peppers (make sure they're not waxed). You can also use any hot peppers you'd like instead of habanero peppers.

2 onions

10 garlic cloves

4 tablespoons (20 g) Korean chili powder (you can use any chili powder—some are hotter than others)

Salt

Water

Procedure

1. Chop the ingredients very roughly, removing the seeds from the habanero peppers, then place everything into a clean jar or other glass container.
2. With clean hands, pack everything tightly in the container. If you're using very hot peppers, you should use clean latex or rubber gloves.

   I usually place a bunch of large leaves on top so the chopped material does not float around on the surface later on.
3. Make a brine composed of 1 tablespoon (17 g) salt for every 2 cups (473 ml) of water. I needed around 8 cups (1.9 l) of brine in this 1-gallon (3.75 l) recipe. As you gain experience and do more research on the subject of fermentation, you may decide to use less salt, but this brine has worked very well for me and I've never had a ferment go bad.
4. Place a weight on top of the ingredients to keep them under the brine. I used a pasteurized stone (placed in boiling water for over 10 minutes) to do so. Remove any small pieces that may be floating around.
5. As with the Basic Wild Kimchi, cover your container or, if you used a jar, place the lid and secure the band, but make sure it isn't too tight. The idea is to prevent any potential bacteria or flies from getting into your hot sauce while still allowing fermentation gases to escape. If you screw the band on too tight your jar may explode due to the pressure, and you will end up with a grand mess.

   It's also a good idea to place the jar onto a plate during the fermentation process because bubbles will form inside your ingredients and the contents may expand a little, causing excess liquid to escape.
6. Once or twice a day, remove the lid and push the stone down to let gas bubbles inside the ingredients escape. You'll see that there are a

lot of them! Always make sure your hands are clean before you do this.

I usually let my ingredients ferment from 7 to 10 days. The speed of fermentation is to a large degree related to temperature. In the hot summer months in Southern California, I've sometimes stopped the process after just 4 or 5 days. Basically, taste the concoction periodically and stop the process when you're happy with the flavors. You can ferment much longer, too; once I made this sauce in a fermenting crock and let the ingredients ferment for 4 weeks. It's really all about flavors.

7. The final step is to take your fermented concoction and blend it thoroughly. But you're not done yet . . . Here is where it becomes interesting and you have a lot of room for creativity. Once you've blended your ingredients, taste it again. Does it need more chili powder or salt? Would you like to add some sugar or honey to make it a bit sweet? What about adding some aromatic powders or herbs? Personally, I like my hot sauces to have some nice vinegar flavors and, due to the fact that I make my own "wild" vinegars, I have a wide array of additional tasty choices. The last time I made a fermented hot sauce I added 2 cups (473 ml) of mugwort beer vinegar after blending, but you can also use a wide variety of commercial vinegars for flavor, such as apple cider, rice, or wine vinegars.

8. You can store your sauce in the refrigerator and it should last for many weeks. You can also opt to pasteurize your hot sauce and bottle it (see Bottling Your Sauce on page 297).

Basically the idea is to use the fermented liquid as a base to make the hot sauce that *you* like. Some people may say that you kill the good stuff (probiotics) by adding vinegar, but it's really your choice. On my side, working with chefs and restaurants, I tend to err on the side of flavors.

This sauce will be quite liquid in nature and the ingredients will usually separate after a while—this is easily resolved by shaking the bottle before serving. If you want to make it thicker and have less separation, you can add some chia seeds. Start with 1 tablespoon (10 g) of seeds per cup (236 ml) of hot sauce, let it rest for 10 minutes, and check the consistency. Add more seeds if necessary. Don't forget to stir while pouring the seeds so they don't stick together. *Note:* I've only used chia seeds with cold/raw sauces so far, so I don't know what would happen if you boil or pasteurize your sauce.

Another solution to make a thicker hot sauce is to add 100 percent pure cornstarch or xanthan gum. I've not used cornstarch myself yet, but based on my research I would start with 1 tablespoon (10 g) of cornstarch for every cup of sauce. When using xanthan gum, I start with ½ teaspoon (1.2 g) per ½ gallon (1.9 l) of sauce. Xanthan dissolves better in hot liquid, so I set aside some hot sauce, bring it to a simmer, and add the gum bit by bit while stirring with a spoon. Then I whisk it thoroughly (you can also use a blender), let it cool, and pour it back into your batch of (cold) hot sauce and whisk or blend everything one more time. From there you can store in the fridge or pasteurize and bottle the sauce.

If all this sounds a bit complex, here is the simplicity of it. Ferment your ingredients, then blend them to make a liquid sauce. Taste it and add vinegar or spices if you want. You also have the option of using thickeners to make your sauce less liquid. Store it in the fridge as is, or you can boil it, then store in the fridge. I like to enjoy my sauces within a month.

If you're a pro at canning, you can also calculate the pH, add more vinegar if necessary, and then can it or bottle it to make it shelf-stable.

Fermenting hot sauce with wild greens.

Making Jams and Syrups with Wild Ingredients

I'm a bit peculiar with regard to jams. I had never heard of using pectin to gel them until I came to the United States. As I was growing up in Belgium, my mom made a lot of strawberry and rhubarb jams with the bounty of our garden, and the usual method was to cook the sugar and fruits over the boiling point, until the mixture reached the "set point" at 220°F (104°C).

Over the years, I've made a lot of jams using both methods (adding pectin or high temperature), but the more I started using wild ingredients, the less I was interested in either of these methods. I think boiling up to 220°F is excessive and not optimal for flavors.

I have a different philosophy, and I always tell this to my students: Let the plants talk to you. If you want to create a true original and native cuisine, your cooking ideas and recipes should come from the ingredients themselves and their environment. Presently I use the same philosophy with my "jams"; they're often more like syrups, and I like to let the ingredients do their own thing.

My method is simply to create a somewhat heavy syrup (3 parts sugar for 4 parts ingredients) for wild berries such as blackberries, wild currants, gooseberries, and elderberries. Some berries, such as elderberries, will be cooked whole while others, such as our local wild currants, will be juiced first, due to the large amount of seeds they contain. I don't overcook the syrup—I simply bring it to a temperature of 200°F (93°C) for 12 minutes, then place the contents in half-pint (250 ml) jars and process them for 15 minutes in a boiling-water bath. For pint (500 ml) jars I process for 20 minutes.

My elderberry jam never sets properly; it's a thick syrup with lots of berries, and that's completely fine with me. It's delicious with game birds such as quail or pigeon. Other ingredients, such as our local passion fruit, will set properly like a regular thick jam if I use the whole fruit, including the skin.

I also like to add interesting wild aromatics to some of the jams or syrups I make. Very often they come from the same location. A leaf of mugwort or black sage in elderberry syrup adds a lot of subtle flavor. The same is true with a tad of white fir needles when making a manzanita berries syrup.

Native Chia Seeds Jam

You can make a solid jam without overcooking or adding pectin by using chia seeds and (probably) plantain seeds—although I've not tried the latter yet. Both seeds have gelatinous properties.

The technique is simple. Heat berries and sugar in a saucepan as explained above. If necessary, depending on the berries you have locally and use, you may need to lightly crush the berries with a fork.

Add the chia seeds (foraged or purchased) into the hot syrup at the end of the cooking. Start with 2 tablespoons (20 g) per cup (236 ml) of liquid; cook for another couple of minutes while stirring the seeds. Remove from the heat and let the jam sit for 5 minutes, then check the consistency. If necessary, add more chia seeds, but usually 2 tablespoons (20 g) is enough. Place in a jar and close the lid. This jam should keep in the refrigerator for up to 2 weeks.

There are many recipes available online for this type of jam, some using fresh fruits or juice and honey instead of sugar.

Wild passion fruit and mugwort beer jam.

FALL
The Seeds Time

Fall Recipes

Fall is an interesting season in Southern California with a wide range of unusual wild foods available. When the season starts, we're pretty much in a desert-type climate. The temperature can still reach as high as 110°F (43°C) during the day, which makes it pretty much impossible to forage comfortably. I adjust my schedule accordingly and start my foraging as early as 5 a.m., and by 11 a.m. I often have to call it a day. The rest of the day is spent preserving, canning, making beers and vinegars, and so forth.

The beginning of fall is what I call the "seeds time." It's when a considerable amount of seeds can be collected although I collect many during the summer, too. Pine nuts and white sage and black sage seeds in the mountains, and in the vicinity of the city we have countless other seeds coming from various plants—wild fennel, curly dock, evening primrose to name a few sources.

In order to get edible greens such as watercress or curly dock, I have to do water foraging, which means that I put on my boots and walk through the water. You'll still find a considerable amount of wild food near water and in the shade. The streams are really the highways of the forest. I can go to locations that would otherwise be impossible to access or too tedious due to rocks and vegetation. The temperature is also cooler near the water, which is a bonus.

If we have a rainy year, by the end of fall we're going back to having a wide variety of wild edible and aromatic plants available in the form of delicious and tender sprouts emerging all over the place. Once the rain comes I can also start looking for mushrooms. Southern California is definitely not the best place for foraging them, but we do get a decent quantity of interesting edible fungi, such as oyster, chanterelles, honey, inky cap, split-gill, and turkey tail mushrooms.

I'm sure there are many, many more delectable mushrooms, but I'm not an expert in that area so I tend to stick to what I know very well. If I were living in a different location, such as Northern California or Oregon, I probably would be much more interested in mushrooms.

With the rain, we also have an interesting downtime, a sort of "dead zone" between the time the rain washes out the wild edibles that were available on the stream banks and when the new sprouts emerge in another 2 to 3 weeks.

It's really the only downtime I experience during the year, and it makes it difficult if I forage for restaurants, but I like the challenge; each year I get better at finding new culinary uses for whatever is available. For example, if I see that rain is coming, I collect as much as possible of the plants I know will be gone shortly and start doing some fermentation projects such as making wild food kimchi, hot sauces, dehydrated plant powders, and infused salts so that I can still provide interesting foodstuffs to my chefs in those couple of weeks.

It's also a good time to make some forest beers and other interesting alcoholic concoctions using tree leaves, mushrooms, and various forest aromatics.

In terms of climate change and these somewhat extreme seasons, the main lesson I have learned as a forager is that, no matter what, with proper research, hard work, and a dash of creativity you will always find plenty of interesting ingredients to keep you very busy, and it only gets better every year as you learn more.

Appreciating Olives

Olives are quite common in Southern California. They're not native, but can be found growing in the wild quite frequently.

Originally planted by Spanish missionaries in the late 1700s as a source of food and oil, their crop success was followed quickly by large commercial plantations once it was discovered that the climate and soil were ideal for growing them. Where I live, there used to be some large plantations up until the early 1900s, which slowly have been displaced by the expansion of Los Angeles and are now buried under concrete and asphalt. Of course, nature always finds a way to survive, and olive trees are quite abundant in the wilderness surrounding the city.

The period for foraging olives ranges from October up to December, though each year is a bit different. In early fall you can pick up the green olives. Over time they will mature and turn purple.

Olives are terribly bitter and need to be processed before you can eat them. There are several methods for processing, ranging from leaching to salting and fermenting. Some people even use lye, but I avoid that process, preferring to use slower and more gentle methods. (I suppose I could make some lye water using ashes, and I may do that in the future.) The type of process I generally use to make the olives edible is somewhat dependent on the stage they're foraged at: green, ripe, or in-between.

While I can recognize olives, I'm not an expert in determining which exact types they are. There are hundreds of different olive trees with fruits of different sizes and flavors. Some are mostly used for oil production and others are used as food. I suspect the main variety we have around here are Mission olives, although I've also found some other ones that I think are Sevillano, Kalamata, and Greek olives. Unlike commercial growers, I don't have much choice in choosing specific varieties; I pick up whatever is available and prepare them with basic methods.

To forage them, I usually pick them directly from the branches—if possible, I'll climb up the tree as well, although as I get older I tend to stay at ground level. Falling from a tree while you're by yourself in the middle of nowhere is not a very safe foraging strategy.

The traditional method of collecting them involves using a ladder and a large comb and letting the olives fall onto a net or tarp, but it's difficult, to say the least, for me to walk around the wilderness with a ladder, and, besides, I get plenty by just picking them up by hand. In a good year I can easily forage 40 pounds.

The flavors I get by preparing my own olives are different from the taste of the olives you buy at the local store, which are usually commercially processed using lye; the olives I process are not as strong tasting and their flavor is more subtle. You can definitely tell the difference, and I think it's in a good way. There are more methods of preparing olives than the ones I'm using, so don't hesitate to do your own research and experiment.

Photo courtesy of Mia Wasilevich.

Fermented olives preserved in brine.

OLIVES SICILIAN-STYLE

I use this method with green-ripe local olives. You don't want them too young (that's why they're called green-ripe), and an effective way to check if they're not unripe is to take one from the tree and press it. You should get a sort of cloudy, milky juice that will let you know it's ready for picking.

This method, involving simple fermentation, is probably the easiest way to process olives. You simply place the olives in a jar or fermenting crock with brine, leave it alone for several months, and voilà! The olives are ready to eat. The end result is olives that can be quite bitter, but with a lot of layered flavors due to the various herbs and spices you add to them while they're fermenting.

Traditionally the herbs and spices used to flavor the brine include dill, fennel seeds, oregano, thyme, dried chili peppers, chopped garlic and onions, and peppercorns.

For my part, to have olives that are a reflection of my terroir I usually use a mix of regular and wild aromatics and spices, such as wild fennel seeds, sages, pequin chili peppers, California bay leaves, wild celery, black mustard seeds, and so on. I don't have a set recipe; it will vary based on what's available and what I have managed to store in my pantry during the year. In essence, the flavors will be influenced by that specific year and the forage that's available.

Procedure

1. Forage, sort, and clean your olives. Remove any olives that are bruised or possibly infected with olive fly larvae. (These are quite visible—inspect the olives and look for obvious brown spots and/ or a small indentation or lump on the surface of the fruit.) You want perfection for your homemade olives!

2. Mix the clean olives with the herbs and spices of your choice and pack them into your fermenting vessel. You can use 1-quart (1 l) or ½-gallon (2 l) jars or a fermenting crock.

3. Make a brine composed of 1½ cups (410 g) of sea salt per gallon (3.75 l) of water. Don't use tap water, which may contain chlorine. For each gallon of brine, add 2 cups (473 ml) of vinegar (5 percent acidity). I like to use apple cider vinegar. In the future I plan to use my own homemade wild vinegars, but, technically, using your own homemade vinegar is not recommended, as you don't exactly know the acidity level and you'll

need a bit of experience to supervise the fermentation and check for potential spoiling. If it's your first time, play it safe.

4. Pour the brine into the jars or fermenting crock. If you're using jars you need to make sure the olives will stay under the brine. I usually place a large leaf (such as cabbage or curly dock) on top, then add a pasteurized stone (placed in boiling water for more than 10 minutes) to keep the olives under the brine if it is necessary.

   Close the lids, but not too tight—you want to enable the fermentation gases to escape.

5. Store at room temperature (70°–90°F/21°–32°C). Within a couple of months the initial fermentation should be done; you can then close the jar lids. Go by flavor—taste your olives after 3 or 4 months and, if you're happy, place the jars in the refrigerator or a cool, dark place. If you used a fermenting crock, pour the olives and brine into jars and place in the fridge or a cool, dark place.

Stored properly in their brine, these olives should last a year. My friend is still enjoying his homemade fermented olives after 2 years, but I like to use my fermented olives within a year for freshness and added food safety.

Although it has never happened to me with this process, if I saw any signs of mold growth in the jar I would discard it.

GREEN CRACKED OLIVES

You can use the same kinds of olives (green-ripe) as the Sicilian-style olives for this process. It's also very simple to make. You have to cure them in water a few times to remove the bitterness; the chemical compound that makes them bitter, called oleuropein, will leach into the water over time. When they're ready, you place them in brine (vinegar, salt, and water) and you're done!

The only supplies you'll need for this method are salt, vinegar, a glass or plastic container (jars are okay if you do a small quantity), and something to crack the olives (a stone or mallet). You will also need jars for storing.

Procedure

1. Forage, sort, and clean your olives. Remove any olives that are bruised or possibly infected with olive fly larvae. (Inspect the olives for obvious brown spots and/or a small indentation or lump on the surface of the fruit.) As with any foraged olives, you want perfection!

2. Take your clean olives and, one by one, crack them open using a mallet or a stone. Use a cutting board, as it's a bit of a messy business. The pits are meant to stay intact with the olive so don't worry about them.

3. Place the cracked olives in a food-grade plastic bucket or a glass container and cover them with water. You can use regular tap water for this part if you want. Leave them in the water for a day and then drain the water.

4. Pour new water into the container and repeat the procedure of changing the water daily. Taste the olives after 10 days or so. If they're still too bitter, continue changing the water for another week or more if necessary. You really go by taste on this

process, but you don't want them to lose all their bitterness. Some of the bitterness will mellow when you put them in the final brine. Tasteless olives are not what you want, and some bitterness is part of their flavor profile.

5. When satisfied with the taste, prepare a brine composed of ¾ cup (205 g) of sea salt to ½ gallon (1.9 l) of springwater or distilled water (not tap water), and add 1 cup (236 ml) of apple cider vinegar with 5 percent acidity (some people prefer white or red wine vinegar). This should be enough for around 5 pounds (2.27 kg) of olives.

6. Drain the water and place your olives in jars. You can mix them with various aromatic herbs and spices at this point such as dill, oregano, chili peppers, garlic, onions, thyme, or lemons. I often use all kinds of wild ingredients such as fennel seeds, pequin peppers, chervil, and California bay leaves. In a recent batch I just added a bit of California sagebrush, dehydrated pequin pepper, and a couple of lemon rings in each pint-sized jar.

7. Pour the brine into the jars containing the olives and herbs, close the lids tightly, and place in the refrigerator or a cool, dark place. I like to wait 3 weeks before enjoying them. Stored in the fridge, they should last for at least a year.

KALAMATA-STYLE OLIVES

I use this method for ripened black olives; the ones I have found are usually Mission olives, but it has worked as well with bigger ones as well. The color will change somewhat during the process and the beautiful black will turn to a more faded, somewhat purple/brown color. I kind of like the fact that they're not as pretty as the ones you can purchase at the store; they look "rougher" and have the same color palette as the local chaparral where I most often find them. You can tell they're homemade and wild.

The leaching process is a bit more tedious than the process used for the green olives. You'll need a food-grade plastic or glass container, a sharp knife, sea salt, vinegar (red wine vinegar is what's used traditionally, but I've also used my own elderberry wine vinegar), and olive oil. You'll also need jars for storing.

Procedure

1. Forage, sort, and clean your olives. Remove any olives that are bruised or possibly infected with olive fly larvae. (Look for a small indentation or lump on the surface of the fruit.) Again, you want perfection!

2. Using a sharp knife, make two cuts in each olive (lengthwise), about ⅛ inch (0.3 cm) or a bit more into the olive and on each side. If my olives are really tiny, I only make one cut.

3. Place your cut olives into your container and pour some water in it (tap water is okay). To avoid potential spoiling, the olives must stay under the surface of the water, so you'll need something to keep them down. I usually use a plate that fits the container. Your local thrift store can be a great resource for cheap plates of various sizes.

4. After a day or so, drain the water and replace it with fresh water. At this point you'll need to change the water every couple of days until you reach the de-bittering level you like. This can take anywhere from 1 to 3 weeks, so you'll need to taste the olives from time to time. You don't want to remove all the bitterness, which is characteristic of olives. Some of the bitterness will still mellow a bit in the brine later on.

5. Prepare a brine composed of 2 cups (473 ml) red wine vinegar and ¾ cup (205 g) sea salt to ½ gallon (1.9 l) of water, which is enough to cure around 5 pounds (2.27 kg) of olives. Change the proportions if you have more.

6. Place the olives in jars. You can add aromatics such as oregano, crushed garlic, dill, onions, peppercorn, bay leaves, thyme, dehydrated chili pods, or wild aromatics. For a taste of Southern California I like to use California bay, juniper berries, and even a tad of California sagebrush.

7. Pour the brine into the jars to cover the olives. Some may have a tendency to float. To avoid oxygen exposure and potential spoiling, cover the brine and olives with ¼ inch (0.6 cm) or a bit more of olive oil. Close the lid firmly.

8. Store in a cool, dark place and enjoy after a month. I usually keep them in the refrigerator, where they will last up to a year.

Step 2

Step 3

Step 4

Step 6

SALTED OLIVES

This is probably the easiest method of preserving nicely ripe and soft larger black olives. I've tried it with smaller ones, but they usually end up too hard.

The idea is to leach the bitter chemical into the salt and to dehydrate the olives at the same time. You end up with somewhat shriveled, soft, and very salty olives that are packed with flavors. The process takes around a month, sometimes a couple of weeks more. Again, you'll need to taste as you go, and stop when you're happy with the flavors.

The traditional method is to use plain sea salt, but I like to add dehydrated wild herbs and spices to my salt during the process. You can achieve incredible flavors by doing so. For my last batch, I mixed in some of our Chaparral Wild Spice Blend (see page 158) and the result was truly delicious.

You'll need a burlap bag or clean pillowcase and sea salt. The spices are optional.

Procedure

1. Forage, sort, and clean your olives. Remove any olives that are bruised or possibly infected with olive fly larvae. (These are quite visible—inspect the olives and look for a small indentation or lump on the surface of the fruit.)

2. Place the olives in your bag and add the sea salt. For every pound (450 g) of olives, you'll need ½ pound (225 g) of salt. Mix the salt and olives by shaking the bag thoroughly. Add your dry spices if you want. When done, add a layer of salt around 1 inch (2.5 cm) thick on top.

3. Hang the bag in a location where the temperature is between 60° and 80°F (16° to 27°C). Don't do it inside your house, as the contents may leach a bit. If you do it in a garage, place a container below the bag or pillowcase, just as a precaution.

4. Leave it alone for 2 or 3 days. Then you'll need to establish a routine whereby you shake the bag vigorously every couple of days, for about 10 seconds or so, to really mix the ingredients.

5. After 3 to 4 weeks, taste the olives. If they're to your liking you can stop right then and there; otherwise continue the curing process and taste every 3 or 4 days. This salt curing should not take more than 6 weeks.

6. When done, you'll need to remove as much salt as possible from the olives. You can clean each one by hand, but I usually place them on a homemade framed screen and shake. Once most of the salt has been removed, mix the olives with new salt (¾ cup or 205 g for every 5 pounds or 2.27 kg) and place in airtight containers or jars. Store in a cool, dark place for a month or in the fridge for up to 6 months. You can also freeze them for up to a year.

7. When you want to eat them, marinate the olives overnight in fresh olive oil with some spices if you want, such as thyme, oregano, garlic, rosemary, dehydrated chili peppers, or wild spices, although these may not be necessary if you added dehydrated herbs and spices to the original salt mix.

Backwoods Olive Oil Extraction

This somewhat crazy experiment started when I wanted to make my own olive oil for a workshop so I could serve a sort of olive oil–balsamic bread dip to my students. It was a really good year and we had an abundance of olives, so I decided to go ahead and try.

The research was rather disappointing: I concluded that I needed to purchase an oil press. But with my forager's earnings, purchasing a piece of equipment that could cost well over $1,000 didn't seem worth it. If I had my own plantation and the ability to collect tons of olives each year I would probably do it, but I really don't collect enough to warrant such a purchase. In a great year I may be able to collect 80 pounds and, frankly, olives are just one of the many edibles I forage. They don't have greater priority than other things.

With the option of purchasing an oil press set aside, I started looking for primitive techniques. The original old presses were very simple—similar to primitive grain mills. The olives were pressed using a large circular vertical stone wheel that ran around a circular stone track or trough, drawn by a wooden pole or "sweep" using animal or human power. Then the pulp was collected and placed into thick baskets made of twisted cord, which were then closed and placed on top of one another. The actual press is similar to a regular grape or apple press, but instead of the fruits you have the baskets loaded with pulp. As the baskets were pressed, the oil would exude from the tight fibers and the thick pulp would remain inside.

Well, I thought, I don't have a mill to make the pulp, but I can use my stone grinder or blender to do it; and I may not have thick cord baskets, but maybe I could use several layers of cheesecloth instead.

And so I proceeded. I made a pulp with the olives using a blender at low speed and placed the pulp inside several layers of cheesecloth. It was a lot of hard work squeezing the pulp by hand and not very effective, but I ended up with a very fine liquid pulp that, as I could feel between my fingers, was mostly composed of oil. No success, though—the opaque oily stuff could not compare to pure olive oil. It was also terribly bitter.

After so many hours of work foraging and working with those olives, I was determined to somehow get some olive oil. Since oil floats in water, I poured my olive pulp into a 3-gallon (11.25 l) fermenting bottle and added water so the liquid would nearly reach to the top, around 80% water and 20% pulp. I shook the bottle as much as I could, then let it rest overnight in the cold garage. In the morning I checked the bottle and—Eureka!—I had a couple of inches of pure olive oil. The oil had separated from the organic compound (pulp) and floated to the top. I collected the oil using a brining syringe, added a bit more water to the bottle, and shook the vessel again as much as I could for a few minutes to repeat the process.

In a couple of days, I managed to collect ⅓ cup (78 ml) of pure olive oil from around 4 to 5 pounds (2.27 kg) of olives.

Was it worth it and would I do it again? Nope, it was just one of my crazy experiments, and maybe useful in a survival situation. On the positive side, I did manage to serve my cold hand-pressed foraged oil as a dip using my fermented black walnuts (blended) with a sourdough crouton, California sagebrush, and wild mint, but I don't think anyone really understood how much work went into making it. It was really good, though!

Top left, after blending the olives, the pulp is strained through several layers of cheesecloth. *Top right*, the pulp is poured inside a 3-gallon bottle. Water is added: around 20% pulp and 80% water. After shaking the bottle, it is left overnight. Oil forms on top. *Bottom*, priceless! Homemade olive oil dip with black walnut sauce and sourdough crouton.

Foraging Wild Seeds

When I began foraging in Southern California, seeds were not really high on my priority list. I sometimes tell my students that if you don't know that a plant or a specific wild ingredient exists then you won't see it, but once you know it, you'll realize how abundant it is. It's quite true; I have received many emails from students telling me how the new plant they just learned about is suddenly appearing everywhere! In fact, it was there all the time, but not knowing what it was made it invisible to them.

To some degree, I went through that with seeds when I learned about foraging. They're not really obvious. During early fall you see a lot of sun-parched, dried, dead-looking plants that don't seem very appetizing or even edible until you realize that those tiny dried and sad-looking pods on their stems are loaded with seeds.

The real problem with foraging wild seeds and grains is time; it's not like foraging regular wild greens, where you can collect two large bags of watercress in 15 minutes. When collecting seeds you can spend a whole morning shaking chia pods into a plastic bag and end up with maybe a cup of actual seeds. If you take into account the 30 mph (48 kph) winds and temperatures close to 100°F (38°C) in the desert, you'll realize that it's hard work!

During the terrible drought we had in 2014 and 2015, there wasn't much to collect in terms of wild food. It's a real problem if you're a forager for chefs and restaurants. On the plus side, though, we had tons of seeds available, and I decided to start collecting as many as possible and see what creative culinary uses I could find for them.

It wasn't the first time I had played with seeds. Every year I collect a bunch of black mustard seeds to make my own spicy mustard with homemade wine and vinegar, but I usually didn't bother to collect others such as stinging nettle seeds or evening primrose seeds.

So that year I went to town researching as well as collecting them and ended up with over 30 different kinds. Some, such as curly dock seeds, are super easy to collect, while others were insanely time consuming— white sage and black sage seeds fall into that category. The research I did into native edible seeds and potential culinary uses was utterly fascinating; it was like discovering a new universe of super-nutritious and tasty little things. Seeds are really a kind of superfood!

I thought I was doing great with my 30 different seeds until, doing some research online, I came across a pdf document from the Natural Resources Conservation Service titled "Edible Seeds and Grains of California Tribes and the Klamath Tribe of Oregon in the Phoebe Apperson Hearst– Museum of Anthropology Collections, University of California, Berkeley."

Photo courtesy of Mia Wasilevich.

This 216-page document (available free online) was a real eye-opener for me about the bounty surrounding us, but also how we have lost touch with nature. Most of the edible native seeds named in the document—and we are talking about well over a hundred types of wild seeds—are no longer collected and eaten. Even the chia purchased at the store is not the same as the one growing wild locally.

It's a sad statement about how the modern world has truly limited our food supply and the lack of variety that's been forced upon us. What is presently available is basically what's economical to produce in somewhat large quantity. Some wild seeds, which were relished by native peoples for their unique flavors and high nutritional value, are nowhere to be found in local stores or supermarkets. The only place you can still find them is where they've always been . . . in the wilderness.

On the plus side, from a forager and culinary explorer's perspective, it's a whole new world to discover and experiment with. Even after 16 years of foraging in Southern California, I still feel like a kid in a candy store.

There are numerous unique culinary creations you can make with seeds. If you take into consideration that hundreds of edible seeds with various flavors are available, a simple ethnic dish such as pinole (a sort of porridge using a mix of flour, ground seeds, and herbs) has thousands of possible variations.

Seeds can be ground into flour to make unique breads and crackers, or added to other ingredients to make tasty fried cakes. You can pickle them or use them in sauces and stews for flavors, add them to infusions and other drinks, ferment them, make interesting porridges, and use them in an infinite number of other ways.

As I've worked with local chefs, wild seeds have slowly made an appearance again in the Los Angeles food scene, but only in a very few places. Recently, I made some pickled seeds for a restaurant that included some very obscure native ones that had probably not been eaten for over two hundred years. I don't think the customers realized that part, but the feedback in terms of flavors was very positive.

Although I already use many wild seeds, I'm really in the beginning of my research on this subject. I look forward to learning much more and experimenting with what I'm able to find and collect as I go along on this fascinating forage journey.

SOME OF THE FORAGED SEEDS, NATIVE AND NON-NATIVE, I'VE USED SO FAR INCLUDE:

Amaranth (*Amaranthus retroflexus*)
Black mustard (*Brassica nigra*)
Black sage (*Salvia mellifera*)
Broadleaf plantain (*Plantago major*)
California sunflower (*Helianthus californicus*)
Canary grass (*Phalaris canariensis*)
Caraway (*Carum carvi*)
Chickweed (*Stellaria media*)
Common madia (*Madia elegans*)
Curly dock (*Rumex crispus*)
Elegant clarkia (*Clarkia unguiculata*)
Evening primrose (*Oenothera* spp.)
Field mustard (*Brassica rapa*)
Golden chia (*Salvia columbariae*)
Lamb's quarters (*Chenopodium album*)
Longleaf plantain (*Plantago lanceolate*)
Miner's lettuce (*Claytonia perfoliata*)
Nasturtium (*Tropaeolum majus*)
Purslane (*Portulaca oleracea*)
Red maids (*Calandrinia ciliate*)
Saltbush (*Atriplex Canescens*)
Sedge (Cyperaceae)
Smoothstem Blazingstar (*Mentzelia albicaulis*)
Stinging nettles (*Urtica dioica*)
White sage (*Salvia apiana*)
Wild celery (*Apium graveolens*)
Wild fennel (*Foeniculum vulgare*)

Some of the Plants I Collect Seeds From

Black sage (*Salvia mellifera*).

California buckwheat (*Eriogonum fasciculatum*).

Clarkia (*Clarkia exilis*).

Evening primrose (*Oenothera* spp.).

Curly dock (*Rumex crispus*).

Lamb's quarters (*Chenopodium* spp.).

Black mustard (*Brassica nigra*).

Nettles (*Urtica* spp.).

Golden chia (*Salvia columbariae*).

Broadleaf plantain (*Plantago major*).

California sunflower (*Helianthus californicus*).

White sage (*Salvia apiana*).

Wild fennel (*Foeniculum vulgare*).

Field mustard (*Brassica rapa*).

Amaranth (*Amaranthus palmeri*).

Miner's lettuce (*Claytonia perfoliata*).

Foraged wild seeds.

PICKLING WILD SEEDS

The flavors you can achieve with this type of condiment are truly amazing, and there are hundreds of subtle variations you can create by combining wild seeds with infused or homemade vinegars, as well as wild aromatics and spices. Aside from acquiring the knowledge of which seeds are edible, understanding their flavor profiles, and spending the time to forage for them, it's a very easy process to pickle them. Some blends can taste like a somewhat strong mustard if you've put in a lot of black mustard seeds, while others may have more floral qualities. It all depends on the seeds you use.

A mix with a lot of wild fennel seeds works very well with fish. Caraway or wild celery seeds will also create very distinctive flavors, which can be used nicely in stews.

Here is a blend I made recently for chef Ludo Lefebvre (Trois Mec restaurant), which had somewhat strong spicy mustard and subtle pine flavors.

Pickling solution

1½ cups (354 ml) Mountain-Infused Vinegar (see page 244), or you can substitute apple cider, rice, or champagne vinegar
1 tablespoon (17 g) salt
3 tablespoons (50 g) sugar or honey

THE SEEDS I USED IN PHOTO ON PAGE 326:

Black sage seeds
White sage seeds
Broadleaf plantain seeds
Black mustard seeds
    (25% of the mix)
Field mustard seeds
    (15% of the mix)
Stinging nettle seeds
Evening primrose seeds
Lamb's quarters seeds
Sedge seeds
Miner's lettuce seeds

Procedure

Fill around half of a 1-pint (500 ml) jar with wild seeds. A quarter of the seeds should be black mustard to make it a hot mustard-like condiment. Add the vinegar, then the salt and the sugar. Make sure to leave ½ inch (1.25 cm) headspace. Place in the refrigerator for a week before consumption. Shake two or three times daily for the first 4 days. The seeds will expand, and some seeds may expand more than others. If you've put in too many seeds, just remove any excess.

The mix is always a bit different for me: It varies with what I've managed to collect and store as well as what's in season.

Wild aromatics such as sages, California bay, mugwort, or eucalyptus leaves can also be added as flavoring agents. In this case, I added half a California bay leaf to the jar.

Note that you can make interesting mixes representing the flavors of whole environments. Recently I made one using pine-infused mugwort beer vinegar with wild seeds foraged in the local mountains—it was like tasting the mountains themselves. I tend to avoid using chia seeds when pickling seeds due to their mucilaginous properties.

Note that it is better to wait and taste your pickled seeds after a week or so. Some seeds such as black mustard can be bitter in the beginning, but the bitterness will dissipate after a few days.

PICKLED OYSTER MUSHROOMS WITH WILD SEEDS

The texture of these mushrooms is entirely dependent on the type of mushroom you use. I usually dice my pickled oyster mushrooms and add them to other condiments.

Ingredients

¾ pound (338 g) oyster (or other) mushrooms
Water
⅓ cup (around 50 g) mixed wild seeds—
    black mustard, field mustard, nettles,
    white sage, black sage, lamb's quarters,
    evening primrose, sedge, et cetera
⅓ onion, sliced
2 garlic cloves, chopped
½ teaspoon (1.5 g) wild fennel seeds
1 teaspoon (5.5 g) salt
2–3 teaspoons (12 g) honey or sugar
½ California bay leaf (you can substitute
    1 regular bay leaf)
2¼ cups (530 ml) Mountain-Infused Vinegar
    (see page 244), pine needle vinegar, or
    apple cider vinegar with 5% acidity

Procedure

1. Wash and slice the oyster mushrooms.
2. Place the mushrooms in salted water, bring the water to a boil, and simmer for 10 minutes.
3. In another pot, combine all the wild seeds and other ingredients with the vinegar. Bring the solution to a boil and simmer for 4 to 5 minutes. Taste it, add salt, and more honey or sugar to your liking.
4. Drain the mushrooms and place them in the jar.
5. Pour the vinegar solution (with the wild seeds, onion, et cetera) into the jar and leave ½ inch (1.25 cm) headspace. If necessary, add more vinegar.
6. Wipe the rim and close the lid.
7. Let it cool, then place the jar in the refrigerator; it should keep for several weeks.
8. If you want to can it, use the water bath method (see page 38) and process the jar in boiling water for at least 35 minutes (for a 1-quart [1 l] jar).
9. Remove the jar, let it cool, and make sure you have a good seal, then store. It should be good for up to a year.

The $350 Energy Bar

Most people don't realize it, but you can actually find influences of native foods in the aisles of modern supermarkets in the form of what we presently know as energy bars. Local natives used to create a similar type of power food with ground native dates, berries, nuts, and seeds. In the North, where the colder climate dictated a much higher fat content, pemmican was made using fat, animal protein, and berries.

The recipes would vary immensely based on the regional ingredients and the seasons. Locally, ingredients such as acorns, pinyon pine nuts, dates, wild seeds, and berries (elderberries, manzanita, currant, and so forth) would be mixed together in a thick mush, while in the North, pemmican was made using available meat and fat from such animals as elk, buffalo, bear, moose, deer, and the local berries.

The story of the $350 Energy Bar is a bit funny. *Los Angeles* magazine was putting together a feature article about 25 of L.A.'s most influential tastemakers, and somehow I ended up being one of them. I was asked to bring wild ingredients for a photo shoot and I decided to create a truly unique one by making an energy bar using foraged ingredients. While at the photo shoot, the writer was tasting the bar (it was delicious); I proceeded to explain what it was made of and gave her an estimate of the cost if someone had asked me to make one for them. Based on a somewhat low salary of $25/hour, the cost ended up being around $350 for the foraging time, preparation, and related expenses (travel and so forth). The bar never made it into the article (they used photos of wild plants), but a month later I was talking to a chef about local edible plants and, out of the blue, he asked me if I was the creator of the "$350 energy bar." We had a good laugh about it, and since that time, this is what I call it.

NATIVE "POWER FOOD"—THE ENERGY BAR

This power bar is really not complicated to make—you can even use purchased seeds and dates—but to make the "real" $350 energy bar, you shouldn't cheat: You'll need to forage the ingredients. If you don't forage you can buy commercial chia seeds, pine nuts, and other seeds such as sesame, fennel, and flax, as well as dates or even dry figs

Ingredients

6 large dates (such as Medjool) with
    pits removed
½ cup (80 g) chia seeds
1 teaspoon (4 g) pine nuts, ground
¼ cup (40 g) mixed edible seeds
2 tablespoons (30 ml) olive or other oil
A bit of dehydrated berries such as currants,
    blueberries, or elderberries (optional)

Procedure

1. Using a stone pestle and mortar (*molcajete*) or blender, mix all the ingredients into a thick paste.
2. Using clean hands, roll the paste into balls or form into a rectangular shape similar to commercial energy bars. It's a bit of a messy and sticky business, but you don't have to do a perfect job shaping the thing.
3. Place it in the refrigerator for a few hours or overnight. After chilling, the texture will be harder and you can shape it again more easily.
4. Wrap it parchment paper, and voilà! Your power bar should keep for many weeks in the fridge.

To make the $350 version, you'll need to forage native dates, pinyon pine nuts, and golden chia seeds, then add ¼ cup (40 g) of mixed wild seeds such as nettles, evening primrose, and plantain (I used around 16 types of wild seeds), then use homemade olive oil and local berries such as dehydrated elderberries or currants. Now that I think of it, this should really be a $700 energy bar!

Wild seeds power bar wrapped in giant reed leaf.

FERMENTING WILD SEEDS

This is another way to add some interesting funky spicy flavors to seeds. It's the same method for making wild kimchi (see page 119).

Honestly it's not for everyone but I like them and I'm sure people who are into fermented and spicy food can do some amazing creations with flavorful seeds.

Procedure

1. Fill one-third of a 1-quart (1 l) jar with edible wild seeds. I'm going for a hot and spicy condiment, so I would say that half of my seeds are composed of black mustard and field mustard seeds. The rest of the seeds are from white sage, black sage, stinging nettles, lamb's quarters, evening primrose, clarkia, plantain, and frankly whatever else I have available that day.

2. Add a layer of thinly chopped garlic, onion, and cabbage—around ⅓ of a cup or 4 tablespoons (around 45 ml by volume).

3. The next layer is composed of 3 tablespoons (20 g) of hot chili peppers. The choice of chili powder is up to you; some are mild and some are super spicy.

4. On top of everything, place 6 or 7 large cabbage leaves to keep all the ingredients under the brine.

5. Make a brine composed of 1 tablespoon (17 g) of sea salt for 2 cups (473 ml) of springwater or distilled water. Don't use tap water, which contains chlorine. Slowly pour the brine into the jar, and with clean hands push down and try to remove any air bubbles in the ingredients.

6. Place a lid and screw band on the jar. Don't screw it down tight—you want the gas produced by the fermentation to escape. If it's too tight the pressure could break your jar and create a mess.

7. This is a fermentation you want to supervise. The seeds will expand and the gas emanating from the fermentation will have a tendency to push the ingredients upward. Place a plate under the jar in case some liquid comes out of the jar. After the first 24 hours, check your fermentation two or three times a day and, with clean fingers or a clean spoon, push down the ingredients and remove any debris floating on top of the brine. As much as possible you want to keep everything under the brine. On day 2 and 3 I even shake the jar a bit to make sure the seeds are loose in the brine.

8. Let the fermentation go for a few days. Usually around 5 days is enough, but you can also let it ferment longer, which will increase the flavors. When I'm happy with the smell and taste, I place the jar in the refrigerator for another couple of days. The fermentation will slow down considerably due to the low temperature, and I think it's good to let the seeds soak in all the flavors.

9. The final step is to remove the large cabbage leaves from the fermented solution. You're basically left with the seeds and the finely chopped garlic and onion. I typically end up with 2 cups (473 ml) of seeds.

10. Taste it. This is all about personal flavor preference. If you like it as is, just place all the seeds and the brine into a new jar and put it back in the fridge. Personally, I like to replace the brine with vinegar, usually apple cider vinegar or one of my infused vinegars, such as pine vinegar. I also add 1 tablespoon (17 g) of sea salt and 2 tablespoons (34 g) of sugar or honey. I let it rest in the fridge for an additional 2 or 3 days before it's ready to serve. I try to use the seeds within a month, but they probably would keep much longer.

PRIMITIVE GOURMET CRACKERS

For our private dinners, I often make primitive-looking crackers using a wide variety of wild ingredients such as aromatics, herb powders, seeds, acorn or cattail flour, and so on. One time we used them with a soup and another time with a sort of salsa topping with roasted foraged crickets.

The basic recipe changes all the time based on what I have in the pantry. These crackers are not all wild; I also use regular flour to make them.

Ingredients

2½ cups (325 g) whole wheat flour (use all-purpose flour if you don't have whole wheat)

¼ cup (32 g) curly dock seed flour or acorn flour

¼ cup (32 g) California buckwheat flour

1 tablespoon (17 g) sea salt (homemade or purchased)

⅓ cup (78 ml) olive oil, plus more for brushing

1 cup (236 ml) warm water

Wild toppings such as aromatics, herb powder, cattail pollen, and wild seeds

Procedure

1. Place the flours in a bowl. Add the salt and olive oil. Using a whisk, wooden spoon, or clean hands, start stirring while slowly pouring in the hot water. Once done, place the dough on your table and knead it for at least 10 minutes.
2. Using your hands, make a large dough ball and wrap it up in a clean wet towel or plastic wrap. Let it rest 30 minutes.
3. Preheat the oven to 450°F (232°C).
4. Now you're ready to make your crackers. With your fingers, pick up some dough and make a ball around 1 to 1½ inches (2.5 to 4 cm) in diameter. Roll it out (you want it quite thin), then place on your baking sheet. It helps to roll the dough on a large cutting board sprinkled with wheat flour so the dough doesn't stick to the board. You may also want to spray the baking sheet very lightly with oil beforehand to ensure the crackers won't stick to it.
5. When the baking sheet has enough crackers, brush the surface of each one lightly with olive oil. Sprinkle with additional salt if you want (optional) and your wild toppings. This is where the fun comes in: You can add dry California sagebrush, herb powders, a tad of chili powder for heat, wild seeds, and so on.
6. Place your pan in the oven and bake for 10 minutes or until browned. Watch closely as the crackers can burn quite quickly.

Can you make primitive crackers with just wild seeds and flours? Of course. I once made some using the following ingredients and cooked them on a flat stone over a campfire:

1 cup (130 g) acorn flour
     (hot leached flour; see page 54)
⅓ cup (43 g) curly dock seed flour
     (or other appropriate flour)
⅓ cup (43 g) California buckwheat flour
¼ cup (32 g) edible leaf powder
     (such as nettles or lamb's quarters)
¾ cup (177 ml) cattail root juice
     (see Extracting Cattail Starch on
     page 274)
3 tablespoons (47 g) rendered fat
2 teaspoons (34 g) foraged sea salt

The Neanderthals probably really loved these but the *Homo sapiens* I made them for were less excited and were so-so about the flavors and texture. This truly wild recipe still needs some work on my part, but it was fun to make.

Note: To make California buckwheat flour, simply crumble the dried brown flowers into a coarse flour. I usually forage them in late summer and early fall.

Foraged Pinole

While doing research on edible wild seeds and flours, I often came upon statements such as, "Natives used the ground seeds to make pinole." After reading so much about all those seeds used to make it, pinole sounded great, whatever it was, so I decided to make some. The only thing I needed was to find a recipe, right? Oh boy! Easier said than done, but in the end, I finally understood what a pinole is.

The origin of the word *pinole* comes from the Aztec word *pinolli*, which means "flour, ground maize, or chia." My initial confusion stemmed from the vast amount of somewhat conflicting definitions of pinole.

Then it gets even more fun. Some definitions say it's coarse or fine flour, a beverage, gruel, porridge, or even a cake. A couple of recipes even included dried rabbit meat.

The more I was trying to figure out what it was, the more I got confused until Eureka!—I saw the light.

All the definitions are actually correct: A pinole is a reflection of the environment and culture. If you are living in central Mexico, a traditional pinole would be made with corn combined with local seeds and herbs, but in Southern California, acorns were the main staple, and so a porridge made with wild seeds, acorn flour, and local herbs could have been called a pinole as well. The Ohlone and Tongva recipes I found listed acorn as part of the pinole recipe instead of corn. Like the French dish known as ratatouille (a sort of stew with mixed vegetables and herbs), it's highly probable that recipes would vary from tribe to tribe, across the seasons, and even between family units.

So what's a pinole? It's a mixture/flour made of seeds (wild or commercial), ground acorn or maize, and various seasonings (herbs, spices, berries, et cetera), with the possible addition of a sugar base (honey, mesquite beans, sugarcane, or others). You can eat the dry flour, make porridge or cakes with it, and even drink it mixed with water. It's all good! If you go to Mexico, they may not recognize your acorn-and-seed concoction as a pinole, so you may need to call it a gruel or porridge.

My pinole changes all the time depending on what I am able to forage and store during the year. There are hundreds of variations that can be made. Because I'm more into flavors, what's important for me is that it tastes great. (If I were an athlete, I would likely be more concerned with nutrition than with flavors.)

I made a coarse flour using my stone grinder, placed the flour in a pot, and added 1½ cups (354 ml) of water. I simmered it for 10 minutes and let it rest for 20 more. I like it cold.

HERE ARE SOME OF THE MANY DEFINITIONS I FOUND DURING MY RESEARCH:

Coarse flour made from maize, herbs, and ground chia seeds
Pounded seed mixtures
Toasted cornmeal mixed with natural sugar, spices, and water
A meal, made from acorns, seeds, and wild grain
Toasted ground corn combined with cocoa, sugar, cinnamon, or vanilla
Wheat or corn, dried, ground, and sweetened, usually with the flour of mesquite beans
Maize corn that has been parched and powdered

THE PINOLE SHOWN IN THE PHOTO ON PAGE 337 WAS MADE WITH THE FOLLOWING FORAGED INGREDIENTS:

1 tablespoon (8 g) acorn flour (cold leached)
1½ tablespoons (15 g) golden chia seeds
1 tablespoon (7.5 g) various roasted wild seeds (white sage, black sage, sedge, plantain, evening primrose)
2 tablespoons (14 g) lerp sugar and 1 teaspoon (5 ml) raw honey to sweeten it
1 tablespoon (10 g) mixed berries (dehydrated manzanita, toyon, and elderberries)

Top, grinding wild seeds, berries, and lerp sugar to make pinole. *Bottom*, after 10 minutes of boiling, this seasonal pinole flavored with black sage is ready.

Sourdough with Wild Yeasts, Seeds, and Aromatics

Although I'm definitely not a prolific baker, in my quest for local flavors I had to try making sourdough using local sources of wild yeasts.

As with many other foods, there is something special about creating an ingredient in which you can incorporate the flavors of your own terroir. Sourdough bread made in New York will taste different from one made in San Francisco or Paris, France. If you think about it, it's quite amazing to be able to taste your own local wild environment—once you've gotten used to the flavors, wild yeast will make the local bread bought at the store taste bland and "civilized." There is something definitely untamed and wild in the flavors of good sourdough bread. It's complex, sour, and sometimes carries hints of cheese.

Once you've tamed the wild yeast, your role becomes that of a guardian and keeper of the sacred flavors, which means you have to take care of it and keep it alive. This requires careful monitoring and feeding.

I've tried to make sourdough from scratch before, essentially just making a dense dough by mixing equal parts of flour and water, then leaving it outside, hoping for wild yeasts from the air to magically end up in it and start a fermentation.

But that never worked. Granted, I used plain everyday all-purpose flour that you can buy at the local supermarket, and I'm sure organic artisanal flour would work better, as wild yeast is probably already present in the flour, but that yeast isn't local either. If the organic flour comes from North Dakota, you're not going to taste your true local flavors, although it probably will change over time and incorporate the local wild yeast.

Plain, all-purpose flour was what I had to work with in the pantry. So, instead of waiting for the wild yeasts to magically appear from nowhere and face a disappointing failure, I decided to use the same local sources of yeast I use for my wild brews. Despite the fact that it was early fall, I was extremely lucky and still found some very ripe elderberries in the mountains that had a nice bloom (composed mostly of wild yeasts). I threw them into the dough and it worked beautifully—with the ambient temperature being quite high, I had a very nice fermenting and bubbly sourdough starter at the end of 3 days. Since that first experiment, I've used all kinds of wild sources of yeasts to make my sourdough starter, including California juniper berries and organic grapes, to name a few.

MAKING A SOURDOUGH STARTER WITH WILD YEASTS

Making a sourdough starter is a little like leaching acorns: There are various methods and lots of (sometime strong) opinions about the right way to do it. What's important is that it works. This is just the method I used. Once you've made a sourdough starter, you can use it with other flours such as wholegrain, rye, and so on.

Making a good starter usually takes 4 to 5 days. During the hot summers of Southern California, I have even had a beautiful fermentation at the end of 3 days, whereas in the winter it generally requires the usual full 4 or 5 days. If you live in a very cold place, it may take a bit longer.

Procedure

Day 1. Make an equal mix of flour and springwater or distilled water (not tap water), and stir to create a nice thick dough. Add a bunch of wild berries (unwashed, with bloom on them) or fruit skins that have a nice bloom, such as organic grapes or plum skins. I use 1 cup (236 ml) of water and 1 cup (130 g) of all-purpose flour.

Stir the berries in the dough, then place a clean towel on top of the container. Three times a day remove the towel and stir vigorously for a couple of minutes using a clean spoon, then place the towel back over the dough.

Day 2. Check your starter. If you're lucky and the temperature is quite warm, you may see a few bubbles, but don't expect it—it's probably too soon. Feed it a little bit, making a dough by mixing ½ cup (65 g) of new flour and ½ cup (118 ml) of water and stirring it into the original starter. Cover the container with the clean towel.

Day 3. Your starter should start bubbling and grow somewhat larger in volume. Feed it again by making more dough, but this time with 1 cup (236 ml) of water and 1 cup (130 g) of flour. Stir. If the starter is not bubbling yet, don't panic, just keep going. You can smell it, too, if it's fermenting properly; it should have a bit of a sour and cheesy smell.

Day 4. Your starter should be bubbly and the dough texture more "loose." The volume can double, but that's not always the case; most times I experience maybe a 25 percent rise. The sour and cheesy smell should be more pungent. It's all good. Feed the dough again by mixing ½ cup (65 g) of new flour and ½ cup (118 ml) of water, and stirring it into the now bubbly starter.

Day 5. Your starter should have risen another 25 to 50 percent and should now be ready to use. It should be very bubbly, and the sour/cheesy smell should be more intense.

You have two choices at this point: Make your sourdough bread with it, or store it in the refrigerator for later use.

For my part, I decided to go ahead and bake the bread at this point. I mixed the bubbling/fermenting dough with the same amount of regular dough/water mix, so it's 50 percent sourdough and 50 percent regular dough. I kneaded it for around 20 minutes. The dough was then placed in the garage with a somewhat humid/wet towel on top of the container (it gets quite hot in Southern California). After 10 hours, the dough had risen well but it wasn't excessive (maybe 30 percent greater volume).

I decided to bake my bread inside a clay container. I could have done it inside a cast-iron Dutch oven, but I also had a beautiful tagine, so I went with the tagine.

I placed the dough inside the tagine. Of course, I'm always keen to add some wild ingredients and flavors.

One of my favorite herbs to use when roasting is Wright's cudweed (also sometimes called rabbit tobacco locally). It really infuses interesting flavors. I placed a bunch on top of the dough and also sprinkled a bunch of California sagebrush, wild fennel seeds, cattail pollen, and lerp sugar on the dough. I closed the tagine and left it in the oven at 475°F (246°C) for 30 minutes, then removed the lid and left it in the oven for another 15 minutes.

The end result was beautiful and really tasty bread; it had hints of cheese (from the wild yeast) and outstanding smoky flavors from the cudweed. The rise wasn't too extreme, maybe 30 percent increase in volume, and I was quite happy with the texture.

MAINTAINING YOUR STARTER

If you don't want to bake your bread right away, it's relatively easy to maintain your sourdough.

When your starter is ready you can place it into a clean jar or container. If you have too much, you can get rid of the excess or give it to a friend. Feed it with a new dough made from ½ part water and ½ part flour, increasing the volume of the starter by 40 or 50 percent. So if you had 1 cup of sourdough, you would make a cup of new dough by mixing ½ cup of flour and ½ cup of water. Stir the new dough, cover, then let it rest 8 hours or so at room temperature, then place

back in the fridge. You will need to repeat this process once a week (remove any excess if necessary).

When you're ready to use the starter, take it out of the fridge. I usually leave it alone for 12 hours at room temperature, then start feeding it again as per the regular procedure. It may take 3 days to get the quantity you need to bake new bread.

As a note, I'm definitely not an expert baker—there may be better ways to feed and maintain sourdough starter and to make sourdough breads of all sorts. If there is only one thing I would like you to take away from this, it's the fact that you can use wild berries and other sources of wild yeasts to help initiate the fermentation and create sourdough breads with your own local flavors. Foraged aromatic herbs can also be added to the bread or sprinkled on it. As I did in this example, you may even try placing wild aromatic herbs on top for "smoking" the bread.

You can find a lot of information online, in books, or from more experienced local bakers. I just purchased a great book on the subject titled *Classic Sourdoughs, Revised: A Home Baker's Handbook* by Ed Wood and Jean Wood, and their recipe for No-Knead Sourdough sounds very interesting.

I can't wait to make more sourdough breads, pizza dough, pitas, and so forth following some of the interesting recipes from that book, but using wild ingredients.

Sourdough bread in a tagine ready to be placed into the oven.
Wild aromatics are placed on top for flavoring.

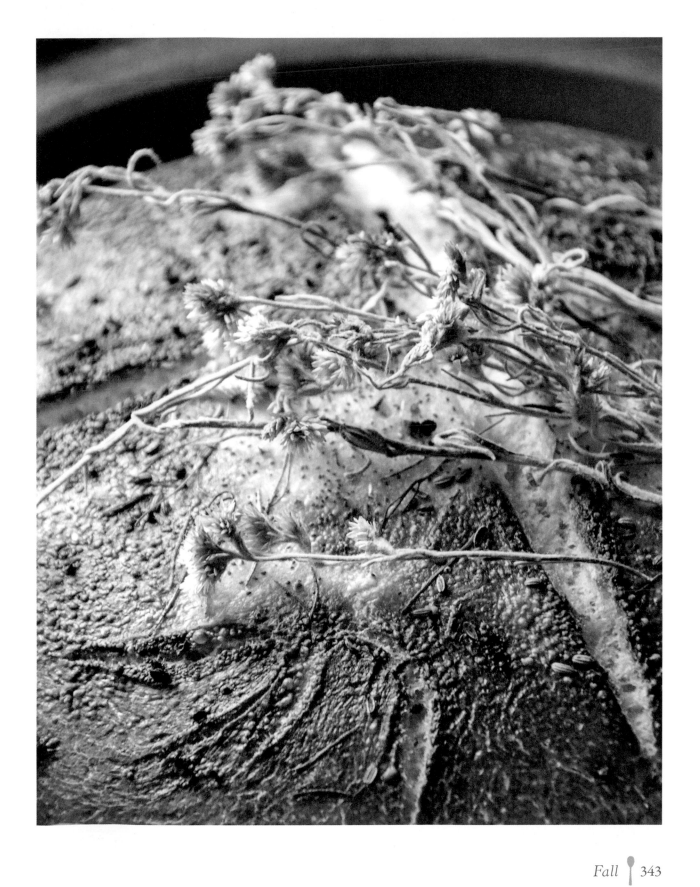

Wild golden currants preserved in alcohol with a tad of mugwort.

Preserving Fruits and Wild Berries in Alcohol

Preserving in alcohol is another great method to capture the intrinsic nature of a terroir. By mixing foraged fruits and berries with wild aromatics, you can obtain some very interesting and unique flavors. My approach to this is very similar to making beer: I like to use various inspiring components found in one particular environment and try to re-create the essence of it through taste. For example, I can mix dry elderberries from the local mountains with a bit of white fir, juniper berries, and pine needles. I have preserved wild golden currant with a tad of mugwort that was found nearby. I also made another batch that was flavored with some black sage. Of course, the blends can be quite complex, but in the beginning you can keep them simple with excellent results.

There are many interesting culinary uses for your boozy delicacies: desserts, ice cream, cocktails, and even cooking. I once added some currants preserved in brandy to rabbit cooked in a forest beer, and the fruity notes were a perfect addition to the dish.

You'll need a strong alcohol (80 to 110 proof) for this method, the idea being that bacteria that could spoil the food won't survive in that sterile environment. Sugar is added to bring out flavors, but it also has an osmotic effect. In other words, there is an osmosis or exchange of solution between the content inside the berries, which has less sugar, and the alcohol and sugar solution outside. This creates a balance, and alcohol going inside the berries will also ensure that spoiling won't occur. If you're more interested in creating cocktails, sugar is not always necessary.

There are no real rules as to which alcohol to use. Traditionally rum, brandy, cognac, or kirsch were used for their inherent flavors, but if you also add some aromatic ingredients you can use gin, vodka, or whiskey. It's really a matter of preference, and the fun is to play with various recipes. It's hard to go wrong.

If I use fruits, I cut them in smaller pieces. A somewhat large fruit may spoil inside before the osmosis effect and the alcohol have time to stop bacterial growth.

A basic recipe, such as for preserved wild currants, would be as follows:

1. Use enough (cleaned) berries or fruit pieces to fill around three-fourths of a jar.
2. Add sugar, around half of the fruits' volume.
3. Insert some aromatics of your choice. (I used the peel of 1 lemon and 2 mugwort leaves.)
4. Fill the jar with alcohol to the top, then shake a bit to dilute the sugar in the alcohol.
5. Close the jar and store in a cool, dark place for 3 to 4 months before enjoying it.

Living in the hot climate of Southern California, I often place the jar into the fridge. It can last for a very long time; I've enjoyed berries preserved with this method after 2 years.

As a forager, you have a tremendous amount of ingredients and aromatics to play with. Living in Southern California, I use this method with wild currants, blackberries, figs, dehydrated elderberries, redberry (*Rhamnus crocea*), wild cherries, and many more. Typical flavoring plants would include mugwort, various mints, sages, pine needles, white fir, wild fennel, California juniper berries, yarrow, California bay leaves, and so on.

Don't discard the alcohol after you've extracted and eaten the fruit! When you do your wild experimentations, you'll sometimes find that the infused alcohol is the best part and can make very tasty drinks. Simply pour a small amount in a glass, add some chilled fizzy water, and enjoy!

Transforming Ingredients

As you learn and forage new plants it is important (and fun) to take the time to experiment with them. It's one way to get to know how the plants can be used in various dishes, but also how their flavor, texture, and even appearance can be altered or enhanced.

I like to research and try every part of the plant, from leaf to stem and roots. You'll be amazed at what you can discover. Many new cooking techniques have not been used yet on some wild plants simply because the plants were pretty much absent from the kitchen for the last century, and the people who were still cooking with them have often followed only traditional recipes.

A good example would be some of the large yuccas we have locally. Instead of boiling and sautéing the flowers, you could try frying them. The young shoot makes decent chips. It also makes delicious pickles (see the Pickled Yucca Shoot on page 261). Preserving in vinegar wasn't a native preservation technique, so I could not find any record of the tender shoot being used in that way.

Plantain can be turned into "seaweed" (see the Broadleaf Plantain "Seaweed" on page 116); stinging nettles are beautiful and crunchy once fried and sprinkled with wild spices. Some tree leaves are really beautiful when they're candied (see the Crunchy Candied Tree Leaves on page 85). Mallow leaves can be transformed into seaweed chips with the proper Asian condiments, and curly dock leaves can become sushi wraps. If you want a plant-based alternative to caviar, take some field mustard seeds and marinate them in fish sauce for a while.

I tell my students that they don't have to think outside of the box but can simply eliminate the box altogether. Think freely! Many edible foraged plants have culinary uses that are begging to be discovered. Once you've done your research about edibility and you're good to go, by all means start exploring the possibilities! Fry, dehydrate, and ferment the foraged plants, see how they react in cold water over time, make some infusions, candy them, see how they taste as a powder, and so on.

Go Asian! Curly dock leaves can be blanched and used as sushi wrap. Fermented wild edibles replace the fish inside. Serve with a black mustard leaf "wasabi" sauce.

As you discover new culinary uses, your creativity will also expand. You'll be able to create new and unusual dishes as well as flavors that are completely unique and cannot be found anywhere else. For example, when I introduced the technique for smoking meat or fish with a local cudweed (Wright's cudweed) to some of the chefs I'm working with, the local food critics really took notice because the flavors were so unlike anything else they'd ever experienced.

A good example of transformation is curly dock stem "fried octopus," which is very easy to make. Curly dock can be found pretty much anywhere in North America.

Just take a large stem and cut it into 3- to 4-inch-long (7 to 10 cm) pieces. Using a knife, make a few notches here and there on each end—there is no need to go deep. Place the stem in cold water and put in the refrigerator overnight.

The next day the stems will have curled into what look like small octopi. They're beautiful as is in a salad, but you can even go further by making some interesting batter and frying them. People will swear they are being served fried octopus until they take a bite. The inside is soft and lemony tasting.

Fried curly dock "octopus."

Herb Powders

Herb powders are one of those ingredients that you don't see very often and yet there are so many uses for them. The flavor profile of a plant often changes once you dehydrate it and reduce it into powder. I don't see that as a bad thing; in fact, it makes it more interesting and a nice addition to your pantry. It's also a lot of fun to experiment with these powders.

While doing research on wild seeds and flours, it came to light that natives didn't have the same modern definition as we do for flour, that is, a powder obtained by grinding grain. If you read ethnobotany books, you'll find out that various plants were dehydrated or baked and made into powders to be used as flour. For example, the tender shoots of *Hesperoyucca whipplei* were baked and then reduced into flour. I've made it myself, and it is a very nice sweet, fine flour that can be used in combinations with other ingredients to make flatbreads or pinole.

Aside from added nutrition, many interesting and colorful breads can be made by adding plant powder to the flour. A couple of years ago we made some nettle and lamb's quarter breads. The deep-green color of the slices was quite striking and the flavor of the bread was excellent.

Other uses for herb powders include:

* As an additive to sauces, soups, cheeses, infusions, and other various drinks for flavor and added nutrition
* Sprinkled on food to add some taste and pizzazz
* Mixed into spice blends
* To create dehydrated wild soup mixes

To make the powders, you just need to place your dehydrated herbs into a coffee grinder and push the button. I usually use the espresso setting. Alternatively, you can also use a hand-crank coffee grinder or a stone grinder. Dehydrating your plants properly is crucial for achieving maximum flavor (see Preserving by Dehydrating on page 134).

Plant Chips

This is a fun way to add style and flavors to a dish, or you can simply eat the chips on their own as snacks.

They're very easy to make. You gather some edible plants (wild plants, such as watercress, curly dock, or stinging nettles, or garden-grown edibles), add some spices, and blend them to turn them into a paste. The plants can be either fresh or cooked before blending.

There is room for *a lot* of experimentations here. For example, you can add lime or lemon juice, chili peppers, and very flavorful herbs such as nasturtium, watercress, or chervil.

Taste the blended "pesto" and add salt and pepper if necessary. Don't make it too salty, as the dehydration process will increase the saltiness.

The next step is to spread the paste on parchment paper or a silicone sheet and place it in the dehydrator. You can also use your oven at the lowest setting. Dehydrate until fully dry, and enjoy!

CURLY DOCK "NORI"

Ingredients

1½ cups (100 g) curly dock, chopped
1 garlic clove
½ cup (118 ml) water
2 teaspoons (10 ml) soy sauce
¼ teaspoon (1.5 g) salt

Procedure

1. Place all ingredients into a blender and mix to a paste-like consistency. Using a spatula, spread on a silicone sheet, a large flat plate, or on parchment paper.
2. Dehydrate at 160° to 170°F (71° to 77°C) until fully dry. Use your fingers to create the chips by breaking the dry paste into small parts.

California Buckwheat

Along with California sagebrush, California buckwheat (*Eriogonum fasciculatum*) is one of the most common plants found in our local chaparral. It's a shrub that looks a bit like rosemary, albeit without the aroma. In spring and early summer it is adorned by countless and beautiful white flowers, which turn dry and rusty brown in fall. You want to forage the flowers at that stage (when they're brown), and before the first rains. I usually forage them by the handful; using your open fingers to grab them helps separate the flowers from the stems. I place them in bags on location, twigs and all. Once home, where it's much cooler than outside, I clean them and remove the twigs. It can be a bit tedious, but it's quite easy.

These are not like the buckwheat you purchase at the store; the seeds are very tiny and it's a nearly impossible task to separate them from the flower. We use the whole thing—dehydrated flowers and tiny seeds. When they're clean and ready to use, I soak the quantity I need in water for a couple of hours. This cleans them up, removing any dirt and dust, but also eliminates some of the inherent bitterness. The flower mush is then dehydrated again in the sun or oven. At that point it is ready to use.

When I began to learn foraging, the main use I made of California buckwheat was as an additive to flour when making bread. It's great in primitive flatbreads as it makes the bread less hard and crunchier, and thus more palatable. It gives a beautiful texture to leavened bread and give it a "wild" look. A local chef I know adds around 15 percent of dehydrated buckwheat flowers to his bread.

However, the secret for gourmet uses of California buckwheat is roasting. I usually roast the buckwheat in olive oil in a cast-iron pan. My favorite recipe is to add salt, chili powder, lime juice, and garlic powder during the roasting process, and then sprinkle the crunchy condiment on fish. Mia roasts them with butter and brown sugar for sprinkling on desserts. It's a bit tricky, but she basically roasts them until they are nearly, but not quite, burnt—it takes a bit of practice. The texture of the dry flowers changes from mealy to crunchy.

White Sage Cider Granita
(and Other Frozen Creations)

If you make wild infusions, sodas, beers, meads, shrubs, wines, or any other liquid concoction, you have the potential to make some tasty, refreshing desserts that are really appreciated during the hot summer months.

Granita is a sort of semi-frozen dessert originating from Italy. The texture is a bit more rough and granular than a sorbet or slushy and it is usually made with sugar, water, or juice and added flavorings. Some recipes can be quite elaborate, with the addition of vanilla extracts, cream, and so forth.

The method for making granita is super simple. There are various techniques to achieve the same effect, but the idea is to take your liquid concoction and add some sugar or honey if necessary. Pour it into a flat pan and freeze it. When you're ready to serve it, scrape the surface with a fork or spoon and place the shredded ice into an appropriate serving container, usually a chilled bowl or a glass.

You can create some very beautiful and tasty granitas by adding garnishes and other ingredients, such as fruit powders, edible flowers, or fresh berries.

When I make my white sage cider granita, I simply add some sugar to my white sage cider (see White Sage–Lime Cider on page 66) and freeze the liquid. I garnish with elderberry powder, sour oxalis flowers, a bit of shredded pinyon pine nuts, and one leaf of California sagebrush. The bitterness of the California sagebrush is nicely balanced by the sugar, and one leaf is enough to deliver plenty of aromatics and flavor.

I've also made granitas with my mountain infusions, elderberry wine, and fresh berries.

Edible Roots

Roots have many culinary uses, but here in Southern California we don't have that many edible roots we can forage. From my local experience and attested by countless students, the evening primrose root listed as edible in many East Coast books is downright inedible locally. The sensation is painful, like tiny sharp needles prickling your tongue and mouth. I suspect that's due to the presence of oxalate crystals (which are very bad for your kidneys), possibly due to soil conditions, location, and who knows what else. That's why you can't just trust books but must also rely on your own experience or the know-how of experienced foragers. If something doesn't feel right, trust what your body is telling you.

I don't see a lot of burdock in my area, either. I'm sure I will find more uses for local edible roots as I gain experience as a forager, but for now I've only played with the roots from cattail, wild radish, various mustards, dandelion, and curly dock.

Roots are not always edible per se. Unlike the carrots or radishes you purchase at the store, wild radish or mustard roots are too tough and fibrous to eat as is. You can use them as a flavoring agent in soups and stews, though, and remove them later on.

Another technique is to clean the roots thoroughly, then grate them. The resulting paste can be mixed with vinegar, wine, and other ingredients to be used as a condiment. Black mustard or wild radish root paste is a nice addition to fish dishes.

Young and Tender Stems

I think young and tender stems are too seldom used by foragers and chefs. There are many interesting culinary and aesthetic possibilities. The tender stems I have used so far include watercress, various thistles, wild radish, various mustards, wild celery, burr-chervil—and the list goes on.

There is really nothing complicated about foraging tender stems. You want young plants, but even some older plants will stay quite tender in the right location (shade and water). I usually feel the stem with my fingers—if it's obviously soft and delicate, it's good to go.

One of my favorite uses is to cut the stems finely and pickle them. This technique works very well with tender sow thistle stems, and the little tasty rings are quite beautiful in salads or various dishes.

You can also remove the leaves from watercress stems; use the leaves for salad and the stems for plating. They're very good and look quite interesting as well.

Palo verde beans.

Mexican Palo Verde Beans

Wild beans are fairly rare in my vicinity. I recently planned to go forage for more in the local desert as well as in Arizona, and to also look for mesquite pods, screw beans (*Prosopis pubescens*), tepary beans (*Phaseolus acutifolius*), and ironwood beans (*Olneya tesota*). Unfortunately, my old Jeep needs some serious repairs and, from experience, I know it's not wise to go exploring deep into the desert by yourself if you're not completely prepared. I once experienced a flat tire in 120°F (48.89°C) weather, and I had to stay in the shade and wait for sunset and the temperature to drop a bit before attempting to change the tire. The excessive heat was too dangerous and exhausting.

Anyhow, you have to make do with what you've got, and thus I ended up pretty much stuck with foraging local Mexican palo verde beans (*Parkinsonia arculeata*). Not that it's a bad thing; they're pretty delicious when picked up in late summer or sometimes early fall. You want to pick them up when the pods are still somewhat green and the green beans inside are quite delicious and sugary. Within a few weeks the pods and beans will dry and you end up with some terribly hard brown beans. Needless to say, from a culinary perspective it's easier to deal with them when they are still green and raw.

By the way, there are other types of palo verde trees from which you can collect the beans or even the edible flowers: the foothills palo verde (*Parkinsonia mycrophyllum*), the blue palo verde (*Parkinsonia floridum*), and the palo brea (*Parkinsonia praecox*). Some have delicious edible flowers, too, but the ones from our local Mexican palo verde are not really edible (they're too bitter). *Palo verde* means "green stick" in English, and one of the main striking features of these trees is the obvious green bark.

Foraging the beans is somewhat easy; the pods are usually quite abundant, but it is wise to use working gloves due to the large needles present on the branches. I'm usually able to collect two large grocery bags of pods in an hour or so. Once home, I shell the pods just as you would with peas. The beans are really good eaten raw and make a nice addition to salads or any dishes in which you would use raw peas.

If you want to preserve them for a short time, blanch the beans in boiling water for a couple of minutes. Place them in ice water to cool, then drain and store in the refrigerator or freezer.

Processed in this way, they should keep for a few days in the fridge. My favorite recipe is to cook the beans with cream, garlic, and wild greens. Sprinkled lightly with Chaparral Wild Spice Blend (see page 158), it is quite heavenly in terms of flavors.

The dry pods can be collected later in the year. The shelled beans are terribly hard and the usual technique for using them is to let them sprout first, then roast them. I have made flour without sprouting them, but it required some serious Neanderthal tools such as a heavy pounding stone and an extremely robust mortar or large flat rock. The experience taught me that foraging the beans while they are green is *much* easier.

Exploring the World of Edible Insects

Fall is also an interesting time to forage for some unusual goodies—insects!

Insects are pretty much available during most seasons, aside from winter. I tend to focus more on foraging insects in fall because of the lack of lush edible greens and the fact that insects are quite plentiful in this season.

There is a substantial amount of cultural bias in North America against eating insects. I had to go through that myself. It's kind of interesting when you think of it: Lobsters and crawfish look like giant scorpions, but the idea of eating a scorpion is repulsive to most people. Shrimps are as bizarre looking as crickets or grasshoppers, but we've been used to eating them since we were kids so, in our minds, they're "okay."

My one rule for insects is don't eat them raw. Although some, such as ants, have been served live in some famous restaurants, the fact is that even ants may contain parasites, which could create some serious health problems. I usually freeze my foraged insects first, then cook them thoroughly by boiling, frying, or roasting. I do the same with their eggs.

I'm sure I will find more insects to include in my culinary creations as I continue discovering what's available around me. Some, such as dragonflies and praying mantis, are so beautiful and fun to watch that I've not tried them yet.

THE LIST OF LOCAL EDIBLE INSECTS I'VE IDENTIFIED OR EATEN SO FAR INCLUDES THE FOLLOWING:

Acorn grubs	Hornworms
Some ants (some are delicious and lemony, while others, well . . . didn't taste so good)	Jumiles
	June bugs
Bees	Mole crickets
Cockroaches	Praying mantis
Crickets	Scorpions
Dragonflies	Sowbugs/pillbugs
Earwigs	Tarantulas
Emerita (sand fleas)	Termites
Grasshoppers	Wasps
	Water bugs

LOCAL NON-INSECTS (MOLLUSKS) THAT I'VE FORAGED AND EATEN INCLUDE:

Garden snails	Black mussels
River clams (Asian clams)	

Boiled acorn grubs, salsa, and guacamole.

Acorn Grubs

In a good year I can easily collect 50 pounds of acorns or more. I usually pick the good ones from the tree or the forest floor. I like to travel to my acorn foraging area after a windy day, and often the ground is just littered with them, making for easy picking!

Not all acorns are good to eat; quite a few are infested with grubs. The "bad" acorns are easily identified by the fact that there is a small hole, or a few holes, going through the shell. The hole is made by a small insect called the acorn weevil.

I rarely see the little brown insects themselves—they have a very long beak, which the female uses to bore holes into developing acorns and deposit eggs. The eggs turn into larvae/grubs, which feed on the acorns. Once they're done feeding, they exit through the same hole and bury themselves in the ground for a year or two, until they reach maturity and emerge as adult insects.

If you were to find a caterpillar instead of a grub inside the acorn, it just means that the grub has left already and was replaced by the offspring of the acorn moth, which usually uses the already bored hole to deposit her eggs inside the now vacant acorn. Isn't nature amazing?

In my early foraging days, picking up acorns from the ground was a slow process of inspecting each one for holes in the shell before placing them in a paper bag. These days I'm not that fastidious—I simply load several paper bags of what I see as edible acorns. I estimate that 10 percent or less will not be edible because the grub has eaten the inside.

Once home, I usually leave the acorns in the bag for a few hours, then place them in a large basket to inspect them and sort out the "bad ones." The advantage of this method is that I can take my time to inspect the acorns in the comfort of my own home,

usually with some relaxing music and a good coffee. The other advantage is the fact that the bottom of the paper bag is usually loaded with cute, moving little acorn grubs. They look very much like maggots, but unlike maggots they have been fed a nice rich vegan diet for a few weeks, not rotten meat.

The grubs are completely edible and have a very nice, nutty flavor. Originally I thought that the grubs would taste bitter due to the tannins that most of our local acorns have in their flesh, but that isn't the case at all. It is as if the grubs somehow process the food so as to keep all the good nutrients and flavors while getting rid of the tannins.

Over the years I have tried various cooking methods with acorn grubs, such as sautéing, roasting, frying, and so on, sometimes with great success, but just as often with great failure. If you try to fry or sauté the grubs, for instance, they just seem to melt in the high temperatures. The current method I use is to freeze them first, then clean them briefly, which also helps thaw them out. Then I place them in very hot water, bring the water to a boil for a minute or two, and—voilà!—I have boiled grubs, giving me a base for other preparations.

The transformation in this process is like what happens when you cook an egg—once boiled the flesh is dense and compact, and then you can use other cooking methods without the risk of the grubs melting down into nothingness. Try sautéing them lightly with chili, garlic, lime juice, and salt, then serve with salsa, or cook them briefly in a hollandaise sauce with truffles for an unforgettable culinary experience. As a dessert, I like to sprinkle the boiled grubs with white fir sugar and eat them as is.

Cooked properly, they're quite chewy, creamy, nutty, and highly nutritious due to their high fat and protein content. It's really gourmet food!

Boiled acorn grubs and white fir sugar.

Yummy Crickets

Foraging crickets is not a leisurely activity, it's a challenging sport! There are many ways to catch wild crickets—the easy way is to build traps, and there are countless ingenious ones you can make yourself if you do some research online. Personally, I like the plain old method of using a butterfly net. The net works great if you have a large population of crickets where you live, and it can be quite entertaining if you can get your friends to help. The crickets usually start coming out right after sunset and show up on my porch in large numbers. With the net, I can easily forage around 30 per hour.

Once I've foraged them, I place them in a specialized cricket pen I purchased at the local pet store. Raising crickets is outside of the realm of this book, but basically I feed them for a few days to make sure they have a healthy diet before they're ready for consumption. Then I scoop them into a jar and place them in the freezer. After an hour or so, I move them from the jar into a plastic freezer bag to join their old friends from earlier forages. In a rather short time I can collect a substantial quantity.

My cooking methods are very basic. (I've been so busy foraging and playing with edible and aromatic plants that insects have been neglected a bit.) Once they're removed from the freezer, I briefly rinse my crickets with cold water and pat them dry. I then sauté them for a few minutes with salt and a small amount of olive oil. Sometimes I also use garlic and soy sauce. I take the additional step of dehydrating them in the oven at 170°F (77°C) until they become really crunchy. Most of my students and guests seem to enjoy them better as a crunchy snack. They also make a wonderful topping for tacos, pizzas, or salsa.

You can also roast them in a pan with spices and a small amount of oil. Roast them in the oven at 250°F (121°C) for about 15 to 20 minutes and shake the pan every 5 minutes or so. Once they're done, taste and sprinkle on some additional spices if necessary. I've served them as an appetizer with homemade goat cheese on primitive crackers and in wild food salads.

Delectable Ants

I started investigating edible ants a few years ago, but it was during the terrible drought we had in 2014 and the scarcity of possible forage that I really took a look at them as a valid and quite delicious ingredient.

It may come as a surprise to some readers, but most ants are edible. I say *most* are edible because some of them simply don't taste very good. Ant eggs and larvae are even considered a delicacy in some countries, such as in Mexico (*escamoles*) or Thailand.

Foraging ants is a bit tricky; some species can inflict pain while others are harmless. Fire ants are a good example. If you're serious about investigating the flavors of ants, you probably should purchase or make a device called an insect aspirator or "pooter." Search online and you'll see many interesting such devices for sale. For ants, you will also need a good filter so you don't inhale fine dirt. Trust me . . . I know!

Although it's tedious, it's actually a lot of fun to forage ants, and quite rewarding. By doing so you'll discover that while some ants are rather flavorless or unpalatable, some have really awesome lemony and even floral qualities. Don't eat ants raw, though, as some can carry very unhealthy parasites.

My method for collecting and preparing ants is very simple. Armed with my mighty pooter, I wander in the unforgiving wilderness to stalk and find my prized prey. Over time I have learned about the type of habitat, the activities, and the flavors of my local delicacies, which makes foraging them much easier. As I "vacuum" them in the field, I transfer them to a larger jar if necessary and, once I'm back home, I place the jar in the freezer for an hour or so. By the way, some ants are able to climb on the side of glass jars, so don't think foraging them is a boring activity.

After freezing them, because I don't want to eat them raw I have two choices: either boiling or roasting. Often I will boil them in lime or lemon juice with chili powder to accentuate the flavors and let them infuse for a few hours in the refrigerator before serving. When I use them as an ingredient in my beers, I simply crush my frozen ants with my stone grinder, then place them in the boiling herbal solution.

Most of the time I roast them in a pan with the addition of spices. You can add lemons, limes, chili powder, and garlic, but you can also use all kinds of regular or wild aromatics and spices. Brown sugar works great too. The roasting usually takes around 2 to 4 minutes. I use a cast-iron pan and drizzle my ants/spices with a very small amount of extra-virgin olive oil or butter, bring the pan to a medium heat, then stir the contents by moving the pan back and forth.

Once roasted, the ants are used as a condiment, usually sprinkled on food.

These were the tastiest ants I've ever foraged: They fed on aphids' nectar, and the aphids themselves were feeding on mugwort. The flavors were extremely complex—a bit lemony, yet floral and highly aromatic.

Mia foraging waterbugs.

WATER BUGS

A couple of years ago I was foraging watercress in the local forest. As I was picking plants from the stream, I noticed a large amount of water bugs.

I had never eaten water bugs before, but being on the list of edible insects, I had to try them. They are considered something of a delicacy in Thailand, where they are eaten lightly boiled or deep-fried with salt (*maeng da*). Foraging them is easier said than done, though: You *don't* want to forage them by hand, as their bite is reportedly the most painful bite that can be inflicted by any insect. Indeed, their method of catching dinner involves injecting a powerful digestive saliva into their prey, such as small fish, and sucking out the liquefied remains. Imagine your finger instead of a fish, and you can be sure that the "digestive saliva" will cause some real pain. That said, once the excruciating pain subsides, there is usually no need for special medical attention aside from a good cleaning of the wound.

Our method to catch them involved using a simple mesh strainer and scooping them up in the water, then placing them in a jar filled with water. Once home, I cleaned them thoroughly with clean water, then froze them. I made a batter of garlic and chili powder with lime juice and deep-fried them for a couple of minutes.

Eating water bugs is a process in itself. To eat them, go through the following steps:

Procedure

1. Remove the wings.
2. Separate the head from the body, squeeze the juice out, and suck the meat inside the body. Alternatively, you can also munch on the whole thing and spit out the leftovers (the exoskeleton) as we did, but we're not expert water bug foodies—we just didn't know any better at the time.
3. In Thailand, they also munch on the head, but we skipped that part.

On a scale of 1 to 5 in terms of overall experience and taste, I give water bugs a 2, but it's not the insect's or the recipe's fault; it's just our own lack of experience and the fact that I still have to get used to eating such large insects without any cultural bias.

Next time I'll try to make a Thai condiment called *nam prik mang da*, for which my friend David George Gordon has a great recipe in his book *The Eat-A-Bug Cookbook*.

Emerita (Sand Fleas, Sand Crabs, Sea Cicadas, Mole Crabs)

Mole crabs are well known by fishermen, who use them as bait, but they are rarely eaten in North America. The people I've seen foraging them in California are usually immigrants from South America, who told me they used them as a flavoring in soups. One person told me that he fried them, added spices, and ate them as a crunchy little snack.

Of course, I had to try them because they're so abundant. The best time to catch them is in summer or early fall. They're really easy to forage. You can purchase a mole crab rake at stores selling bait, but even by just using your hands you can get plenty of them if you understand their habits and lifestyle.

These little creatures have large feathered antennae that are used to filter plankton and other nutrients from the seawater. You find them living in colonies under the sand; when an incoming wave shows up, they quickly rise to the surface and use their antennae to filter the water and collect their food. If you look closely you can see a slight V-shaped disturbance in the receding wave, indicating a colony. It's easier to find them at low tide and at the edge of the water.

Once you've located a colony, use your hands or a shovel to quickly grab a bunch of sand when the water recedes and place it in a bucket. When your bucket is full, filter the sand through a strainer—you'll be amazed at the quantity of these little guys that you can forage in a very short time. They come in various sizes, ranging from ½ inch (0.65 cm) to over 1½ inches (4 cm).

I transport them home in a container with a few inches of sand and lots of seawater. Once home, I remove the sand, set aside some seawater, and give the little buggers a nice clean, cold shower. I then place them in clean seawater and leave them in the refrigerator overnight; this will clean them a bit more.

Once the crabs are prepared you have a lot of culinary options. For one thing, you can use them fresh to flavor soups; their flavor is a bit of a cross between shrimps and crabs.

I like to steam them with my own wild beers and homemade vinegars, then sprinkle them with some of my wild spice blends, but you can find your own recipes to experiment with. An online search will bring up lots of recipes for cooking crabs—and if it works for regular crabs, it will work with mole crabs. You will just need to adjust the cooking time, due to their small size.

To preserve crabs, I usually steam them and place them in the freezer for later use. I don't try to remove the shells; instead, I munch on them as is, the same way I used to eat shrimps growing up in Belgium. The small ones are better as their shells are softer; the big ones are best used to flavor soups and sauces.

Wood Shrimps

Wood shrimps are not really shrimps, but prepared properly they will just taste like them.

Yes, take a look at the accompanying photo: I'm talking about pill bugs, wood lice, or roly-polys, the cute little bugs many of us liked to play with as kids.

If you didn't know it already, pill bugs are crustaceans and belong to the same family as saltwater shrimps, which explains the flavor. You will find over three thousand species worldwide.

Before you get too excited (as I'm sure you are right now!) and go forage some in your garden, you have to know that not all of them have the same flavors. Some taste great and some are, well . . . not so great. You want the ones with a dark-gray color (*Armadillidium vulgare*) that will actually roll themselves nicely into a ball if you poke or grab them—not all of them do this, but the common pill bug will. You will find them in large numbers in the northern United States and in Europe. They are possibly numerous in other places, too—I'm just not that familiar with wood lice distribution.

I stick to foraging *Armadillidium vulgare*, since they are so abundant here in California that I didn't need to experiment with others. Being a forager, I like my food to be super organic—the best place for me to find pill bugs is the local forest, under rocks and bark. They're usually not my main forage, as I'm mostly interested in plants, but if I find a location where there are a lot of them, I'll take the time to grab a bunch. As a tip, they love humidity, and so in the hot months of Southern California they will be found under rocks in dry streams or near flowing water.

There are a lot of culinary experiments you can do with them, but for my part, I pretty much prepare them like shrimps.

Once they are foraged, I want to make sure they're clean and have a healthy diet for 2 or 3 days. After all, you don't know where your roly-polys were before you picked them up, so who knows what they ate. Their diet in the wild consists of pretty much anything that is decaying, as well as some fresh stuff. This means they could be feeding on scat, perhaps old rotting poison oak leaves, and who knows what else. Most likely they had a healthy diet of yummy decomposing greens, but I never assume anything.

After giving them a clean shower, I place them in a container with a bunch of healthy ingredients, such as fresh grass, fruits, and vegetables, and rocks for them to hide underneath.

After 3 days I pick them up and clean them quickly one more time. I bring water to a boil and add some crab boil spice blend, such as Old Bay Seasoning, to the water. Alternatively you can also make your own spice blend, but I have a fondness for Old Bay.

Your final step is to drop them into the boiling water; it's a humane instant death. Interestingly, unlike shrimps and other crustaceans, they will not turn red as you would expect. They're so little, you don't need to cook them for long, usually 2 to 3 minutes.

Remove them, add a bit more spice to them if you want, and serve as is or with other condiments. Roly-polys in a traditional white sauce with mushrooms and pasta can make a truly gourmet dish. You can substitute roly-polys for shrimps in any dish that calls for small shrimps.

Garden Snails

Did you know that garden snails (*Cornu aspersum*) are not native to California, or even to North America, and that they are edible?

They were apparently imported to our area by a Frenchman during the Gold Rush as a source of food, and I can see how he might have thought he would strike it rich. In French cuisine, garden snails are known as *petit gris* and considered a gourmet food. An adult garden snail is usually three-fourths the size of the large escargots de Bourgogne, which are usually the ones you eat in restaurants, but they are nevertheless excellent eating once prepared properly.

Unfortunately for our poor Frenchman, this highly regional delicacy wasn't appreciated by the gold miners or local residents, and so the little beasts got released, and now they feed happily on your garden vegetables.

To this day they're still not considered a delicacy—they're considered a pest. It's really too bad that more people don't appreciate them as an excellent food source, but it's okay with me. In fact, I often get requests to remove snails from someone's garden, which makes my foraging very easy.

Preparing and cooking snails properly is extremely important. Wild or garden snails can carry bacteria or parasites that can make you sick or even kill you. One parasite (*Angiostrongyliasis* spp.) is known to cause meningitis if the snail is ingested raw or improperly cooked.

Don't let this scare you, though; the same principle of cooking food properly to kill bacteria or parasites and avoid their ingestion applies to many wild and non-wild ingredients, including such domesticated foods as pork.

HOW TO PREPARE AND COOK SNAILS

Before you forage your local delicacies, you should make them a nice cozy home. Because your snails are "wild" you don't really know what they've been eating. I'm sure snails are smart, but who knows if they ingested some plants that could be toxic to humans. I've never seen them nibbling on poison hemlock or mushrooms, but I don't assume anything.

So you need to provide them with a nice home, make some water available, and feed them proper food for a while. Because I forage snails every year, I've put together a cage with window screen mesh, but I've seen people use a cheap birdcage or even a mousetrap to

keep their snails. It all depends on the quantity of snails you forage. If you intend to collect a lot, you may need to build a cage yourself. You want to build it so that it will be well aerated. Don't store your snails in jars or make a cardboard cage; the snails may eat some of the cardboard, which can contain toxic chemicals.

In the cage I place a small container with water and a flat plate with cornmeal or oatmeal. Some people use fresh green ingredients (celery, salad greens, and so forth) and aromatic herbs such as basil or parsley. Both methods work. I like to use oatmeal; it's easy to see when the snails have cleaned their system as their fecal excretion turns white instead of the usual dark green. Keep the cage clean; I remove the snails and clean the cage every couple of days.

After 7 to 10 days, I remove the food and water and let the snails fast for 48 hours.

Once they have fasted, you're ready for the next step. In Belgium, we used to put the snails in a cold brine solution so they would "purge" themselves and eventually die, but I found the method a bit inhumane and it didn't make a difference in terms of flavors. Instead, I opt for throwing them (without purging) in boiling salted water for 2 to 3 minutes.

Transfer the snails to cold water. Using a toothpick, large needle, or small fork, remove the snails from their shells. I like to remove some of the guts, but most people don't do this.

You may need to rinse them if you have bits of shells here and there.

The final step is to cook them for around 30 minutes. It's an important step: You need to cook them long enough to make sure potential parasites that can make you really sick can't survive. Some people cook them even longer, up to an hour.

This is also the step where you imbue your delicious snails with flavors. I like to simmer them in white wine with a bit of minced garlic and aromatics (chervil, parsley, thyme, salt, and pepper) and from there I can freeze them for future use. If I intend to eat them right away after cooking, I strain them and do a final sauté in butter, garlic, parsley, and lemons for a few minutes.

An alternative method after the initial boiling is to place them back in the shells with a compound butter composed of minced garlic, parsley, salt, and pepper. Preheat the oven at 350°F (177°C), arrange the shells upright on a tray, and roast for 10 minutes.

Wild Tapas

I've never thought of myself as a chef or a cook. I have no formal culinary training aside from having taken the Master Food Preserver program a few years ago and attending native cooking classes. To be honest, I would not even know how to make a simple mayonnaise without looking for the recipe first. I've been so deep into foraging and creating with wild ingredients for so many years that it's pretty much the only type of cuisine I'm proficient with.

That said, I have learned a lot from the various extremely skilled chefs I work with, the classes I have taken on native cooking, and, of course, my soul mate, Mia Wasilevich, who is probably the most talented chef I know. Without her input and her constant creativity with wild and commercial ingredients, this book would not be what it is. Mia inspires me to continuously research new edible plants, find ways to create unusual tasty preserves, and investigate possible culinary uses.

In some odd ways, I think that my lack of culinary background is probably an asset. I'm neither stuck within nor trying to use a specific type of cuisine—such as French, Italian, or any other—with my wild ingredients. Not being able to rely much on past training and experience, my only option is to let the ingredients and their flavors talk to me. I think that's what allowed me to think outside the box so often when I'm working with wild edibles.

Foraging has become trendy in the last few years. In order to maintain a fresh approach with my terroir, I have deliberately avoided reading many of the recent culinary books related to foraging or the uses of wild plants from extremely talented chefs and restaurants. The only exception may be the book *Fäviken* by chef Magnus Nilsson, because his approach and environment are so unique. They're not even remotely duplicable in Southern California, but his creativity is inspirational.

If I had to put a name to what I do, I could call it wild culinary alchemy. *Alchemy* is defined as "a seemingly magical process of transformation, creation, or combination"—a nice description of my activities. There is definitely something magical about exploring the wilderness—researching, foraging, and finding ways to use nature's bounty.

Wild food is gourmet food. Not only are the flavors truly unique, but foraging some ingredients such as pine sap, insects, lerp sugar, wild seeds, and many others is extremely time-intensive. Chefs simply don't have the necessary time to do it, and the cost to pay someone else to search and

Roasted oysters with sweet white clover,
smoked with rabbit tobacco.

provide it for them is too prohibitive. It's also not very sustainable for the usual large volume needed to serve in restaurants.

To study flavor combinations, experiment with new preserves or ingredients, and find a way to share them with others, I began creating wild food tapas. *Tapas* are little snacks used in Spanish cuisine to feature specific ingredients and flavors. The approach is perfect for what I do and also for many of the dishes Mia creates. Rare, unusual, or extremely time-intensive foodstuffs can be nicely presented and experienced in small amounts. You're able to serve quite a few people and get instant feedback from the guests. Serving tapas also allows me to be more adventurous and go more deeply into wild flavors. I sometimes tell people to keep an open mind, that they're about to encounter some unusual textures or flavors, and it's possible that they may dislike some of them. This type of food is better enjoyed with a context, and I always explain the ingredients, where they come from, and how they were prepared. This approach is well received by the guests—they expect that their experience will not be just like eating regular food. Instead they're prepared for a culinary adventure into the true flavors of our terroir.

Summer salad: cactus pear vinaigrette, sweet clover, watercress, mustard, and sprouted palo verde beans.

Black-sage-infused yogurt, foraged currant berries, preserved unripe figs, ants, lerp sugar, fennel, and fermented blueberry juice.

Roasted local mackerel, pickled wild seeds with foraged olives.

Fall salad: watercress, willow herb, black nightshade berries, monkey flowers, and pickled quail eggs in vinegar and black nightshade juice.

Unripe figs in syrup, lerp sugar, goat cheese curdled with fig sap, water mint, and mugwort beer syrup.

Roasted baby squids and boiled wild greens with wild spices.

Rabbit cooked in mugwort beer, honey, and forest mix (grass, leaves, and various aromatic plants).

Cricket croquette with seasonal wild greens and forest grass vinaigrette.

Preserved sardines in mountain vinegar, pickled wild seeds, wild currant capers, and white fir sauerkraut.

Quail au vin: quail cooked in elderberry wine, foraged mushrooms, wild hyacinth bulbs, elderberries, wild onions, local mustard seeds, chervil, garlic, and carrots.

Ants, fennel, pickled yucca shoot, wild radish pods, mustard flowers, and unripe elderberry capers.

Steamed sea bass with sweet white clover and homemade sea salt, served with wild radish flowers and fermented unripe elderberry capers in wild food kimchi broth.

Oyster mushrooms, roasted dandelion, and wild radish sprouts.

Broiled forest snails with sweet clover and garlic compound butter, smoked with pearly everlasting.

I'm one of the luckiest foragers on this earth as I get to live with a very talented chef. My partner, Mia Wasilevich, is currently a private chef who caters for private parties, artfully merging cultivated and wild foods and flavors. We met serendipitously over six years ago, and ever since then our life has been centered on what we love the most: cooking and food.

While my approach is to stick as much as possible to what I'm able to forage and wild ingredients, over the years Mia has developed a very unique cooking style using foraged and commercial organic food. She has an incredible ability to merge the unique tastes of the wilderness, produce from local artisan growers or the farmer's market, and exotic ingredients and spices.

Having traveled and experienced the food of many countries, she also has the skills to blend various flavors and cooking styles from pretty much any part of the world. It's a very useful skill when you're discovering new local edibles, as some may work better with Asian spices or French cooking techniques.

A hundred chefs could visit a farmer's market and pick up the edibles and spices they wanted, and each one would come up with different dishes based on their style of cooking or background. What I like about Mia's approach is that she is not "stuck" in specific types of ethnic cuisine, such as Thai, French, or Italian, but will use the appropriate style and method of cooking based on the ingredients she's working with and their flavors. Unlike some of the chefs who've

attended my classes, it's what makes her style unique. It's a very different approach than my own, which tends to stick as much as possible to wild food and extremely simple, often primitive, cooking techniques. Her style of cooking is completely free of barriers, wildly creative, and loaded with flavors that I've not found anywhere else.

In the quest for the true flavors of Southern California, her interpretation and approach are very much in touch with what our modern state is: multi-ethnic, multicultural, and fusion-based.

Needless to say, living and working alongside Mia on a daily basis has brought my foraging and quest for local ingredients to a new level. Not only do I eat a lot of her excellent food, but I also learn a lot about cooking methods from various countries, how to blend unusual flavors, and plating techniques. Her educated input is also extremely valuable when I'm creating my wild preserves, from beers and wines to jams and pickles. In many ways, she is my inspiration and mentor.

We're very much a dream team: I love foraging and researching new plants and flavors as well as creating interesting preserves and simple dishes with wild food. Through her culinary experience and her own knowledge of wild edibles, Mia is able to take those ingredients and perform her culinary magic. She's a talented food stylist and photographer as well, so her dishes are always a visual delight.

Mia is currently working on her own book, but I asked her to share a few recipes featuring wild edibles and preserves. Enjoy!

CACTUS PAD AND LIME MINT PALETAS WITH BAY-INFUSED TEQUILA FILM, LERP SUGAR, AND AUSTRALIAN BUSHBERRIES

One of the beautiful things about where we live is the variety of ingredients we can get when the weather is on our side. However, what brings us the most joy is finding creativity and inspiration when the weather isn't in our favor. Cactus is one of those ingredients that can be challenging, yet extremely versatile. It's available during most of the year and, with a little preparation and know-how, it's a rewarding wild food to play with.

A *paleta* is a sort of Latin American ice pop usually made with fruits and fresh juices. This dish is a great accompaniment to a hot day. It's refreshing, easy to make, and can be complemented by so many different flavors. With a few flourishes and your imagination, you can use this basic recipe and make it your own. I like to sprinkle on lerp sugar and add a few Australian bushberries or other berries when serving.

This recipe calls for raw, washed organic sugar. Raw, washed sugar is basically made with the juice of the sugarcane with no additives. You can use regular caster or confectioners' sugar if that's what you have on hand. Agar agar is a natural, seaweed-based thickening agent sold in most health food stores.

The honey or rice bran syrup and agar prevent the paletas from crystallizing and melting too quickly and give an unctuous, slightly softer mouthfeel, but aren't necessary if you prefer an icier pop. Cooling the mixture completely in the fridge before freezing is also key.

If you are using wood or bamboo sticks or even branches (we've used cleaned and soaked mulefat or oak sticks) in your mold, soak them in water for at least 5 minutes first. This will prevent them from releasing from the paleta in the mold.

Photo courtesy of Mia Wasilevich.

Ingredients

3 cups (709 ml by volume) cactus pads, cleaned and roughly chopped (remove any tough skin, but peeling is not necessary)

10 tablespoons (148 ml) water, divided

A few sprigs of fresh mint leaves

Zest and juice of 4 limes

¼ small jalapeño pepper, seeded (optional)

¼ cup (56 g) raw, washed organic sugar (see note)

1 tablespoon (15 ml) honey, brown rice syrup, or corn syrup (to prevent crystallization)

1 tablespoon (9.25 g) gelatin powder or 1 teaspoon (3 g) agar agar powder (see note) or Vegan Jel (to prevent rapid melting, but you may omit)

A pinch of salt

A small amount of lerp sugar and a few Australian bushberries or other berries for plating (optional)

Procedure

1. In a high-speed food processor, blend the chopped cactus pads with 2 tablespoons (30 ml) of the water, plus the mint, lime juice and zest, and jalapeño, until smooth. Reserve in the food processor. Add a bit more water if you need to loosen the mixture.

2. In a small saucepan, combine the remaining ½ cup (118 ml) water with the sugar and honey or rice or corn syrup; dissolve over medium-high heat. Once dissolved, rapidly whisk in the gelatin, agar agar, or Vegan Jel until dissolved and bring to a boil, then turn off the burner and remove from the heat. Whisk for a few minutes to cool the mixture.

3. Pour the warm mixture into a food processor with the reserved cactus pad mixture and a pinch of salt and blend until very smooth. Pour immediately into molds and chill in the refrigerator for at least an hour before freezing to prevent crystallization.

Photo courtesy of Mia Wasilevich.

Tequila Film

Ingredients

¾ cup (177 ml) bay-infused tequila (or any other flavored liquid of choice)

2 grams agar agar powder

Preparation

1. In a small saucepan, bring the alcohol and agar agar to a boil over medium-high heat, whisking rapidly. Boil for 1 minute. Once the agar agar has dissolved—and before it thickens—pour the alcohol mixture over a large flat plate or platter and swirl the plate gently to create an even, thin layer.

2. Refrigerate for 15 minutes, then cut the film on the plate with a sharp knife and gently lift the film pieces off. Place on top of your paleta and enjoy with a squeeze of lime and some good flake salt or habanero salt (see Salts with Wild Herbs on page 173).

Cactus-n-grits by chef Mia Wasilevich.
Photo courtesy of Mia Wasilevich.

CACTUS-N-GRITS

Another new classic in our home is Cactus-n-Grits. The addition of a fresh egg from your backyard would be perfect along with some smoky pork. You can use speck, which is a smoked pork belly, but bacon or prosciutto would go just as well. You can enjoy the cactus two ways—poached and fried. With its citrusy flavor the cooked cactus resembles bell pepper. It pairs well with smoky and bright flavors.

The grits, a type of hominy porridge, are such a nice, comforting, and creamy base for this dish. We used coarse-cut grits here, but you could also use cornmeal mush or polenta.

Ingredients

Cactus flower buds

Stock, broth, water

Onion

Garlic

Cilantro

Spices

Citric acid (optional)

Clarified butter or butter/oil combination

Cactus pads

1 cup (170 g) cornmeal

1 cup (136 g) all-purpose flour

1 egg, beaten with 2 tablespoons
(36 ml) water

Salt (optional)

Pepper (optional)

Chili powder (optional)

Preparation for Cactus Flower Buds

1. After you prepare and dehydrate your cactus flower buds (see page 104), simmer them in a stock or broth or even water with the addition of onion, garlic, and cilantro. I simmer them in chicken stock, onion, garlic, peppercorns, and Mexican oregano for about 25 to 30 minutes. I add a little bit of citric acid (you could use lemon) so that they don't discolor and remain green, but it's not necessary.

2. Drain and cool them, then hard-sear in clarified butter or butter mixed with a little oil.

Preparation for Cactus Pads

1. Clean and trim the cactus pads and run a sharp knife parallel to the pad to remove bumps where the glochids once were. You should have a smooth pad. You'll notice that the pad itself splits in two (top and bottom layer). This is great for stuffing them like a bell pepper, and for baking as well. Split them and then stamp out circles using a pastry or cookie cutter to make rounds or "chips"—or you can just rough-cut with a knife.

2. Blanch in acidulated water (add a little citric acid, lemon, or vinegar to your water) for a few minutes to remove some of the mucilaginous properties, then pat dry and let cool.

3. Prepare your dredge with cornmeal in one bowl, all-purpose flour in another bowl, and a beaten egg mixed with 2 tablespoons of water in a third bowl. Season each bowl with a little salt, pepper, and chili powder, if desired. Dust the cactus pad rounds in the flour first, then egg wash, then cornmeal. Fry at 350°F (177°C) until browned. Salt slightly immediately after frying and store on kitchen paper or paper bags to drain and cool slightly, then serve.

SAVORY "PUMPKIN" PIE WITH CANDIED, SPICED BUCKWHEAT FLOWERS AND RUM RAISIN SAUCE

Buckwheat flowers are another one of those ingredients that beg for some creativity and that, like cactus, can be quite abundant despite the weather conditions. Touted as a "survival food," buckwheat is fibrous, and collecting the minuscule buckwheat berries inside is virtually impossible. However, using the whole flower once it's been dried and processed (see California Buckwheat on page 350), can yield some interesting textures, and the dried flowers can be crisped and flavored in many different variations.

Ingredients

California buckwheat flowers, dried and processed

Water

2 tablespoons (28 g) plus 1 teaspoon (5 g) butter

Cinnamon

Nutmeg

Allspice

Pepper

Salt

1 teaspoon (4 g) brown sugar

4–5 cups (approximately 450 g) dried fruit soaked in rum

1 cup (225 g) sugar

4 tablespoons (60 g) butter

Photo courtesy of Mia Wasilevich.

Preparation

1. Pick the California buckwheat flowers and remove any stems. Soak the flowers to dislodge any debris. (They collect a lot of dust in the wild.) Once soaked, drained, and rinsed again, place them in a pot of boiling water for 5 minutes, then drain.
2. Dehydrate the flowers on low for at least 12 hours, or at the lowest setting in your oven with the oven door slightly ajar. You can prepare a large quantity this way and then use them for piecrusts or as part of your batter coating for fried foods to add a nutty and crispy texture.
3. Melt 2 tablespoons (28 gr) of the butter in a cast-iron skillet, then add ¼ cup (60 ml by volume) of the processed and dried buckwheat flowers, along with a pinch of cinnamon, nutmeg, allspice, pepper, and salt. Using a wooden spoon, make sure to coat the buckwheat flowers thoroughly and stir frequently to prevent burning. The buckwheat flowers will darken after about 3 to 4 minutes. Follow with 1 more teaspoon (5 g) of the butter and 1 teaspoon (4 g) of brown sugar and combine with the flowers, stirring rapidly. The buckwheat flowers will basically candy in the butter-and-sugar mixture after another minute.
4. Remove from the pan immediately and place on kitchen paper until cool. The heat toasts the buckwheat and allows the fibrous flowers to "pop" and become lighter in texture.
5. We used a rum raisin sauce with this dish, but you can use foraged dried currants if you have them, and we've even used dried foraged elderberries with port instead of rum. This sauce consists of 4 to 5 cups (approximately 450 g) of dried fruit soaked in rum and then drained (save the rum to flavor other dishes or drinks), with 1 cup (225 g) of sugar and 4 tablespoons (60 g) of butter. In a pan, add a ratio of 2 parts sugar to 1 part water and cook over medium-high heat until it forms a caramel. Off the heat, add your dried fruit and whisk in the butter. Use your judgment for sweetness—not sweet enough for you? add more sugar—and consistency (add more butter). Simple. There's no hard-and-fast recipe for this.

Feasting:
A Friends-and-Family Affair

Every year we put an event together featuring the bounty local nature is giving us, a true taste of what Southern California can offer in its pure, wild, and unaltered state, from the mountains to the desert. It's also an occasion to meet with friends and some of our online fans. Usually around 30 to 40 people attend this private dinner, and we are blessed with a large number of talented volunteers who help us in the kitchen, sometimes as many as 12 people.

The work to create this dinner starts many weeks in advance, but you could say that it takes a whole year if you take into account the preserves we use. Two months before the dinner I will forage the ingredients to make some of the drinks, such as the white sage cider or the forest beer. We have several meetings to figure out what we will have to play with in terms of fresh wild edibles and the preserves in our pantry, so that a menu can be put together.

Being a fantastic organizer and talented chef, Mia creates the menu. Figuring out the various dishes and recipes is not a simple task; in a typical dinner, I estimate that we use over 70 wild ingredients that could not be found or purchased anywhere—at least in the usual food channels. Even the salt we use is foraged from pristine seawater. A simple spice blend can incorporate over 10 local aromatic plants. We also like to use interesting local exotic foods, such as ants and other various edible insects. For those attending, it is truly a unique wild culinary experience.

I usually create a couple of dishes, but I'm much better at foraging and creating preserves than cooking. This is Mia's time to shine and perform her incredible culinary magic. Once a menu has been set, Mia will test each recipe, determining the amount of work that's needed to prep all the ingredients and how to plate them. Based on that information, I'll know what to forage and when. The making of some ingredients, such as duck prosciutto infused in chaparral sages (see page 162), needs to be timed precisely. The initial menu is not set in stone, because we deal with highly seasonal products and Mother Nature can throw us a few curveballs, as was the case in 2014 when some forages were unavailable due to the terrible drought that year.

The week before the event is when the most intense work happens. I have a precise list of ingredients I have to forage on a daily basis. Some of them, such as fresh white fir or juniper berries, may require a trip to the mountains or the local desert. Mia is pretty much working 18 hours a day in the kitchen prepping the food with volunteers until the final day. For my part, the 3 days prior to the event can be quite brutal, with countless hours of hiking and foraging fresh edible plants in various locations.

On the final 2 days, we pretty much run on pure adrenaline. Mia assign tasks to the kitchen staff, organizes the kitchen and pantry as well as the timing for each dish, and, if she's lucky, manages to get a few hours of sleep. Without the help of our wonderful volunteers, talented home cooks, and chef friends, we could never make this kind of culinary experience possible.

The dinner itself is always memorable. It usually comprises 10 or so courses, and Mia always adds some interesting snacks on the side. My greatest pleasure is watching people discover those incredible new flavors and get a new understanding of what wild food really is . . . gourmet food. For some people it is truly an emotional revelation, and at times we've seen people with tears in their eyes as they taste some of the dishes.

Our last dinner was hosted at the fabulous Zane Grey Estate in Altadena, owned by our friends Steve Rudicel and Gloria Putnam, who also did a fantastic wine pairing with some of the dishes, organized the service, and provided some amazing artisanal products from their goat farm.

Wild Food Lab Dinner Series #2

MENU

Duck prosciutto infused in chaparral sages
Seasonal wild food salad

———

Green lamb's quarter seed canederli, wild greens sauce

———

Raw goat milk and roasted garlic pudding with fried yucca blossoms
Wild seeds mustard

———

Acorn burger, charcoal bun, elderberry ketchup, wild spicy
black mustard, glass potato chips, and juniper pickled onions

———

Quail confit with elderflower beurre blanc

———

Roasted cactus flower buds with speck and charred corn

———

Local trout cooked in clay with sweet clover,
white fir, and rabbit tobacco

———

Forest floor goat stew

———

Cactus pad paletas, lime and habanero salt

———

Elderberry entrement with California buckwheat,
flower crust, lemon ants, and wild currants

DRINKS

Local mountain infusion
(white fir, California juniper berries,
wild mints, manzanita and
toyon berries, yerba santa,
pearly everlasting)

———

Wild sodas
(California wild rose hips,
elderflower)

———

White sage cider

———

Forest beer
(mugwort, elderberries,
and forest ingredients)

———

Local black walnut nocino and
white fir aged in our own oak barrel

———

Special wine pairing by our hosts,
Gloria Putnam and Steve Rudicel

Photo courtesy of Seth Joel.

Cleaning and prepping the wild ingredients.

Our friend Sue helping us in the kitchen.

Primitive crackers with wild seeds, pickled black walnuts, foraged olives, seasonal wild edibles, and raw goat cheese. *Photo courtesy of Seth Joel.*

Artisanal products and foraged plants.

Acorn burger, charcoal-grilled bun, elderberry ketchup, wild spicy black mustard, glass potato chips, and juniper pickled onions.

My daughter Felicia helping us plating. She also foraged most of the table decorations.

Raw goat milk and roasted garlic pudding with fried yucca blossoms. Wild seeds mustard.

Mia plating the acorn burgers.

Wild brews—white sage cider is being served. *Photo courtesy of Seth Joel.*

The table is set and decorated with material foraged from the local forest by my daughter. *Photo courtesy of Seth Joel.*

The chef doing her magic plating. *Photo courtesy of Seth Joel.*

Forest floor goat stew.

Buckwheat flower and ants cookies.

Trout cooked in clay with wild aromatics.

Quail confit with elderflower beurre blanc.

Three hours and 10 courses later—the end of the day.
Everyone is delighted, and now it's time to share wild stories.
Photo courtesy of Seth Joel.

APPENDIX

Some Winter Forage

Acorns (Oak family—Fagaceae).

Black mustard (*Brassica negra*).

Burr-chervil (*Anthriscus caucalis*).

Cleavers (*Galium aparine*).

Curly dock (*Rumex crispus*).

Dandelion (*Taraxacum* spp.).

Horehound (*Marrubium vulgare*).

Lamb's quarters (*Chenopodium album*).

London rocket (*Sisymbrium irio*).

Mallow (*Malva* spp.).

Milk thistle (*Silybum marianum*).

Spearmint (*Mentha spicata*).

California mugwort (*Artemisia douglasiana*).

Stinging nettles (*Urtica dioica*).

Broadleaf plantain (*Plantago major*).

Wild celery (*Apium graveolens*).

Mediterranean mustard (*Hirschfeldia incana*).

Field mustard (*Brassica rapa*).

Sow thistle (*Sonchus* spp.).

Toyon berries (*Heteromeles arbutifolia*).

Watercress (*Nasturtium officinale*).

White sage (*Salvia apiana*).

White fir (*Abies concolor*).

Canaigre, or wild rhubarb (*Rumex hymenosepalus*).

Inky cap mushrooms (*Coprinus comatus*).

Miner's lettuce (*Claytonia perfoliata*).

Hairy bittercress (*Cardamine hirsuta*).

Pine sap.

Cactus pads—nopales, prickly pear, cactus pear (*Opuntia* spp.).

Split gill mushrooms (*Schizophyllum commune*).

Pine nuts.

Willow herb (*Epilobium ciliatum*).

The New Wildcrafted Cuisine

Some Spring Forage

Giant reed (*Arundo donax*)—leaves used as wrap.

Ash keys (*Fraxinus* spp.).

Thistles (*Sonchus* spp.).

Blue dick (*Dichelostemma pulchellum*).

Little bittercress (*Cardamine oligosperma*).

Prickly pear cactus buds (*Opuntia* spp.).

California sagebrush (*Artemisia californica*).

Cattail (*Typha* spp.).

Pineapple weed (*Matricaria discoidea*).

Unripe currant berries (*Ribes* spp.).

Elderflowers (*Sambucus mexicana*).

Unripe elderberries (*Sambucus mexicana*).

Wild fennel (*Foeniculum vulgare*).

Filaree (*Erodium* spp.).

Nasturtium (*Tropaeolum* spp.).

Purslane (*Portulaca oleracea*).

Soaproot (*Chlorogalum pomeridianum*).

Garden snails (*Cornu aspersum*).

Unripe figs (*Ficus carica*).

Unripe black walnuts (*Juglans nigra*).

Wild radish (*Raphanus raphanistrum*).

Yerba santa (*Eriodictyon californicum*).

Cholla cactus flower buds (*Cylindropuntia acanthocarpa*).

Some Summer Forage

Blackberries (*Rubus fruticosus*).

Cactus pears (*Opuntia littoralis*).

Wild cherries (*Prunus ilicifolia*).

Wild currants (*Ribes* spp.).

Coffee berries (*Frangula californica*).

Mexican elderberries (*Sambucus mexicana*).

Wild fennel flowers (*Foeniculum vulgare*).

Gooseberries (*Ribes speciosum*).

Lemonade berries (*Rhus integrifolia*).

Mexican palo verde beans (*Parkinsonia aculeata*).

Passionfruit (*Passiflora caerulea*).

Purslane (*Portulaca oleracea*).

Redberry buckthorn (*Rhamnus crocea*).

Figs (*Ficus carica*).

Ripe black walnuts (*Juglans nigra*).

Yucca flowers and buds (*Hesperoyucca whipplei*).

Some Fall Forage

Olives (Oleaceae).

Oyster mushrooms (*Pleurotus ostreatus*).

Chickweed (*Stellaria media*).

Pine (*Pinus* spp.).

Wood sorrel (*Oxalis* spp.).

Water speedwell (*Veronica anagallis-aquatica*).

Turkey tail mushrooms (*Trametes versicolor*).

Grasses (Poaceae).

ACKNOWLEDGMENTS

This book would never have been possible without the knowledge and contributions of many people and friends from whom I learned so much over the years.

Wild Food

I learned a lot about local wild edibles from many gifted teachers in Southern California. Over the years I've probably attended over 400 classes and workshops given by various wild food experts, botanists, survivalists, native people, and herbalists. My friend, author, and wild food expert Christopher Nyerges was a major influence in my education. I probably attended over 200 of his classes and learned priceless information about our local flora.

Many other wonderful teachers also contributed to my education. I would like to thank James Robertson, Alan Halcon, Gary Gonzales, Paul Campbell, Dude McLean, and Timothy Snider.

The online world is also a source of wonderful teachers and friends who are a constant source of knowledge and inspiration. Thank you Marie Viljoen, Wendy Petty, Leda Meredith, Maury Grimm, Green Dean, Hank Shaw, Bibi Snelderwaard, John Slattery, Julie James, Rebecca McTrouble, Ken Albala, David George Gordon, Dave Gracer, and countless others.

Cooking and Culinary Art

I would like to thank the following individuals for sharing their knowledge of native food and cuisine: Barbara Drake, Abe Sanchez, Deborah Small, and Craig Tee.

Foraging for and working with extremely talented chefs has helped me in countless ways, from being motivated to research more and creating unique ingredients and preserves to observing and learning from them through their creative uses of local wild edibles and plating. Each one was an inspiration. I would like to thank the following chefs: Ludo Lefebvre (Trois Mec restaurant), Josiah Citrin and Ken Takayama (Melisse restaurant), Sergio Perera, Ari Taymor (Alma restaurant), Michael Voltaggio (Ink restaurant), and Chris Jacobson (Girasol restaurant).

Thank you Ernest Miller for teaching the Master Food Preserver program and food safety in Los Angeles—your passionate teaching was priceless.

This book would have never happened without the contribution and culinary artistry of the incredibly talented wild food chef Mia Wasilevich, my partner in life and culinary arts. Thank you for being a constant source of inspiration and putting up with me.

Many other talented friends and artists have contributed to this book and my life. Thank you Melissa Brown Bidermann for helping me with your incredible artistic and pottery skills and Seth Joel for the superb photos.

To my kids, I love you tremendously and hope we can spend more time together now that this book is done! Thank you both for being in my life.

Photo courtesy of Seth Joel.

DISCLAIMER AND NOTES

Dealing with wild food requires experience and a good understanding of the plants used in recipes. Always exercise caution when foraging: Only use plants that you can positively identify with complete certainty. This book is not meant to be used for plant identification; from experience it is best if you find a local expert to teach you the local plants. Books on plant identification and online groups are also a good resource for you to learn foraging.

While I have shared the wild ingredients and preserves I've created with countless people with no ill effects, there is always the possibility that some people may experience an allergic reaction to a new food source. Always exercise caution and make sure you research each plant properly before consumption. Starting with a small amount first is always good advice.

Some wild edibles such as curly dock, wild rhubarb, lamb's quarters, and others can have higher levels of oxalic acid than similar plants found in local stores; thus, voluminous and/or extended consumption of these plants may have adverse health effects on some individuals. The same principle is true with various wild plants. For example chickweed (like celery) has a rather high amount of nitrates. I view wild food as gourmet food and advocate a varied diet.

Exercise caution if you are pregnant, elderly, or have an impaired immune system. It is your responsibility to study and know the plants and their potential effects, thus the strong advice to learn from a local expert. For example, yarrow and mugwort are not recommended for consumption if you are pregnant.

Be aware that, while I have done my very best to follow food-safety protocols based on my training and experience, some recipes in this book are more traditional and some are experimental. Thus I would strongly recommend everyone to get well educated on food preservation techniques and use your own judgment before attempting some of my recipes, or even any recipes that have not been tested in a lab. The National Center for Home Food Preservation (http://nchfp.uga.edu) is a good resource for learning about food safety, preservation techniques, and tested recipes. Unfortunately there are no "tested" recipes for wild food, hence the need to really understand food-safety and preservation techniques.

As a general rule, I don't serve wild food to young children unless the foods are deemed and proven extremely safe—for example, nettle soup or wild currant or blueberry juice.

With many traditional preservation methods such as fermentation, hygiene is extremely important. Keep your environment and equipment very clean at all times. Also, it's a good idea to get well educated on the signs of food spoiling, such as smell, mold, bubbles, cloudiness, scum, change in color, and so forth.

As a final note, when dealing with wild plants there is no such thing as enough research. If you find a new potential culinary plant or ingredient, take the time to research it thoroughly, not just from a culinary perspective but also from the perspective of traditional medicine (herbalism) and modern medicine. Also check for potential allergies. Just because a plant was used in recipes three hundred years ago doesn't mean it is now considered safe. Modern testing has sometimes proven that plants used in the old days are in fact not too healthy for you. Some plants can also be medicinal or safely used as an aromatic or spice in small quantities but are toxic in larger amounts. This is true of wild plants, but is also the case for some commercial ingredients that can be bought at local stores. Nutmeg is a good example.

Within all these parameters, there is a tremendous amount of culinary fun and experimentation awaiting you.

Photo courtesy of Seth Joel.

RESOURCES

Books about plant identification in the United States

This list includes a few books I'm familiar with, but it is very incomplete. A simple online search will give you titles of plant identification books that you can use to learn about your local wild edible plants.

SOUTHWEST

Foraging California: Finding, Identifying, and Preparing Edible Wild Foods in California by Christopher Nyerges (Falcon Guides, 2014).

The Forager's Harvest: A Guide to Identifying, Harvesting, and Preparing Wild Edible Plants by Samuel Thayer (Forager's Harvest Press, 2006).

California Foraging: 120 Wild and Flavorful Edibles from Evergreen Huckleberries to Wild Ginger by Judith Lowry (Timber Press, 2014).

Nuts and Berries of California: Tips and Recipes for Gatherers (Nuts and Berries Series) by Christopher Nyerges (Falcon Guides, 2015).

NORTHEAST

Northeast Foraging: 120 Wild and Flavorful Edibles from Beach Plums to Wineberries by Leda Meredith (Timber Press, 2014).

Edible Wild Plants: A North American Field Guide to Over 200 Natural Foods by Thomas Elias and Peter Dykeman (Sterling, 2009).

SOUTHEAST

Southeast Foraging: 120 Wild and Flavorful Edibles from Angelica to Wild Plums by Chris Bennett (Timber Press, 2015).

NORTHWEST

Pacific Northwest Foraging: 120 Wild and Flavorful Edibles from Alaska Blueberries to Wild Hazelnuts by Douglas Deur (Timber Press, 2014).

Foraging the Mountain West: Gourmet Edible Plants, Mushrooms, and Meat by Thomas J. Elpel and Kris Reed (Hops Press, 2014).

CENTRAL

A Field Guide to Edible Wild Plants: Eastern and Central North America (Peterson Field Guides) by Lee Allen Peterson and Roger Tory Peterson (Houghton Mifflin Harcourt, 1999).

Food preservation

Preserving Food Without Freezing or Canning: Traditional Techniques Using Salt, Oil, Sugar, Alcohol, Vinegar, Drying, Cold Storage, and Lactic Fermentation by The Gardeners and Farmers of Centre Terre Vivante (Chelsea Green Publishing, 2007).

Pickled, Potted, and Canned: How the Art and Science of Food Preserving Changed the World by Sue Shephard (Simon and Schuster, 2000).

So Easy to Preserve by Cooperative Extension Service, the University of Georgia (1988).

Mouneh: Preserving Foods for the Lebanese Pantry by Barbara Abdeni Massaad.

Wild Fermentation: The Flavor, Nutrition, and Craft of Live-Culture Foods by Sandor Ellix Katz (Chelsea Green Publishing, 2003).

The Art of Fermentation: An In-Depth Exploration of Essential Concepts and Processes from Around the World by Sandor Ellix Katz (Chelsea Green Publishing, 2012).

Primitive beers and wines

Sacred and Herbal Healing Beers: The Secrets of Ancient Fermentation by Stephen Harrod Buhner (Brewers Publications, 1998).

Brew Your Medicine: How to Use Basic Kitchen Equipment to Brew Custom Herbal Beers by Kristi Shapla (CreateSpace Independent Publishing Platform, 2012).

The Homebrewer's Garden: How to Easily Grow, Prepare, and Use Your Own Hops, Malts, Brewing Herbs by Dennis Fisher and Joe Fisher (Storey Publishing, 1998).

Wild Fermentation: A Do-It-Yourself Guide to Cultural Manipulation by Sandor Ellix Katz (Microcosm Publishing, 2002).

Herbalism

The Herbal Medicine-Maker's Handbook: A Home Manual by James Green (Crossing Press, 2000).

A Modern Herbal, volumes I and II, by Margaret Grieve (Dover Publications, 1971).

The Herbal Handbook: A User's Guide to Medical Herbalism by David Hoffman (Healing Arts Press, 1998).

Native food and ethnobotany

Chumash Ethnobotany: Plant Knowledge Among the Chumash People of Southern California by Jan Timbrook (Heyday, 2007).

Temalpakh: Cahuilla Indian Knowledge and Usage of Plants by Lowell John Bean and Katherine Silva Saubel (Malki Museum Press, 1972).

Native American Ethnobotany by Daniel E. Moerman (Timber Press, 1998).

Culinary arts

Fäviken by Magnus Nilsson (Phaidon Press, 2012).

Noma: Time and Place in Nordic Cuisine by René Redzepi (Phaidon Press, 2010)

Hunt, Gather, Cook: Finding the Forgotten Feast by Hank Shaw (Rodale Books, 2012).

The Eat-a-Bug Cookbook, Revised: 40 Ways to Cook Crickets, Grasshoppers, Ants, Water Bugs, Spiders, Centipedes, and Their Kin by David George Gordon (Ten Speed Press, 2013).

Where to purchase pine rosin

http://www.rosinproducts.com/Rosin_Baked_Potato.html
http://www.diamondgforestproducts.com

Equipment for collecting insects

Bioquip Products
2321 Gladwick Street
Rancho Dominguez, CA 90220
Phone: (310) 667-8800   Fax: (310) 667-8808
https://www.bioquip.com

INDEX

Note: Page numbers in *italics* refer to photographs.

honey. *See also* raw honey
 in Black-Mustard-Seeds Mustard, 180
 in cold infusions, *146, 148*
 in forest blends, 11
 in hot and chilled infusions, 149, 150
 in mead, 63, 74, 76
 in mustard, 34
 in shrubs, 73
 wild yeast in, 74, 76, 81, 226, *227*
horehound (*Marrubium vulgare*)
 in beer, 64, 68
 foraging, *389*
 in forest blends, 11
 pregnancy precautions, 6
Horehound and California Sagebrush Beer
 (Bitter Beer), 68
hornworms, foraging, 356
horsetail (*Equisetum arvense*), 6
hosrom (green grape juice), 124
hot and chilled infusions, 149–150, *150*
hot-infused vinegars, 243. *See also* vinegars
hot leaching, 50, 51, 54, *55*
hot method for sodas, 212–13
hotness scale, 292
hot sauces, 291–301
 basic procedure, 292, *293*
 canning and bottling, 294–97, *294–96*
 Fermented Hot Sauce with Wild Greens,
  298, 299–300, *301*
 Nasturtium and Watercress Hot Sauce,
  291, 293
 overview, 291
Hydrastis canadensis (goldenseal), 6
hygiene precautions
 beer making, 64
 overview, 401
 soup stock making, 47
 wine making, 206

I

ice cream, with white fir powdered sugar, *84,* 134
infused vinegars. *See also* vinegars
 basic procedure, 243–45, *244*
 in fermented seeds, 333
 in hot sauce, 291
 in pickled seeds, 327
Infused Vinegar Sauce with Wild Berries, 253
infusions
 blends for, *135*
 cold, 146–48, *146, 148*
 hot and chilled, 149–150, *150*
inky cap mushroom (*Coprinus* spp.), 20, *392*

insects, 356–367
 acorn grubs, 51, 356, *357, 358, 359*
 ants, 356, 361, *361*
 in beer, *72,* 73
 collecting, 361, 404
 crickets, *155,* 356, 360, *360*
 emerita, 356, 364, *364, 365*
 in forest blends, 11
 in local cuisine, 5
 overview, 356, *356*
 shrimp allergy concerns, 6
 in spice blends, *155,* 157
 typical species foraged, 356
 water bugs, 356, 362–63, *363*
 wood shrimps, 364, *366,* 367
Italian spice mix
 in Beef Stone-Cooked in Forest Floor, 24
 in Chaparral Roasted Quail, 169
 in mustard, 181
 in nettle soup cubes, 144
 in pickled acorns, 57
 in pickled unripe walnuts, 108, 109
 in pickled wild radish pods, 117
 in unripe currant capers, 129
 in wild cheeses, 24

J

Jacobson, Chris, 12, 167
jalapeño pepper, 293, 377
jams, 266, *267, 302,* 303
jerky, from yucca, 134, 266, *267*
jimsonweed (*Datura stramonium*), 10
Joshua tree (*Yucca brevifolia*), 258
Juglans spp. *See* walnut (*Juglans* spp.)
juices. *See* fruit juices
juicing, unripe currants, 125, *125,* 127
jumiles, foraging, 356
June bugs, foraging, 356
jungle juice, 254
juniper (*Juniperus*)
 in beer, 64, 71
 in clay cooking, 22
 in fish dishes, 22
 in grilling/smoking blends, 90
 inner bark as string, 96
 pregnancy precautions, 6
 in preserves, 41
 in sauerkraut, 288, 289
 in spice blends, *155,* 157
 wild yeast in, 79, *80,* 81, 211
Juniperus californica. See California juniper
 (*Juniperus californica*)

K

Kalamata-Style Olives, 314, *315*
kelp, 41, 64, 71
Kelpie (beer), 71
kimchi
 Dehydrated Wild Kimchi Spice, 138, *139,*
  140, 141
 fermenting elderberry capers in, 131
 recipe for, 119–122, *121, 122*
 with sea bass, *373*
knapweed, as plant rennet, 32

L

Lactobacillus spp., 42, 93, 119
Lallemand Nottingham Ale Yeast, 63
lamb, 16, 87, 90, 161
Lamb Cooked in Forest Floor, 16
lamb's quarters (*Chenopodium* spp.)
 dehydration of, 137
 in dinner series menu, 383
 foraging, *389*
 in Pickled Oyster Mushrooms with Wild
  Seeds, 328
 powders of, 142, 335, 348
 seeds of, 321, *322,* 327, 328, 333
 in wild cheeses, 24
leaching, to remove tannins, 50–54, *53, 55*
leaves. *See also* tree leaves
 in hot and chilled infusions, 149
 in preserves, 41
 for wrapping, 22, 30, 96
leeks, wild. *See* ramps
Lefebvre, Ludo, 146, 189, 327
lemon
 in ash key capers, 114
 in beer, 65, 67, 68, 70, 71, 73
 in candied tree leaves, 85
 in cold infusions, *146,* 147, 148, *148*
 dehydration of, *135,* 164
 in elderflower cordial, 208
 in Green Cracked Olives, 312
 in grilling/smoking blends, 90
 in hot sauce, 292, 293
 in Local Mountain Nocino, 111
 in mead, *75,* 76
 in Sacred Lerp Sugar Fermented Drink, 211
 with shrimp, 99
 in SoBeer, 229, *229*
 in sodas, 214, 217, 218, *223,* 225
 in spice blends, 165
 in unripe currant capers, 129
 in wild cheeses, 27, 32

White Sage-Lime Cider
   in dinner series menu, 383, *386*
   in granitas, 351
   recipe for, 66, *66*
   vinegar from, 237
white snakeroot (*Ageratina altissima*), 10, 97
white wine
   in mustard, 180, 181
   in pickled acorns, 57
   in pickled unripe walnuts, 108
   in pickled wild radish pods, 117
wild beer. *See* beer
wild blends. *See* forest blends; grilling/smoking blends; mountain blends; spice blends
wild celery (*Apium graveolens*)
   dehydration of, 137
   in fermented hot sauces, 299
   in fermented olives, 310
   in pickled seeds, 327
   powders of, 142
   seeds of, 321, 327
   in soup stock, 46
   in spice blends, *152, 155*
   stem uses, 353
wild chamomile. *See* pineapple weed (*Matricaria discoidea*)
wild cheeses, 24–33
   Basic Wild Cheese, *25, 26, 27*
   Goat Cheese with Fig Sap, 33, *33, 372*
   overview, 24
   plant rennet for, 32, *32*
   sweet white clover cheese, 24, *28–29*
   Tiny Cheesy Wild Snacks, 30, *30, 31*
wild cherry (*Prunus ilicifolia*)
   in beer, 64, 71
   foraging, *396*
   preserving in alcohol, 345
   in shrubs, 254
wildcrafting. *See* foraging
Wild Currant Verjus, 127
wild fennel (*Foeniculum vulgare*)
   for alcohol-preserved fruits, 345
   in cheese balls, 30
   in clay cooking, 22
   in cold infusions, 147, 148, *148*
   in compound butter, 170, 171
   dehydration of, 137
   in fermented olives, 310
   in fish dishes, 22
   foraging, *394, 396*
   in forest blends, 11, 12
   in Green Cracked Olives, 312

   in grilling/smoking blends, 87
   in nasturtium capers, *40*
   in Pickled Oyster Mushrooms with Wild Seeds, 328
   in pickled seeds, 327
   in pickled wild radish pods, 117
   pollen of, *56*
   powders of, 142
   in preserves, 41
   seeds of, 321, *323*, 327, 328
   in shrubs, 254
   in sodas, 214
   in sourdough bread, 341
   in spice blends, *153, 155*, 158, 161, 165
   sugary powders from, 160, *160*
   in tapas, *371, 373*
   in wild cheeses, 24
Wild Fennel Seeds Blend, 161
Wild Food Lab Dinner Series, 382–87, *383–87*
wild gardens, 257–58
wild hyacinth (*Dichelostemma pulchellum*)
   foraging, *393*
   powders of, 142
   in quail au vin, *373*
wild mint (*Mentha* spp.)
   in cold infusions, *146, 147, 148, 148*
   dehydration of, 137
   in forest blends, 11
   in mead, 76
   in preserves, 41
   in sodas, 217, 222, 226
   in spice blends, *154*
   in wild cheeses, 24
   for wrapping cheese balls, 30
wild onion
   in clay cooking, 22
   in fish dishes, 22
   foraging, 6, 34
   powders of, 142
   in Quail au Vin, *373*
wild radish (*Raphanus raphanistrum*)
   foraging, *395*
   in forest blends, 11
   in hot sauce, 291
   in kimchi, 119, 120
   pickled, 117, *117, 118*
   powders of, 142
   root uses, 352
   in sauerkraut, 288
   with sea bass, *373*
   sprouts of, *373*

   stem uses, 353
   in tapas, *373*
wild rhubarb (*Rumex hymenosepalus*)
   foraging, *391*
   powders of, 142
   pregnancy precautions, 6
   verjus from, 124
wild rosemary
   in beer, 64
   in Salted Olives, 317
wild yeast
   for beer, 59, 63, 74, 76, 79
   for elderberry wine, 203, 204
   overview, 79, 81
   in raw honey, 74, 76
   for Sacred Lerp Sugar Fermented Drink, 211
   for sodas, 220, 226, *227*
   for sourdough bread, 339
wild yeast starters
   basic procedure, *80, 82*
   for sodas, 220, *224, 225*, 226
   for sourdough bread, 339, 340–41, *341*
Williams Brothers Brewing Company, 71
willow
   allergy safety precautions, 71
   in beer, 64, 70
   candied, *84, 85*
   in forest blends, 11, 12, 16, 18
   in grilling/smoking blends, 87, 90
   inner bark as string, 96
   in SoBeer, 229, *229*
   in sodas, 217
   stem uses, 83
   trout with, *99*
   vinegar from, 248
willow herb (*Epilobium ciliatum*), *372, 392*
wine
   elderberry, *198, 202*, 203–6, *204–6*
   grilling with, 87
   "primitive" flavors of, 199
   resources, 404
   starter for, 82
   sugar for, 63
   wild yeast for, 79, 82
wine vinegar
   in Green Cracked Olives, 312
   in hot sauce, 293
winter
   foraging in, 9, *389–391*
   recipes list, 8
Winter in the Forest Beer, 70, *70*
wiwish (acorn mush), 51

ABOUT THE AUTHOR

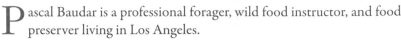

Pascal Baudar is a professional forager, wild food instructor, and food preserver living in Los Angeles.

For the last 16 years, his passion has been to investigate the flavors and possible uses of local wild edibles through extensive research and experimentation into the fields of modern and traditional methods of food preservation, herbalism, and ethnobotany.

A sort of culinary alchemist, he has seen his locally found wild ingredients and unique preserves make their way into the kitchens of such star chefs as Ludo Lefebvre, Josiah Citrin, Ari Taymor, Michael Voltaggio, Chris Jacobson, and many others.

Over the years, through his weekly classes and seminars, he has introduced thousands of home cooks, local chefs, and foodies to the flavors offered by the wild terroir of Southern California.

Pascal has also served as a wild food consultant for several TV shows, including *MasterChef* and *Top Chef Duels*. He has been featured in numerous TV shows and publications, including *Time* magazine, the *Los Angeles Times*, *L.A. Weekly*, the *New York Times*, and many more.

In 2014, he was named as one of the 25 most influential tastemakers in L.A. by *Los Angeles* magazine.

Pascal offers private and public foraging classes through his website: www.urbanoutdoorskills.com.

Photo courtesy of Mia Wasilevich.